therapeutic recreation program design

Prentice-Hall, Inc., Englewood Cliffs, New Jersey 07632

therapeutic recreation program design

principles and procedures

Scout Lee Gunn, Ed.D.
University of Illinois

Carol Ann Peterson, Ed.D.
University of Illinois

Library of Congress Cataloging in Publication Data

GUNN, SCOUT LEE (date)
    Therapeutic recreation program design.

    Bibliography: p.
    Includes index.
    1. Recreational therapy. I. Peterson, Carol Ann
(date) joint author. II. Title.
RM736.7.G86   615'.8515   78-992
ISBN 0–13–914804–3

© 1978 by
Prentice-Hall, Inc.
Englewood Cliffs, New Jersey 07632

Printed in the United States of America

10 9 8 7 6 5

PRENTICE-HALL INTERNATIONAL, INC., *London*
PRENTICE-HALL OF AUSTRALIA PTY. LIMITED, *Sydney*
PRENTICE-HALL OF CANADA, LTD., *Toronto*
PRENTICE-HALL OF INDIA PRIVATE LIMITED, *New Delhi*
PRENTICE-HALL OF JAPAN, INC., *Tokyo*
PRENTICE-HALL OF SOUTHEAST ASIA PTE. LTD., *Singapore*
WHITEHALL BOOKS LIMITED, *Wellington, New Zealand*

kids grow up and do adult things
like writing books,
but still feel small next
to the importance of parents

This book is dedicated to our parents
Ed and Pat Spencer
Don and Grace Peterson

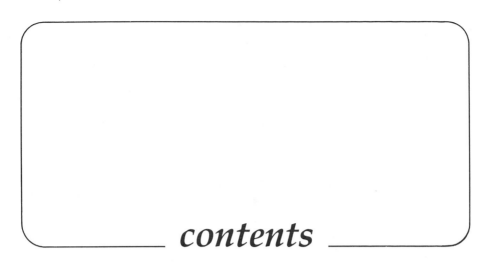

contents

CONTENTS

2

client-centered
program planning

CONTENTS

3

management concerns
in therapeutic recreation

appendixes

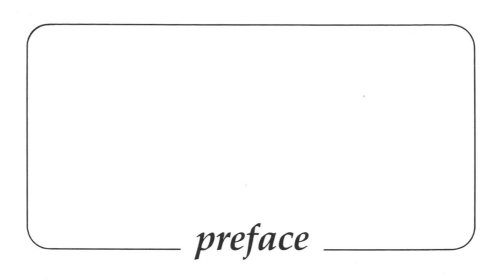

preface

This text was conceived in our classrooms in response to our students. Its birth has been slow and sometimes painful as we agonized over content, process, and writing style. For the past three years we have developed our own lecture notes, transparencies, videotapes, slides, and cassette tapes, and bombarded our students with reams of handouts, in an effort to compensate for the absence of systematic and comprehensive therapeutic recreation programming materials. Although several texts address certain aspects of programming, no one text offers a consistent approach to program conceptualization, design, implementation, and evaluation. Encouraged by colleagues within our department and across the nation, and supported by our students, we plunged headlong into the task of producing such a book, with the hope that our approach will be helpful in every area of therapeutic recreation program planning.

From the onset of this effort we have constantly used our students and colleagues as sounding boards and critics. Perhaps the most insightful assistance we have received came through the persistent and sometimes frustrating questions posed by our students who always insisted on clarity and simplicity. When students responded "I don't understand" or "I'm not sure what you mean," we returned to the drawing boards. We now feel confident that the material presented, although often complex in nature, is expressed clearly and simply.

We have attempted to integrate our own experiences into the examples given in the text, realizing that some specific areas may have been overlooked. However, the principles and procedures for therapeutic recreation programming in rehabilitation, education, and community recreation settings have been consistently discussed throughout the text. Obviously, some aspects of program planning relate more specifically to treatment or education settings, while others relate to community recreation settings.

It is difficult to pinpoint the specific systems approach to program design that we have used. The materials presented reflect our own trial-and-error approach to consolidating methodology into a format most conducive to therapeutic recreation. Knowledge acquired over the years from a variety of sources has become so integrated into our own thinking that it is often difficult, if not impossible, to acknowledge original sources. We therefore apologize for any unintentionally borrowed thoughts for which we can give no recognition. We also want to acknowledge the many teachers, colleagues, peers, students, friends, and clients who have touched our lives and molded our existence.

We would indeed be remiss if we claimed that this book is solely our own creative effort, since the creative process always appears to be stimulated by others. Space limitations prevent our being able to list the hundreds of students who have contributed to this book. We, therefore, offer to our students this gift of our time and energies in appreciation for the numerous times they not only critiqued our material but also granted us additional hours of solitude in order to complete the work.

Our colleagues across the nation also played a large part in the creation of this text. We appreciate their constant support (and sometimes playful badgering!) and willingness to assist us in polishing concepts.

Some people offered special support and assistance and deserve our deepest appreciation. Dr. Joseph Bannon, our friend and department chairperson, believes that creativity and productivity by faculty demand time and encouragement, which he has generously provided. On numerous occasions our friend and colleague, Jerry Burnam, assisted us with piles of paperwork so that we would be free to write. Rosa Lee Brill, our secretary, remained joyful and supportive throughout the entire project, while voluntarily working many overtime hours typing and editing our manuscript.

Finally, we applaud the awesome phenomena of our open and honest communication with each other. Throughout the entire process, we have remained friends!

therapeutic
recreation
program
design

1

*conceptual
overview*

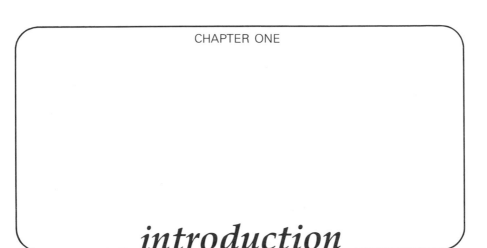

CHAPTER ONE

introduction

PURPOSE: To present a rationale and foundation for systematic program design, program implementation, and program evaluation in various therapeutic recreation settings. The format of the text is presented along with an overview of therapeutic recreation services.

> *I shot an arrow into the air,*
> *It fell to earth, I knew not where.*
> **Henry Wadsworth Longfellow**

The above quotation parallels the quandary that prompted the writing of this book. Therapeutic recreation programming decisions are often random shots in the dark or blasts skyrocketed toward undefined targets. Glibly, we therapeutic recreators have purported that our programs make substantial contributions to the habilitation or rehabilitation of our clients. "Play behavior is a vital part of normal growth and development." "Recreation services reduce delinquency, truancy, aggression, and bizarre behaviors." "Therapeutic recreation programs improve self-concept, socialization skills, cognitive skills, tolerance of authority figures, personal appearance, and physical skills." We believe these statements, altruistically and experientially. We've seen the multiplicity of positive effects our programs have had on our clients. Most of us can sit for hours and share personal, heart-warming accounts of visible successes in our programs. We can also painfully recount the frustrating experiences of not being able to reach certain individuals. However, whenever asked to account for our successes or pinpoint possible reasons for our failures, our responses are all too often vague or accusing of administration, legislation, and other classical scapegoats. Miracles are often credited to the value of play behavior, and failures are often blamed on such nebulous factors as lack of support, inadequate funding, changes in administrative policies, and uncooperative families.

It is often impossible to repeat the process that produced positive changes, because specific procedures either were not designed before implementation or not recorded during implementation. It is also common to read glowing reports about the accomplishments of program participants, but the resulting participant behavior cannot be correlated with entry-level skills because initial assessments were not conducted.

All too often the SWAG technique of programmatic decision making is employed—SWAG stands for Sophisticated, Wild-Ass Guess! Without sufficient supporting data, program assignments are made, treatment techniques employed, numbers of staff hired, volunteers recruited, equipment purchased, facilities designed, and budgets either squandered away or allotted far below the level of actual program needs. However, our guesses have not always been bad. Quite the contrary. Over time our guesses get better and our programs improve—we think But we can no longer afford just to believe our programs are effective. We must *know*!

Today an important issue is *accountability*. We are constantly pressured to give evidence of the results of our programs regarding clients' skills, attitudes, and leadership styles; assessment and evaluation strategies; cost-benefit returns; utilization of equipment and facilities; management strategies and planning techniques; intervention and interaction styles; in-service training strategies; recruitment techniques; and numerous other variables that directly influence the lives of our clients and the philanthropic, philosophical, and financial support for our services. We can no longer afford to be vague concerning our effectiveness. Local, state, and federal funding sources and taxpayers and consumers are demanding evidence of our worth.

It is no longer sufficient to state at the end of a program that "the objectives of the program were attained." More often than we care to admit, participants in our programs do indeed attain the objectives set forth but become so disconcerted by the process that they never return to our or similar programs. Overall program effectiveness is concerned "not only with the results in terms of behavioral changes in people, but also with the proportion of the potential clientele that's reached, the balance in types of people reached, the extent to which the results deal with urgent and continual need, and the care with which participant, agency, and societal resources are used. Program evaluation is as concerned about the value and suitability of the program as it is with whether its purpose is accomplished."[1] We are now asked to be accountable not only for the *product* of the programs but also for the *process* of our programs and the interrelatedness of the two.

Accountability implies *evaluation* and evaluation necessitates *systematic program planning,* two concepts that often incite feelings of inadequacy. Having experienced these feelings ourselves and empathized with numerous other practitioners and students, we felt that part of the challenge of writing this text was to arrive at a format that would comprehensively, yet simply, convey this message: accountability achieved through systematic program design, implementation, and evaluation can be challenging, rewarding, and even fun.

We have shared with you our thoughts, suggestions, concerns, questions, experiences, and feelings—sometimes joy, pain, frustration, or anger. Knowing that this conversational style of writing and sharing is unusual in a textbook, we hasten to claim full responsibility for our words. We hope that we will make a contribution to our commonly shared concern for the leisure life styles of the individuals we seek to serve.

format of materials

part 1

We have attempted to follow the basic principles of program design in the formation and presentation of these materials. Part 1 provides the broad background of program concerns in therapeutic recreation and presents the various philosophical and theoretical premises on which basic programs are developed. This chapter presents a rationale for systematic program design, the format for the presentation of materials, and a brief overview of therapeutic recreation. The last section introduces the nontherapeutic recreator to the field and recaps for the therapeutic recreator the basic rationale for our services. Since several other books adequately cover the historical development of therapeutic recreation we do not attempt to repeat this material.

Chapter two presents a comprehensive therapeutic recreation service model that systematically conceptualizes and defines the roles and functions of services on a continuum ranging from treatment to independent leisure functioning. The model correlates the various expected roles of the therapeutic recreator with the expected leisure functioning of clients. Early in the process of program design, it is important to identify both the general and specific expected outcomes of services. This model helps the programmer to identify the generic purpose of services rendered.

Chapter three presents a biopsychosocial approach to working with program participants, which neither presumes illness nor wellness, but rather views the life situation of the total person. Other approaches are discussed for the sake of comparison.

Chapter four concludes part 1 with a discussion of contemporary factors affecting program design. Included are the concepts of normalization and mainstreaming, integrated versus segregated programming, accessibility, and debilitating attitudes assumed toward and in working with the handicapped.

part 2

Having reviewed in part 1 the philosophical and theoretical premises on which program design is developed, part 2 proceeds to develop sequentially the components of program design, implementation, and evaluation. Chapter five outlines the basic concepts of systematically designed programs and develops a rationale for utilizing a systems approach.

Chapter six presents an approach to individualized program planning. It discusses client assessment strategies and outlines a systematic approach for determining client needs. Having determined needs, procedures are presented for deriving and appropriately stating programming goals and individual behavioral objectives. Material is provided for planning individualized programs.

Chapter seven presents a method of group assessment. Material is provided that enables the designer to select and utilize variables that are of specific concern to different populations. Programming considerations based on group assessment methodology are described.

Chapter eight focuses on determining program direction once individual and group needs have been established. Also presented is how to prepare a statement that specifies the purpose and goals of the program. Several sample program models are provided to illustrate program development and conceptualization.

Chapter nine focuses on program content and process. Detailed procedures are outlined for breaking program goals and behavioral objectives into components for service delivery. Task description and analysis pave the way for specifying the actual content (activities) and process (interaction or facilitation technique) to be used.

Chapter ten presents materials related to activity analysis and applications, including principles of activity selection, modification, and sequencing, as well as techniques to determine an activity's appropriateness and the possible inherent therapeutic benefits of participation.

Chapter eleven discusses the importance of specifying the interaction styles and techniques used by the therapeutic recreator as vital aspects of program design and implementation. Predominant facilitation styles are presented along with criteria for appropriate utilization with specific populations. The chapter presents techniques appropriate for therapy, leisure counseling, activity and social skills instruction, and basic leadership.

Chapter twelve discusses program implementation strategies. It includes a discussion of procedures for the selection and specification of the delivery model as well as practical considerations of program operation.

Chapter thirteen presents the basic techniques of program evaluation based on systems design. Criteria-based performance is given as the basis on which program revision is made. Revision strategies for the improvement of program design and operation are also discussed.

part 3

The final part deals with specific management concerns that are crucial to the effective operation and evaluation of systems-designed therapeutic recreation programs. Chapter fourteen discusses a basic management philosophy that uses all available resources and allows for individual accountability and responsibility in service delivery. A variety of specific principles of effective management are mentioned. Open communication and staff and client motivation are presented as major concerns.

Chapter fifteen presents a rationale and guidelines for ongoing staff development and in-service training as vital components of program design, implementation, and evaluation. Policies and procedures, training needs, and implementation strategies relative to staff development are discussed.

Chapter sixteen discusses the basic principles and appropriate styles of charting, record keeping, and reporting in therapeutic recreation programs. Also included are the basic signs and symbols used in charting.

Chapter seventeen details the various roles and functions of consultants in therapeutic recreation. Guidelines are given for effective consultations in therapeutic recreation.

We have presented basic principles and procedures of programming design in therapeutic recreation that relate to all types of settings and services. Examples of various program-design applications are dispersed throughout the text.

overview of therapeutic recreation

Free time is a problem for many people. Some of us almost laugh at that statement, for we want more time to relax, to forget the hassles of jobs and responsibilities, and to have the opportunity to engage in our favorite activities and enjoy our friends. But for many ill, handicapped, and elderly people, free time is a major problem, if not a dreaded enemy. The profession of therapeutic recreation deals with all aspects of this problem.

As a profession, therapeutic recreation is rather new. It emerged during World War I but had its greatest impact during World War II. During both wars, recreational activities were used with both physically disabled and psychiatrically disturbed individuals in order to speed the recovery process and help them adjust, both to the treatment settings and to the communities to which they would be returning.

Basically, therapeutic recreation is concerned with enabling individuals with physical, mental, emotional, or social disabilities to acquire appropriate socioleisure life styles. However, the process is much more complex than that. Some individuals in treatment settings have conditions that are severe enough that the immediate focus cannot be on how well they play; rather, it must be on assisting them to function better. In these settings, specific recreational activities are used as part of the treatment process to improve physical, mental, emotional, or social functioning.

This therapeutic use of recreational activities is a well-planned process that includes assessing the client's functional problem, stating a treatment goal, selecting appropriate activities, and selecting an interaction or intervention style. Once a client's functional level has improved, the emphasis of the therapeutic recreation program shifts to helping the individual to develop leisure attitudes, values, and skills.

Some people with physical disabilities or conditions of mental impairment live in the community and are not in treatment situations. Free time is a problem for many of them because they have never had the opportunity to acquire recreational skills or engage in recreation programs or activities as other people do. For this group, free time is a burden. Opportunities are limited for self-expression, growth and awareness, and social experiences. Therapeutic recreation programs for these individuals, therefore, focus on providing meaningful experiences through leisure activities. Some may learn recreational skills so that they can choose how to use their free time; others may attend programs that take into consideration their particular handicaps or limitations; and others may learn about leisure and its potentials for self-expression and satisfaction.

Why is there this concern for recreation for the disabled? Certainly more pressing problems face this group. The answer lies within American culture itself. Leisure has become a dominant part of American life. We are concerned about, even centered in, the exercise of our recreative activities. Although we recognize the "work ethic," most of us value our free time highly and the activities in which we engage during that time. Our friends and our leisurely pursuits captivate much of our attention and are often the motivation for "staying with the job." This switch in priorities in the American way of life has been subtle, yet is very real.

Our play behavior allows us to experience values that are all too often negated in the work world. Among these are self-expression, release of tension, opportunities for mastery of self through skills, social interaction and recognition, and development of awareness and human potential. As a result, an individual's self-expression through leisure time is one of the most highly prized, though least acknowledged, possessions.

Disabled individuals, however, have traditionally been excluded from finding meaning within the context of leisure. Their tasks have been to acquire a job, attain acceptance by "normal" people, and achieve functional levels of behavior. Little effort has been exerted in assisting this group to achieve the socioleisure skills so essential to the rest of the culture. Yet, if there was ever a group who needed release from tensions and problems and who needed to find ways for self-development and expression, social interaction, relaxation, mastery of skills, and just plain fun, it is the disabled.

—————————————— *note* ——————————————

[1] Sara M. Steele, *Contemporary Approaches to Program Evaluation* (Washington, D.C.: Capital Publications, Inc., Education Resources Division, 1973), p. 25.

a therapeutic recreation service model

PURPOSE: To present a continuum model that systematically conceptualizes and defines the roles and functions of therapeutic recreation services, ranging from treatment to independent leisure functioning. The model includes the various expected roles and functions of the therapeutic recreator as they relate to the functional level of the client. A basic model of service is introduced, from which specific program designs and content can be derived at different stages on the continuum.

Perhaps one of the most confounding questions asked of our students is in response to their gleeful announcement that they "are majoring in therapeutic recreation." The response is all too familiar: "Therapeutic recreation? What is that? What do you do?" The answer seemed so simple on first enrolling in the curriculum. "I want to be a recreator and work with retarded children!" However, when confronted with the confounding barrage of literature introduced in their first therapeutic recreation course—which attempts to define and explain therapeutic recreation and a multiplicity of services—the student very often feels hard pressed to explain succinctly and systematically what he or she "is all about." Hesitantly the student may begin, "Well, . . . we work in recreation with special populations . . . that is, people not traditionally served by existing recreation programs . . . you know, . . . like the mentally retarded, physically handicapped, mentally ill, and emotionally disturbed. Sometimes we work as therapists in various treatment settings, and sometimes we work as leaders of special recreation programs in the community. By special recreation programs, I mean . . . ." And so it goes. These sometimes prolonged, indirect attempts meaningfully to encapsulate and explain the essence of such a broad field of study and service generally leaves the student feeling somewhat frustrated and the inquirer feeling slightly confused.

This problem is not unique to the student. Listen in on a proud parent trying to explain what her or his child is studying. Even many professionals in the field and allies of the therapeutic recreation movement experience a similar dilemma. We have attempted to cut through the traditional issue of therapy versus recreation by developing a therapeutic recreation service model that allows for a variety of program designs and content, based on the needs of particular clients in a number of settings. This model should facilitate succinct, meaningful explanations of what therapeutic recreators do. The model represents the total range of therapeutic recreation services—a dynamic continuum that strives to facilitate meaningful, independent leisure functioning for the clients that we serve.

We can no longer afford to spend valuable classroom time attempting to defend our existence by debating such issues as (1) "Is all recreation therapeutic?" (And, if so, all recreation specialists are therapeutic recreators.) Or (2) "Can recreation prescribed in therapy really be recreation?" (And, if not, how can we call ourselves recreators?) Although these types of inquiry can provide hours of mental amusement, their resolution in no way affects the important work that has been, is being, and needs to be done in our field. We no longer need to presume that we maintain a subordinate posture in the leisure movement or among other related health professions. We now have a national registration program and are listed in merit-system job classifications. Therapeutic recreators are commonly listed with other recreation and health-related disciplines, such as physical therapy, occupational therapy, social services, and nursing. Interested persons will continue to ask us what we do, just as they do of physiatrists and ichthyologists, and we must be able to throw back our shoulders and describe the services that we therapeutic recreators offer.

therapeutic recreation: a process or a service?

Perhaps the therapy-versus-recreation issue has resulted from attempts to define therapeutic recreation service as a specific *process*, with most of the emphasis placed on therapeutic recreation rather than on service. Therapeutic recreation service is defined as

a process which utilizes recreation services for purposive intervention in some physical, emotional, and/or social behavior to bring about a desired change in that behavior and to promote the growth and development of the individual.[1]

11

One cannot expect the title of any profession to be a philosophical statement about a single, specific process of service delivery. Cosmetology identifies a type of service and utilizes many processes. Orthopedics identifies a type of service and utilizes many processes. Likewise, therapeutic recreation identifies a type of service and utilizes many processes. The specific processes involved in any service depend on the need of the consumer, which in turn identifies the specific role of the producer and the method by which the producer will render the service. Implicit in any service is a population that needs or wants a change that can be facilitated by the skills of the producer. Someone who goes to a beauty shop desires a change in appearance that can be facilitated by the use of cosmetics, a skill possessed by the cosmetologist. The term therapeutic recreation service likewise identifies a population that needs or desires change that can be facilitated by the skills of a therapeutic recreation specialist.

therapeutic recreation services: definition or identity?

Rather than being a philosophical statement of one specific process, therapeutic recreation service identifies (1) a group of professionals who possess recreational activity and facilitation skills and who are interested in using those skills to bring about some type of change with (2) special-need populations, such as the mentally retarded, emotionally disturbed, mentally ill, and physically handicapped. The specific needs of the consumer determine (a) the type of change, whether in a functional-skill area or a leisure-skill area, and (b) the ways that the therapeutic recreator employs his or her activity and facilitation skills to bring about the change. Therapeutic recreation service broadly describes those processes that promote independent leisure functioning for special populations through remedial, educational, and recreational experiences that use various activity and facilitation techniques.

purpose of therapeutic recreation services

The purpose of any service is to bring about a change in the consumer. Thus, the overriding, generic purpose of therapeutic recreation is to bring about a change in a special-population member with the ultimate goal of achieving independent and personally rewarding leisure functioning.

Regardless of the population with whom we work or the setting in which we work, therapeutic recreators have two ideals in common: (1) we hope to facilitate positive change in special-population members, and

(2) we hope to see our clients eventually enjoying independently chosen and personally rewarding leisure activities.

Clients who are profoundly retarded may never be able to function completely independently. However, the belief that most human beings can be personally responsible for their own leisure well-being excites and motivates us to use a variety of facilitation techniques and program content to bring about meaningful, independent leisure functioning.

Some of our clients come to us needing only accessible facilities or adapted programs to be able to enjoy their leisure. For them we need only to provide opportunities to express recreative skills that have already been developed. Other clients ask us for the opportunity to learn new leisure skills, and so we become leisure educators. For still other clients, the demands for leisure-skill acquisition are far less specific because they do not even possess the functional abilities necessary to learn leisure skills. For these clients, we may have to assume the role of therapist along with other health professionals and assist them in acquiring basic functional abilities so that they can begin to acquire new leisure skills and attitudes.

Whether we assume the primary role of therapist, educator, or recreation leader, we are all vital to therapeutic recreation services and we are all ultimately striving to facilitate meaningful independent leisure functioning for our clients.

therapeutic recreation services: a continuum model

Both advantages and difficulties are inherent in presenting a schematic representation of a multifaceted phenomenon. Very often a picture of a phenomenon or concept will make comprehension quicker and more meaningful than stringing together a mass of words. Relationships may be more clearly understood, and movement throughout a process may make sense for the first time. However, the difficulties of a schematic model need to be mentioned so that the reader does not limit it to the two-dimensional characteristics of a page in a book.

The words chosen for schematic models are crucial in that space does not allow for extended explanations. It is also difficult to perceive movement or exact degrees of relationships on a static drawing. Additionally, models may be presumed to encapsulate a total concept when in reality models can, at best, offer a visual clue to the basics of a concept or phenomenon. We acknowledge the limitations of schematic models and ask that our readers be aware that the various domains of therapeutic recreation services are very often not distinctly separate units of service, but in fact, overlap or are conducted simultaneously. Processes may be used in conjunction with each other, and the therapeutic recreation specialist may be required to wear more than one hat at the same time. Due to the ease of misinterpreting the meaning of specific words, we will also define our terms.

focuses of service

Therapeutic recreation services usually fall in one of three domains: (1) rehabilitation, (2) education, or (3) recreation. As a result, the therapeutic recreation student may experience confusion concerning her or his role. "Am I primarily a recreation therapist? Or am I a leisure educator for special populations? Or am I a recreation specialist for special populations?" Again, the problem is not unique to the therapeutic recreation student. Many professional therapeutic recreators work in acute treatment settings and function primarily as therapists. Other professionals work in residential, institutional, and community settings where their primary function is to teach leisure skills. Still other professionals work predominantly in community agencies where their primary function is to provide leisure opportunities for special populations. Quite often, a therapeutic recreator is required to perform all three functions in a given setting. It is important to understand the role of the therapeutic recreation specialist in relation to program planning and evaluation. The Therapeutic Recreation Service Model (fig. 2–1) depicts the three major domains of service and the resulting role implications to the therapeutic recreator.

rehabilitation as a focus of service

The setting is an in-patient psychiatric facility where Sam Spacey has just been admitted with the following diagnostic labels: paranoid schizophrenic, compulsive neurotic behavior, auditory hallucination, and disoriented x 3.

Further investigation into Sam's life and problems reveals that he is twenty-six years old, single, and living with his parents. For the past three days, Sam seems to have totally lost touch with reality—he does not seem to know who he is, where he is, or what time and day it is. He sits alone in the kitchen complaining that men from the CIA are conspiring to kill him by poisoning his food. Apart from washing the dishes approximately twenty times a day, Sam does nothing that could be interpreted as constructive activity. Before becoming ill, Sam enjoyed classical music and oil painting. However, it has been over two years since he actively participated in any leisure activity.

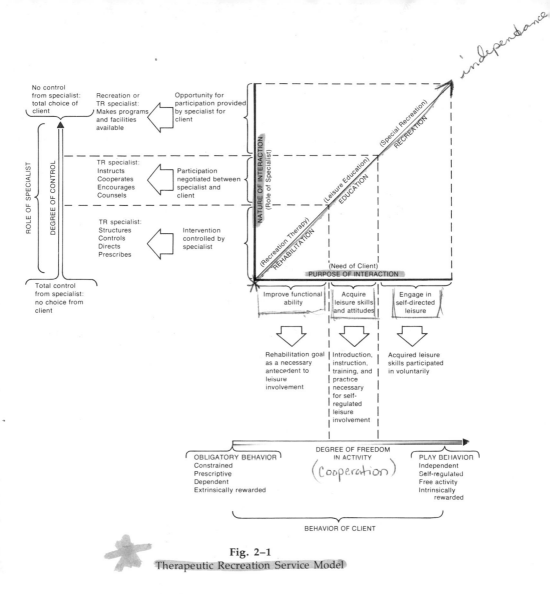

Fig. 2–1
Therapeutic Recreation Service Model

At the time of admission to the psychiatric facility, Sam seems frightened of all social contacts and refuses the assistance or company of anyone. As a part of the treatment team, the therapeutic recreation specialist is asked to partake in an all-out effort to help Sam to demonstrate enough trust in another human being to be able to engage in self-initiated conversation.

The therapeutic recreator would ultimately wish to see Sam again enjoying classical music and painting, as well as participating in other forms of enjoyable leisure activity that did not leave him so isolated. However, before leisure education or leisure involvement can become the primary focus of services, Sam will need to reestablish the *basic functional*

15

ability of conversing realistically about who he is, where he is, and what is going on around him. To begin with then, the therapeutic recreator's primary concern is not with leisure-skills development or expression. He or she is more concerned with helping Sam overcome his fear of others around him, so that he may later learn new or reactivate old leisure skills. This may, however, be accomplished by leaving a classical record with Sam or by sharing a book of art, with the hope that Sam will begin to trust a caring relationship.

client needs

In this instance, the need of the client determines the purpose of the interaction, which is to improve Sam's basic functional abilities—to develop enough trust in another person to be able to carry on a self-initiated, reality-oriented conversation. Here rehabilitation is the primary goal and is a necessary antecedent to leisure involvement (fig. 2–2). In similar cases, recreational activities and facilitation techniques become the means to the primary goal—rehabilitation. When recreational activities and facilitation skills are used in the rehabilitation or the treatment process as a means to a treatment goal, the interaction may be defined as therapy—recreation therapy. In cases such as Sam's, achieving defined rehabilitation goals and objectives and utilizing recreational activities and facilitation techniques becomes a necessary preliminary to the client's future leisure involvement.

The client's degree of freedom in choosing the activities in which she or he participates may be extremely limited and at times even obligatory. In acute treatment settings, clients are often required to attend and participate in recreational events on a prescriptive basis, just at they are required to attend group therapy sessions or spend time in physical therapy. Clients who lack basic functional abilities may depend on the therapeutic recreator and other members of a treatment team to assist them in developing functional skills. Participating in activities may at first be extrinsically more rewarding, allowing perhaps increased responsibility, greater freedom of choice in activity selection, or more privileges in the unit. It is hoped that increased basic functional abilities will encourage the client to learn new leisure skills that will be intrinsically rewarding. The higher the level of basic functional abilities, the greater the chances for the client to learn positive leisure-activity skills and attitudes.

The specific *need* of the client determines the *purpose* of the interaction, which in turn determines the *role* of the specialist (fig. 2–3). This directs the *content* of the program and the *nature* of the interaction, which influences *how* the program will be implemented.

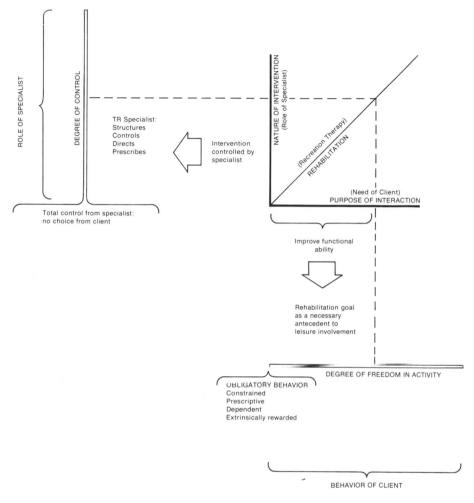

Fig. 2–2
Rehabilitation (Recreation Therapy)

role of the therapeutic recreator

The primary role of the therapeutic recreator in rehabilitation is most often that of therapist. The therapeutic recreator structures the intervention depending on the client's functional ability. The greater the client's functional needs, the greater the control imposed by the therapeutic recreator. Activities and facilitation techniques may be highly structured and even prescriptive, as in the case of Sam Spacey. Other clients' rehabilitation needs may require far less structure and control.

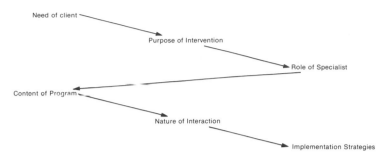

Need of client

Purpose of Intervention

Role of Specialist

Content of Program

Nature of Interaction

Implementation Strategies

Fig. 2–3
Implementation Strategies

Consider the emotionally disturbed child who is allowed to select any recreational activity, while only acting-out behavior (for example, slapping peers) is controlled with a specific facilitation technique, such as behavior modification, life-space interviewing, or reality therapy. The main concern initially may not be with learning new leisure skills, but rather with learning appropriate social behavior with peers. The controlling role of the therapeutic recreator, both in the selection of activities and facilitation techniques, diminishes as the client's basic functional abilities improve.

Effective program design and evaluation depends on understanding the specific client needs and the resulting role of the specialist. While the therapeutic recreator may be considered an important member of the treatment team, the specific needs of the client are not always clearly communicated. The result is role confusion, nonspecifically planned programs, and poor, if any, evaluation. All too often, the therapeutic recreator is only told that the client has "low self-esteem" and has therefore been referred to recreation therapy. The therapeutic recreator may ask, "Am I supposed to try to change this client's behavior? Or, am I supposed to teach activities? Or, am I just supposed to involve the client in diversional recreational activities? What is my role?"

The assumption that participation in recreational activities will automatically result in increased self-esteem is as absurd as dropping a bottle of ink onto a piece of paper and expecting it to fall into the shape of the United States! The relationships, attitudes, and skills developed during recreation may indeed result in increased self-esteem. However, before we can justify the contributions of recreational participation, we must define what lack of self-esteem means for the particular client served, and then define what behaviors indicate to us that self-esteem has been improved. First identifying the basic functional behaviors that the client lacks allows us then to select and structure appropriate activities and facilitation techniques to help the client. (Later chapters detail some techniques for selecting goals and defining behavioral objectives for our clients.) Whenever the primary goal is to improve basic functional behavior, rather than to learn leisure skills and attitudes or to participate in leisure activities, the therapeutic recreator may be considered a therapist, regardless of the setting. This implies greater control. It also implies that evaluation is geared toward measuring basic functional behavior rather than leisure-skill acquisition. Specific behaviors observed during leisure activities often indicate that functional abilities are improving. The skills necessary to assess and effect positive change in basic functional behavior are primarily clinical in nature and differ somewhat from the skills used in leisure education.

leisure education as a focus of service

Some therapeutic recreation programs focus on leisure education. The State Technical Institute and Rehabilitation Center (STIRC) in Plainwell, Michigan, requires leisure education classes for students in the two-year program of vocational training. The teacher covers a variety of specific leisure skills and attitudes. The Leisure Services Department is not particularly concerned with teaching how to improve basic functional abilities, such as increasing range of motion, increasing attention span, and improving communication skills. Many programs do not focus on leisure education, although a vital part of the services offered have to do with specific leisure skills and attitudes. When the focus of service is for clients to acquire leisure skills and attitudes, which are measured, the service is called *leisure education* (fig. 2–4).

When the behavior to be learned is no longer defined as a basic functional skill, attention can then turn toward teaching leisure skills and attitudes. After intensive treatment, Sam Spacey consistently initiates conversation and voluntarily participates in his treatment program; he is now ready to learn new leisure skills and attitudes. Over a short period of time, he is introduced to a variety of new leisure activities and expresses a real interest in learning to play tennis. The therapeutic recreator then provides the instruction, training, and practice opportunities necessary for Sam to learn the basic skills of tennis. In time, Sam will probably acquire the level of ability necessary for him to enjoy playing tennis with new friends.

The role of the therapeutic recreator has significantly changed. She or he no longer acts as a therapist but rather as a teacher and counselor. Sam is counseled concerning the appropriate use of his leisure time and is encouraged to visit the facilities provided by the recreation department or to join a tennis club. Through his recreative experiences, Sam is encouraged to talk about his feelings and any problems he might

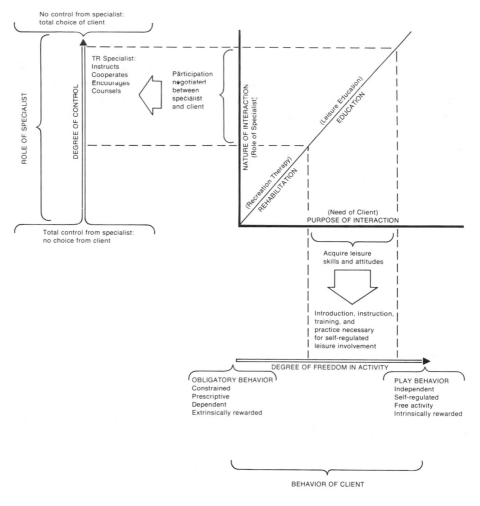

Fig. 2–4
Education (Leisure Education)

be having. Using various facilitation techniques, the therapeutic recreator may help Sam become aware of the problems connected with his past leisure participation and attitudes, and assist him in developing new leisure skills and attitudes. This process is called *leisure counseling* and generally falls under the domain of leisure education. (Later chapters deal with the techniques of leisure counseling.)

The interaction between the therapeutic recreator and the client becomes a cooperative effort. What was once perhaps a dependent relationship takes on the dimension of mature sharing. As the client learns to take responsibility for his or her own leisure involvement, and to develop healthy leisure attitudes, the therapeutic recreator relinquishes control. It is a glad moment for the therapeutic recreator when a client assertively announces, "I no longer have time for your services. I've joined a wheelchair basketball team and I must practice three days a week!"

special recreation
as a focus of service

Many persons with permanent disabilities have developed mature leisure attitudes and skills and are no longer personally handicapped by their disabilities. That is to say, they have developed adaptive skills that allow them to enjoy meaningful, self-regulated leisure activities. The greatest handicap they confront may be the social barriers that prevent them from enjoying their leisure, including inaccessible facilities, the absence of specialized and/or adapted programs, inaccessible transportation systems, and naïve or prejudicial attitudes that either deny or overlook the ability of disabled people to participate in leisure activities. In recent years, there have been concerted efforts to ensure the rights of special-need populations to participate in recreational activities. More and more local, state, and federal legislation mandates that recreational opportunities be made available to the disabled. Today, more than at any other time in history, disabled individuals have the opportunity to enjoy cultural arts facilities, state and national parks, and commercial recreational facilities. Community recreation programs are beginning to realize the importance of providing services to all people, including disabled ones. When specialized programs provide leisure opportunities for special populations, the focus of service is called *recreation for special populations* or *special recreation* (fig. 2–5).

The primary function of service can shift from teaching leisure skills and attitudes to providing opportunities for special populations to engage in self-directed leisure. John had both legs amputated as a result of an automobile accident. After six months of rehabilitation, John attended a state vocational rehabilitation school to learn to be a draftsman. During his two and one-half years of physical and vocational rehabilitation, he became interested in several leisure activities, including wheelchair sports and photography. It can be hoped that the city in which John will work will have recreational programs to meet his needs. Because John will not be able to participate in many sports events with able-bodied individuals, he will need special or adapted recreation programs, such as wheelchair basketball, archery, and track. However, John can join photography classes attended by able-bodied persons, provided the facility is accessible to him.

21

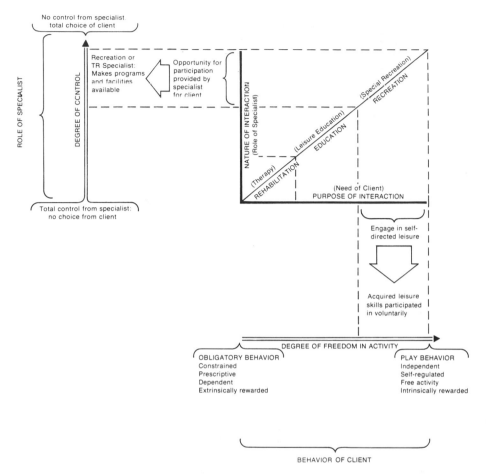

Fig. 2–5
Recreation (Special Recreation)

Not all persons with disabilities need specialized programs. Facilitating opportunities for leisure may only require that a building or area be made accessible, such as for those who are blind or in wheelchairs. Other simple provisions may allow some disabled persons to enjoy the same recreational activities as the able bodied, for example, providing a person who can sign for the deaf.

Other persons, for a variety of reasons, may not be able to participate in on-going community programs and may require sheltered experiences or specialized programs. Such would be the case for John if he is to continue to play wheelchair sports. Most often, low-functioning retarded individuals also need specialized recreation programs. Likewise, those who live in residential settings—long-term health-care facilities, sheltered-care facilities, and state institutions—often need specialized programs. Regardless of the setting, all persons who are capable of participating in intrinsically rewarding, self-regulated leisure activities deserve the opportunity to do so.

When the service is directed toward providing recreational opportunities, the therapeutic recreator's role shifts from a therapist or educator to a recreator for special populations. The specialist is responsible for making programs and facilities available to special populations. The program is no longer primarily concerned with improving basic functional abilities or acquiring new leisure skills and attitudes. Program evaluation is based on whether or not the clients are receiving adequate opportunities for the expression of leisure interests. Rather than attempting to change behavior through the therapy or education, the specialist is concerned with maintaining behavior and providing opportunities for increased leisure involvement. The therapeutic recreator working in special recreation programs is no longer specifically attempting to control behavior. He or she is, instead, mostly interested in controlling the variables that may prohibit the provision of programs—budget, public attitudes, facility accessibility, transportation, etc.

overall implications for program evaluation

Even though all therapeutic recreation services must be concerned with such problems as budget, public attitudes, and accessibility, evaluation concerns vary depending on the focus of service. If the focus of service is rehabilitation, the primary evaluation concern is whether or not the client has acquired the basic functional skills that the therapeutic recreation services have addressed. Variables that influence adequate services may indeed include such administrative issues as budget, facilities, staff, and techniques used. However, evaluation basically measures the client's basic functional ability.

When the service is primarily leisure education, the main evaluation concern is whether or not the client has acquired new leisure skills and attitudes. Again, a variety of questions may need to be answered regarding adequate budgeting, staff, and procedures. But they are asked with one concern in mind, "Did the client acquire the expected leisure skills and attitudes?"

When recreation is the focus of service, the evaluation should determine whether or not programs are adequate and accessible to meet the needs and interests of clients. At this level of program evaluation, questions such as these may be asked:

1. Has the number of participants increased?
2. Has the number of successful programs increased?
3. Is a larger number of interests being met?
4. Has public support improved, as indicated by increased budget, more volunteers, etc.?
5. Are there adequate facilities in terms of numbers and condition?
6. Do participants express satisfaction with the programs?

Evaluation is based on the provision of leisure opportunities rather than on attempting to measure specific, individual behavior changes. (Techniques for individual, group, and total program evaluation are detailed in later chapters.)

implications for program planning

Programs are designed to meet the client needs. If a client needs to increase basic functional abilities, then the program is designed specifically for rehabilitation. If the client needs to learn new leisure skills and attitudes, then a leisure education program is designed and may include leisure counseling. If the client needs to have the opportunity to express acquired leisure skills, then a special recreation program is designed for this purpose.

Most therapeutic recreation agencies focus on more than one of the three domains of rehabilitation, education, and recreation. For example, many residential facilities focus on all three domains of service. Chronic patients who lack basic functional skills may be worked with on an individual or small-group basis, where the focus may be on "orienting the individuals to reality" or "assisting them to take turns in a group." Other clients who have achieved a high level of basic-skill functioning may be taught new leisure skills and attitudes through activity classes and leisure counseling groups. Additionally, recreational events are planned in which the clients may participate volitionally.

Likewise, most community special recreation programs are involved in both leisure education and the provision of recreation services. A good example is the day camp programs for mentally retarded and physically handicapped children, which teach leisure skills through various classes, such as swimming, and stage recreational events, such as family swims.

Generally therapeutic recreation services in community mental health settings focus on rehabilitation and leisure education. Once the clients have developed basic functional abilities, an attempt is made to expose them to new leisure skills and introduce them to existing community recreation programs and facilities.

Sometimes clients participate in the same leisure activity program but for different reasons. One client may participate in a ceramics class to "increase attention span" or "increase a tolerance of authority figures," while another may participate to "learn a new leisure skill." This is often the case in short-term treatment programs, such as an in-patient psychiatric unit at a general hospital. When this is the case, the activity program should at least be evaluated for its effectiveness (1) in changing basic functional behaviors, and (2) in teaching new leisure skills and attitudes.

In some settings, programs that are designed to be recreational (picnics, dances, socials) provide excellent laboratories in which to observe the behavior of clients who lack basic functional abilities. Weekly dances may be planned for the teenage unit of a mental retardation facility. For many of the teenagers, the dance provides a place to try out newly learned dance steps. For others, it is an experience in learning to ask others to dance or trying new dance steps. For still others, the event may provide a setting in which to practice coping with past problematic behaviors, such as fighting with others and public masturbation. In such cases, the therapeutic recreator must observe the interactions of different individuals for different reasons. He or she may want to evaluate the effectiveness of the dance program as a recreational event. The progress of the clients in other rehabilitation and education programs may be evaluated as well, as demonstrated by their behavior at the dance.

Effective program planning and evaluation requires that the therapeutic recreator understand the individual needs of the clients and their related roles in working with the clients. Since the therapeutic recreator may at times be required to function in more than one role, she or he should be aware of how changing roles affect the processes of program planning and evaluation.

summary

The ultimate goal of all therapeutic recreation services is to enable disabled and obviously health-impaired individuals to make self-directed and personally satisfying choices about their leisure experiences. However, the processes involved in bringing some individuals to the point of being able to choose and participate in meaningful leisure activities can be tremendously complex.

When a client enters the therapeutic recreation service model he or she may receive therapy or participate in educational or recreation programs (fig. 2–1). An individual's personal adjustment to emotional and/or physical impairment greatly affects the degree of freedom the client is given for choosing and participating in meaningful leisure activities. A psychotic individual might be unable to choose his or her own leisure experiences and would begin the journey toward self-directed leisure involvement by first having an activity prescribed in the rehabilitation (therapy) domain for the purposes of assisting the client to focus on reality and to relate to others. As clients are better able to relate realistically, it becomes possible for them to begin learning new leisure skills and attitudes. As the individual learns new leisure skills and attitudes, the need for structure in activity involvement diminishes and the client may need only encouragement, assistance, or counsel. Having acquired leisure skills and attitudes through rehabilitation and education processes, the client may only need available resources with which to express leisure needs.

In rehabilitation and education, the therapeutic recreator has the task of using the goal of leisure involvement (i.e., a specific activity) as an end of its own. For example, creative movement, often considered a high form of leisure expression, may first be used by a therapeutic recreator in a treatment setting to increase muscular coordination or communication skills, so that eventually the client may develop the emotional and physical control necessary to choose satisfying leisure activities (which might be creative dance!).

The therapuetic recreator must be capable of identifying clients' needs and of helping them develop basic functional skills. By coping with individuals and their disabilities through masterful manipulation of the clients' remaining abilities, along with various activity tools and facilitation techniques, the therapeutic recreator attempts to promote, first of all, the clients' adaptation to, or the amelioration of, problematic behaviors and conditions. The therapeutic recreator then seeks, through leisure education, to promote growth toward meaningful, self-directed leisure choices.

The therapeutic recreator is a therapist, an educator, and a recreator. The predominant role will depend on the needs of the clients being served. Students enrolled in a therapeutic recreation curriculum may never have a simple answer to the questions, "Therapeutic recreation? What is that? What do you do?" However, by better understanding the implications of the needs represented by various special populations to the functional roles of therapeutic recreators, students need no longer feel frustrated or confused. Additionally, a clearer understanding of our clients' needs and our roles as therapeutic recreators may facilitate more effective program planning and evaluation. Our roles as therapeutic recreators may differ according to the setting in which we work. However, we all are working in different ways toward the same end: the acquisition of independent, meaningful leisure functioning for our clients.

----------------------- *note* -----------------------

[1] Statement formulated at Ninth Southern Region Institute of Therapeutic Recreation, University of North Carolina, 1969, in Richard Kraus, *Therapeutic Recreation Service: Principles and Practices* (Philadelphia, Pa.: W. B. Saunders Company, 1973), p. 3.

----------- *suggested references* -----------

AVEDON, E. M., "A Critical Analysis of the National Therapeutic Recreation Society Position Statement" (paper presented at a special seminar, Indiana State University, May 21, 1970).

———, *Therapeutic Recreation Service: An Applied Behavioral Approach.* Englewood Cliffs, N.J.: Prentice-Hall, Inc., 1974.

BALL, E. L., "The Meaning of Therapeutic Recreation," *Therapeutic Recreation Journal*, 4, no. 1 (1970), 17–18.

BOYD, W., AND F. HARNETT, "Normalization and Its Implications for Recreation Services," *Leisurability*, 2, no. 1 (January 1975), 22.

CLIFF, J. E., "Family Recreational Therapy: A New Treatment Technique," *Therapeutic Recreation Journal*, 6, no. 1 (1972), 25–27, 36.

COMPTON, D. M., "A Linear Approach for Delivering Individualized Therapeutic Recreation Service," *Journal of Physical Education and Recreation*, January 1976, pp. 27–28.

COX, C. L., AND U. DOBBINS, "Before the Merger: The National Association of Recreational Therapists (1953–1967)," *Therapeutic Recreation Journal*, 4, no. 1 (1970), 3–8.

FRYE, V., AND M. PETERS, *Therapeutic Recreation: Its Theory, Philosophy, and Practice.* Harrisburg, Pa.: Stackpole Books, 1972.

GUNN, S. L., *Basic Terminology for Therapeutic Recreation and Other Action Therapies.* Champaign, Ill.: Stipes Publishing Company, 1975.

KRAUS, R., *Therapeutic Recreation Service: Principles and Practices.* Philadelphia, Pa.: W. B. Saunders Company, 1973.

LINDLEY, D., "Problems of Integrating Therapeutic Recreation Programs into the Community," *Therapeutic Recreation Journal*, 6, no. 1 (1972), 8.

MARTIN, F. W., "Therapeutic Recreation Service: A Philosophic Overview," *Leisurability*, 1, no. 1 (January 1974), 22.

McDowell, C. F., "Emerging Leisure Counseling Concepts and Orientation," *Leisurability*, 2, no. 4 (October 1975), 19–26.

Nesbitt, J. A., "Therapeutic Recreation Service: State of the Art, 1971," in *Therapeutic Recreation Annual*, ed. L. L. Neal, 8 (1972), 1–7.

O'Morrow, G. S., *Therapeutic Recreation: A Helping Profession*. Reston, Va.: Reston Publishing Company, Inc., 1976.

Pomeroy, J., "The Handicapped Are Out of Hiding: Implication for Community Recreation," *Therapeutic Recreation Journal*, 8, no. 3, (1974), 120.

Robb, G., "A New Dimension in Treatment: Therapeutic Recreation for the Emotionally Disturbed," *Therapeutic Recreation Journal*, 4, no. 1 (1970), 13–14.

Rusalem, H., "An Alternative to the Therapeutic Model in Therapeutic Recreation," *Therapeutic Recreation Journal*, 7, no. 1 (1973), 8–15.

Spinak, J., "Normalization and Recreation for the Disabled," *Leisurability*, 2, no. 2 (April 1975), 31.

Stracke, D., "The Role of the Therapeutic Recreator in Relation to the Community Recreator," *Therapeutic Recreation Journal*, 3, no. 1(1969), 29.

Woods, M., "Integration of the Handicapped into Community Recreation Centers," *Therapeutic Recreation Journal*, 5, no. 3 (1971), 108.

a biopsychosocial approach to therapeutic recreation

PURPOSE: To present a comprehensive approach in which the therapeutic recreator is free to treat and/or teach supportively the total person. The theory, assumptions, and operating principles of a biopsychosocial approach are discussed. Two other human service approaches are presented for contrast and comparison.

Before discussing specific principles of program design, it is important to establish a common theoretical base for programming in therapeutic recreation. Traditionally therapeutic recreation services have been housed within the medical model and have rendered support services in the treatment process. The term *model* refers to "the typical way in which a profession or discipline studies and organizes data and devises action plans relative to its domain of concern."[1] Therapeutic recreators have long purported to be concerned with the *total person*. However, the two major models under which therapeutic recreation services are delivered are restrictive: the medical model focuses on illness, the health model ignores it. Both discount an aspect of the total person.

therapeutic recreation within the medical model

Within the medical model, which is still widely used in clinical settings, information is structured within the framework of disease, illness, diagnosis, prognosis, and treatment. The basic assumption of the medical model is that all persons have a right to biological life. That which impairs normal life functioning is considered an illness or a disease, and "treatment is directed at just the disease rather than the whole person."[2] Treatment by definition is the "process of eliminating or minimizing the cause of a disease process or the resulting pathology."[3] Regardless of the setting in which the therapeutic recreator works, the ultimate goal of services is to maximize meaningful, independent leisure functioning. Therefore, it is naïve to assume that the main concerns of the therapeutic recreator are disease origins and pathology. Those persons working within the confines of the medical model may at times be hard pressed to justify socializing activities under any title other than diversional. Services within the medical model are prescriptive and directed toward the amelioration of specific disease symptoms. Often the psychosocial aspects of functioning are overlooked. Disease-oriented models also often do not take into account the environmental functioning of clients after the cessation of treatment. The principles governing the medical model are the diagnosis of disease and specific curative treatment. The therapeutic recreator is concerned not only with treatment but also with leisure education and independent leisure functioning, both within the institution and the community. The therapeutic recreator is concerned with the total person rather than only the presenting illness.

therapeutic recreation within the health model

The other human service model that receives support by therapeutic recreators is the health model. A health model focuses on clients' assets rather than limitations. Traditionally, therapeutic recreators have purported to be more concerned with clients' wellness than with their illness. The concept is indeed noble, but unfortunately it ignores the reality of the clients' dysfunctions. Realistic confrontation and appropriate management of dysfunction is a vital part of total care. Also, traditionally, the therapeutic recreators' limited knowledge of medical and psychiatric disabilities has rendered them subordinate to other health-related professionals. Therapeutic recreators who have knowledge and appreciation of the implications of disabilities are in a unique position to prescribe meaningful activities that support the treatment and rehabilitation process, while also educating clients for independent leisure functioning.

Both the medical model and the health model ignore aspects of the total person. Assessment is primarily limited to either the well or the ill parts of the person, and the resulting programming either focuses on remediation of dysfunction (sometimes with knowledge of the clients' assets) or on remaining assets (sometimes without knowledge of the implications of dysfunction). Neither approach views the total person systematically.

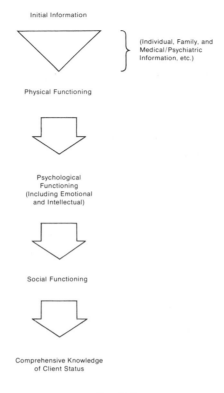

Initial Information

(Individual, Family, and
Medical/Psychiatric
Information, etc.)

Physical Functioning

Psychological
Functioning
(Including Emotional
and Intellectual)

Social Functioning

Comprehensive Knowledge
of Client Status

Fig. 3–1
Biopsychosocial Assessment

a biopsychosocial model

The biopsychosocial model described by Mosey is applicable to therapeutic recreation and does focus on the total person. "The biopsychosocial model directs attention to the body, mind, and environment of the client. It takes these three facets into consideration without any sense of wellness or sickness on the part of the client."[4] Regardless of the setting in which services are delivered, initial assessment considers the total person, including the physical functioning, psychological functioning (including emotional and intellectual), and social functioning (fig. 3–1).

Initial assessments vary depending on the purpose of the services rendered. In acute treatment facilities, sophisticated assessment instruments might be used. In other settings, interviews and brief observation periods may provide adequate assessment information. Regardless of the sophistication of the assessment, it is still directed toward systematically conceptualizing the situation of the total person. (Chapters six and seven discuss specific areas of and techniques for assessment.)

Having gathered sufficient assessment information in the biopsychosocial areas, the therapeutic recreator has a clearer picture of the immediate *status* of the client. Both the positive attributes and the needs of the client become apparent (fig. 3–2). After the presenting needs of the clients are translated into goals (including rehabilitation, education, and leisure participation), the therapeutic recreator is ready to state specific, measurable objectives that can be attained through programming (the logistics of designing individualized plans are thoroughly discussed in chapter six).

Procedurally, the delineation of individual evaluation criteria immediately follows the defining of measurable objectives. Individual evaluation criteria specify the behaviors that will be accepted as evidence that the individual's program objectives have been met. Procedures for defining evaluation criteria are also discussed in chapters seven and nine. After measurable objectives have been defined and evaluation criteria determined, individual program plans can be formulated. Specific learning or treatment activities, facilitation styles, and implementation strategies may be determined. Programs designed to facilitate the total growth and development of the individual may then be implemented and evaluated appropriately. The resulting program design capitalizes on all the information gained about the client. Strategies for designing and evaluating programs are discussed in part 2.

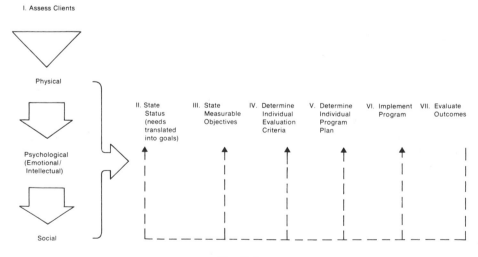

Fig. 3–2
Steps for Applying the Biopsychosocial Model

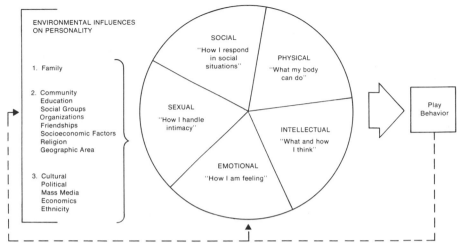

Fig. 3–3
Personality Wheel

rationale for using a biopsychosocial approach

The human personality is a complex structure that intricately weaves together physical, psychological, and social factors to produce a fully functioning individual. The well-adjusted personality is one that has developed adequate coping skills—socially, physically, intellectually, emotionally, and sexually (fig. 3–3). Positive environmental influences have rendered to the personality the skills necessary to be a productive, fully functioning individual.

No aspect of human behavior stands alone. Meaningful social behavior requires some degree of emotional stability, physical and mental involvement, and sexual awareness. Likewise, meaningful intellectual behavior relies on the existence of other aspects of the personality for support. To be lacking in any of the biopsychosocial areas affects the behavior of the total person. For example, the individual with a physical disability usually has concurrent emotional problems. She or he may often have sexual problems or be alienated socially. Adequate educational opportunities have often been unavailable. Mentally retarded persons have often remained secluded from normal social contacts due to the embarrassment or guilt of family members. They have been denied the right of sexual expression and have been isolated from normal peers in educational settings. Work opportunities for retarded individuals have been almost nonexistent, and when jobs have been available, they have usually been menial, degrading tasks for which payment is far below minimum standards. Until only recently, involvement in the creative arts was considered to be beyond the capabilities of retarded persons.

To focus attention on presenting mental or physical limitations is to ignore the residual problems or strengths that often accompany specific dysfunctioning. When play behavior is impaired, usually biopsychosocial functioning is also lacking (fig. 3–4).

When psychological dysfunctioning occurs, the job of the therapeutic recreator may well resemble the task of the frustrated person attempting to locate the one, two, or more burnt-out bulbs on a string of Christmas-tree lights. In order to improve the play behavior of the disabled person, we very often have to plug into every aspect of the individual's personality. The major disability may be obvious, but the resulting deficiencies or strengths are often obscure and require that we assess and deal with aspects of the total person.

summary

A biopsychosocial approach is uniquely valuable to the therapeutic recreator. It does not presume illness or wellness, but rather attempts to determine the strengths and deficiencies of the total person. After assessing the total person, effective programming may be designed to support well-rounded growth and development.

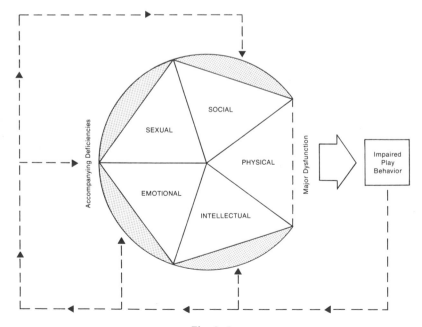

Fig. 3–4
Effects of Disability on Total Personality

notes

[1] Ann Cronin Mosey, "An Alternative: The Biopsychosocial Model," *The American Journal of Occupational Therapy*, 28, no. 3 (March 1974), 137.

[2] Gerald S. O'Morrow, *Therapeutic Recreation: A Helping Profession* (Reston, Va.: Reston Publishing Company, Inc., 1976), p. 162.

[3] Mosey, "An Alternative," p. 138.

[4] Ibid.

suggested references

ADAMS, R. C., A. W. DANIEL, AND L. RULLMAN, *Games, Sports and Exercises for the Physically Handicapped.* Philadelphia, Pa.: Lea & Febiger, 1975.

BRENNER, FERGUSON, AND SUDDARTH, *Textbook of Medical-Surgical Nursing.* N.Y.: J.B. Lippincott Company, 1970.

GRANT, H., AND R. MURRAY, *Emergency Care.* Bowie, Md.: Robert J. Brady Company, 1971.

GUNN, S. L., *Basic Terminology for Therapeutic Recreation and Other Action Therapies.* Champaign, Ill.: Stipes Publishing Company, 1975.

HOLVEY, D. N., ed., *The Merck Manual of Diagnosis and Therapy* (12th ed.) Rahway, N.J.: Merck Sharp & Dohme Research Laboratories, 1972.

KIRK, S. A., *Educating Exceptional Children.* Boston, Mass.: Houghton Mifflin Company, 1972.

KRAUS, R., *Therapeutic Recreation Service: Principles and Practices.* Philadelphia, Pa.: W. B. Saunders Company, 1972.

KRUSEN, F. H., M.D., F. J. KOTTEKE, M.D., AND P. M. ELLWOOD, JR., M.D., assoc. eds., *Handbook of Physical Medicine and Rehabilitation.* Philadelphia, Pa.: W. B. Saunders Company, 1968.

MILLER, K., *Encyclopedia and Dictionary of Medicine and Nursing.* Philadelphia, Pa.: W. B. Saunders Company, 1972.

MOSEY, A. C., "An Alternative: The Biopsychosocial Model," *The American Journal of Occupational Therapy*, 28, no. 3 (March 1974).

O'MORROW, G. S., *Therapeutic Recreation: A Helping Profession.* Reston, Va.: Reston Publishing Company, Inc., 1976.

PETERSON, C. A., AND P. CONNOLLY, *Handicapper Characteristics: A Disability Chart.* Champaign, Ill.: Office of Recreation and Park Resources, University of Illinois, 1977.

STEIN, T. A., AND H. D. SESSOMS, *Recreation and Special Populations.* Boston, Mass.: Holbrook Press, Inc., 1975.

WHITE, R. W., AND N. F. WATT, *The Abnormal Personality.* N.Y.: Ronald Press Company, 1973.

factors affecting program design and content

PURPOSE: To discuss the concepts and issues that influence progressive program content and design. Topics include social and professional attitudes toward the ill and handicapped, normalization, mainstreaming, integrated versus segregated programming, and the impact of labels on identity.

The way in which a society responds to the needs of the handicapped is a good measure of civilization itself. We are more aware today that ever before of the interdependence of human beings. We understand that whatever diminishes anyone, diminishes everyone. [1]

attitudes

A wise person once said, "When people perceived the world to be flat, they feared sailing off the edge. However, when they perceived the world to be round, exploration and discovery became possible." The basic steps in program design are relatively the same in any setting. Differences in program content and implementation strategies depend on the designer's *perceptions* of the tasks and the people served. As program designers in therapeutic recreation, our *perceptions* of the ill and handicapped often dictate the quality and quantity of our programs. The world of the handicapped is not flat; and until perceptions of, and attitudes toward, the handicapped change, progressive programming cannot occur.

The general public's attitudes and reactions toward handicapped persons are timely issues. County and state governments are becoming markedly less inclined to incarcerate the handicapped in institutions. And state and federal legislatures and courts are insisting that handicapped individuals be integrated into regular school classes and community programs. As therapeutic recreators, we may be able to produce highly skillful program designs. We may be instrumental in affecting legislative change that supports the human and civil rights of the handicapped. We may even have the administrative power to issue mandates regarding fair treatment of the handicapped. However, our own attitudes toward the handicapped and the attitudes of all those involved in our programs have the strongest effect on the delivery of services. In the design of our programs, we must be concerned with the attitudes of everyone involved—ourselves, staff, administrators, board members, taxpayers, and political leaders. People's ability to cope is limited by their fear of the unknown, and helping others understand their fear of the handicapped may often precede successful programming.

Historically, this fear of the unknown has crippled well-intended efforts to help ill and handicapped persons. Edwin Martin states,

> *In Augustan England, it was fashionable for presumably sane people to go to "Bedlam" Hospital and pay a keeper to tease the "lunatics" for their amusement. That kind of flagrant torture, that was characteristic of the age of bear-baiting, is not much condoned today; freak shows and public spectacles are dying out. Most abuses of the handicapped today take place on more subtle levels that have not changed much in the last three hundred years.*[2]

Although not terribly prolific, some research has emerged that studies public attitudes toward the handicapped and self-concepts of handicapped persons. German psychologists Gerd Jansen and Otto Esser conducted a survey of society's reactions to visible deformities.[3] Many respondents reacted to the sight of deformity with physically evident revulsion—although with increasing age, obvious rejection tended to be replaced by pity. Very few respondents wanted to become friends with a handicapped person and even fewer wanted to marry or adopt one. Almost 90 percent of the people interviewed were unsure about how to approach a handicapped person and had little appreciation of whether he or she might want help, and, if so, what kind of help.

Often the deepest degree of understanding and appreciation people exhibit toward handicapped people is simply by not staring or by contributing to a charity drive for the disabled. If the handicapped individual is ever to have an equal opportunity for "life, liberty, and the pursuit of happiness," and more specifically for leisurely pursuits, a massive effort must be made to acquaint all leisure specialists and the general public with the needs and conditions of the ill and handicapped. By relating to what handicapped people do not have, rather than to what they do have, by regarding them as incapable of caring about basic rights for themselves, by feeling that they are served out of kindness rather than obligation, society compounds the handicapped person's emotional, intellectual, and economic problems.[4]

attitudinal blocks

As leaders and facilitators of therapeutic recreation programs, we control the ability to have quality programs. We are also professionally responsible to be advocates for the handicapped. Our attitudes toward the handicapped directly affect our effectiveness as leaders and advocates. Dr. John Nesbitt presents these syndromes as familiar attitudinal blocks to quality leisure programming for the handicapped:

The Futility Syndrome. *"What can I do to help? The situation is impossible."* *Laws. Money. Barriers.*

The Leprosy Syndrome. *"If I touch them, I may get it. These conditions, like cerebral palsy, are contagious."*

The Deuteronomic Syndrome. *"They must have done something wrong. God means for them to be punished. If they repent, they will get well." This attitude is classical Deuteronomic Code right out of the Old Testament, which says in essence, "Do good and ye will be blessed; sin, and God will punish you." There are many people whose "gut-level" thinking and feeling follow this line, and for these people, attitudes make them negative facilitators.*

The Punishment Syndrome. *"They are not in jail to be coddled and play games; they're there to be punished." This kind of thinking was inherent in the Nixon/ Agnew/Mitchell "law-and-order" platform. [Karl] Menniger wrote about it in the book* Crime of Punishment.[5]

The Hypocrisy Syndrome. *"We serve the handicapped; that doesn't mean that we have to employ them." This syndrome is characteristic of some individuals and agencies in education, special education, recreation and parks, therapeutic recreation, welfare and social work, rehabilitation, etc. Count the number of handicapped employed in your agency, university, hospital.*

The Charity Syndrome. *"I gave to Cerebral Palsy but that doesn't mean that I want my daughter to marry one."*

The Civic-Pride Syndrome. *"Why sure I am concerned about the handicapped. Our local chapter of the Royal Order of Roosters gives a Christmas party at the rehabilitation center every year." This syndrome is especially pernicious because well-intended people are assisted in deluding themselves into thinking about how they can solve the horrendous problems of disease, disability, poverty, inequality, ignorance, and violence. There is no room for Pollyanna in the fight against prejudice.*

The Me-Me-Me Syndrome. *The handicapped person speaks, "I am here at this meeting with my problem. I want it solved this minute. I refuse to do the staff work, the surveying, or joining with other handicapped persons in order to give really sound advice and guidance to civic-minded citizens or professionals." The role of consumer spokesman is no less demanding than any other professional role.*

The Defense Syndrome. *"I don't see what you recreation-for-handicapped people are squawking about; we are meeting our social and professional obligation by running a once-a-month social night for the mentally retarded and 25 kids show up pretty regular."* Yes, 25 out of a population of maybe 2,500 that need recreation and leisure service.

The All-Those-Others Syndrome. *"I simply can't divert money, personnel, and resources away from the 500,000 able-bodied that I serve to the 500 severely handicapped that I don't serve. I have all those others to worry about and I can't be concerned with a handful of handicapped."*

The Lack-of-Training Syndrome. *"I can't take handicapped people into my program. I don't have the trained staff to handle epileptic fits, convulsions, slobbering, soiled-shitty clothing, poor speech."*

The Smooth-Waters Syndrome. *"I can't have those people in my center [program] because the other participants, the regular people, their parents, the staff, the food suppliers, the janitors, the W.C.T.U.—they would all just quit my program. I can't make waves or the whole thing will just come down on me. We don't want that, do we?"*[6]

People working with the ill and handicapped sometimes also perceive clients in negative ways. The following syndromes are traps to therapeutic encounters in recreation programs for the handicapped:

- **The Bless-Their-Hearts, Ain't-It-Awful Syndrome.** "Since life has been so good to me, I feel obligated to help those poor souls who are less fortunate than I." This syndrome often results in the therapeutic recreator being "hooked" by sob stories, thus becoming extremely vulnerable to manipulation.

- **The Messiah Syndrome.** "My mission in life is to save the suffering masses from their anguish and torment. Let all of the ill and handicapped come to me for help, 24 hours a day, 7 days a week. I'm always loving, kind, and available." Needless to say, this syndrome can be destructive, since energies are quickly depleted and the client never has the opportunity to realize the value of limits being imposed. Modeling "ever-present availability" also subtly asks the client and other staff members to ignore their individual needs for personal time and space.

- **The Great-Guru Syndrome.** "You're always the patient and I'm always the therapist. Your every word and action must be analyzed for their underlying meanings." Obviously, no one is in constant need of therapeutic scrutiny. There is a time to be analytical and a time to simply be!

- **The I-Need-a-Stroke-but-I-Ain't-Tellin' Syndrome.** "Oh, let me help you with that. There's no use straining yourself. You probably need help and I don't mind your being dependent on me." The tendency to be overly helpful, thus precipitating unnecessary dependency, most often occurs when the helper is feeling unloved or unneeded in personal relationships, and thus finds comfort in being needed by clients. Very simply stated, the helper needs a hug and by hugging the client she or he rips off the needed hug (or stroke). The irony is that dependency most often results in hostility.

The Rescuer Syndrome. "I'm guessing that you either need help or a spokesperson, so I'll jump in and help you before you even ask." The person who is constantly rescuing others very often gets blamed for any failure that the client experiences, thus becoming the victim.

The Bubble-Gum-Kid Syndrome. "Life is always bouncy and fun. Everything is wonderful with me. I'm *so* together!" The tendency to feel that we must always portray the happy-go-lucky, rah-rah recreator is not only dishonest, but extremely intimidating to those around us. Even leaders have down days and quiet moments. A bit of personal humanness is therapeutic.

The Tough-Guy Syndrome. "Quit your bellyaching and get moving. I don't care what your disability is. You can do all things well and independently." A firm approach is necessary with many clients, but no one should be expected always to be tough and determined. Occasional gentle and understanding moments are necessary to overcome frustration and discouragement.

Obviously, interpersonal relationships are never totally devoid of preconceived perceptions and assumptions. However, we are becoming acutely aware that the tendency to pigeonhole the ill and handicapped into specific categories with neatly defined problems, weaknesses, and labels is contrary to the emerging emphasis on individuality. We would, however, be remiss in ignoring potential pitfalls in facilitating the therapeutic process. Dennis Edwards, MSW and therapeutic recreator, carefully purports that it may be useful to be aware of these assumptions when confronting clients in therapeutic recreation programs:

Assumptions About the Client. Clients, because of physical or mental dysfunction or stress

1. May risk developing tertiary dysfunctions.
2. May underestimate their potential for leisure involvement.
3. May be unaware of the skills they possess or can develop.
4. May develop a high degree of dependence on others for decision making.
5. May abuse, neglect, or misunderstand the potential of free time as leisure.
6. May forget to use, or fail to remember how to use, previously acquired motor, intellectual, or social skills.
7. May generate self protective ego defenses to relieve anxiety produced by the trauma of loss of function, reduction of capabilities, and the

effect of institutional living on self-assertive and responsible patterns of behavior.

8. May not know how or when to ask for help.
9. Other, as indicated by the unique personality of the client.

Assumptions Clients Make About Us. By virtue of the predetermined therapeutic relationship, clients may assume that

1. The therapeutic recreator is a model of social norms.
2. As therapeutic recreators, we are in touch with reality.
3. Our actions are transmissions of socially accepted behavior and are, therefore, legitimate to model.
4. Our statements are reflective of society and they can expect to hear the same statements outside the therapeutic environment.
5. We are like doctors and nurses and know what we are doing.

Assumptions Clients Make About Any "Authority" Figure. By virtue of the fact that, as therapeutic recreators, we represent authority, clients may make the following assumptions about us:

1. We are "in charge" of the clients and hold some power over their lives.
2. We are not to be trusted until we earn that trust through a number of methods, i.e., continual support, follow through on promises, etc.
3. We are responsible to the system and we, therefore, hold the system or agency above the clients in importance.
4. We have ulterior motives to our every action.
5. We look at clients as statistics rather than people.
6. Working with clients is simply a job responsibility and represents no real emotional investment.
7. They will never get to see us again once they leave the therapeutic environment.
8. We are something to be tolerated.[7]

As therapeutic recreators and leaders it is our responsibility constantly to be aware of preconceived assumptions and attitudes. Procedures for designing programs for the ill and handicapped are relatively simple compared to the Promethean task of changing the attitudes that many still hold about persons who are different. The efficacy of our programs depends largely on our ability to change false attitudes about the people we serve.

mainstreaming

The term *mainstreaming* was first used in public education. "On November 3, Lyndon Johnson signed the Education Amendments of 1966 and the first version of the Education of the Handicapped Act became law as a new Title VI of the Elementary and Secondary Education Act. The new title authorized a program of grants to the states to 'initiate, expand, and improve' educational programs for handicapped children, and created the Bureau of Education for the Handicapped and the National Advisory Committee on Handicapped Children."[8] This gave accelerated impetus to the creation of special programs and special classes for the handicapped in public education. Federally supported special education was born. Separate but equal education programs were supposed to exist for all handicapped youths. In the late '60s and '70s some educators began to question the validity of separate but equal programs, contending that separate programs were inherently unequal. Rather than seeing handicapped children as a small, discrete population with unique learning problems, they began to see the learning needs of all children falling along a continuum of severity, only requiring special intervention at certain times for specific purposes.[9] The mainstreaming concept was introduced as a means of integrating the handicapped child back into as many normal school activities as possible. The concept provides the handicapped child with the least restrictive environment for learning.

Most handicapped persons do not live, work, or play exclusively with other handicapped people. They are an important part of our society and to treat them separately is to deny them the opportunity to join in and enjoy facilities and programs equally. In fact, it is to deny them the opportunity to be a part of the mainstream of Life.

The trend toward mainstreaming now extends far beyond the classroom and is considered as both a process and a goal.[10] The *process* is that of selecting methods of integrating people into programs that are as close to the typical way of doing things as possible. The *goal* has typically been geared toward enabling the handicapped person to live and appear in a way that distinguishes him or her as little as possible from other people. Mainstreaming does not mean that handicapped persons will become normal, but rather that they will be given every opportunity to fit into society to the greatest extent possible and that society will be more accepting of them. Mainstreaming implies that the handicapped individual has a need to be moved as closely as possible to the norm. However, for mainstreaming to be truly effective, nonhandicapped people must be educated about the needs of the handicapped, which tends simultaneously to give them some empathy with the handicapped.

The most important mainstreaming principle is *integration* into regular programs—both physically and socially. For handicapped people to achieve and maintain normative behaviors, appearances, and interpretations and for them to be accepted by society, maximum integration into the cultural mainstream is essential. This is achieved in the field of recreation only when *all* programs and facilities are accessible to the handicapped and totally staffed by persons with some basic knowledge about the needs of persons with handicapping conditions.

Mainstreaming favors increasing the positive interaction between the handicapped and nonhandicapped. The advantages are obvious. The handicapped individual can model positive behavior from the nonhandicapped, while learning to overcome her or his fears of being different. The nonhandicapped person also overcomes his or her fear of the unknown, while losing false assumptions.

The out-of-sight, out-of-mind syndrome does little to precipitate growth and understanding by either the handicapped or the nonhandicapped. Edwin Martin states:

> *Our experience with segregated societal institutions has shown them to be among our most cruel and dehumanizing activities. . . . We have created institutions supposedly for the good of those to be incarcerated or, at least, to provide them with humane treatment. In each, however, there has been a classic pattern of neglect, isolation, rejection, and ultimate dehumanization of the persons on whose behalf society was supposedly acting; and in each there has been further harm done to the individual than if we had left him or her where they were.*[11]

Whenever possible the handicapped should be integrated or mainstreamed into nonhandicapped recreation programs. The individual with paraplegia would obviously be unable to compete on a basketball team for the nonhandicapped and may, therefore, only be able to play on a wheelchair basketball team. However, there is no reason why such a person could not fish, swim, shoot archery, or participate in the creative arts with the nonhandicapped. Integrated programming, when possible, not only deepens the understanding between handicapped and nonhandicapped but also is usually financially expendient, relative to maximum utilization of staff and facilities.

normalization

Little difference exists between the concepts of mainstreaming and normalization. In fact, the terms are most often used synonymously, with little consideration given to the subtle differences. Mainstreaming is the American term for the principle of integration, while normalization is the European term for a similar principle. While mainstreaming implies both normative lifestyles and integration with nonhandicapped populations, normalization (at least in Scandinavian countries) does not always imply integration. Mainstreaming is also most often associated with special education in the United States, while normalization is broader in

43

scope. In 1972, Dr. Wolf Wolfensberger defined the normalization principle as "the utilization of means which are as culturally normative as possible, in order to establish and/or maintain interpretations, personal behaviors and characteristics which are as culturally normative as possible."[12]

Normalization means the total integration of the handicapped person into every facet of life. Walter Boyd and Frances Hartnett explain:

> The most important implication . . . of the principle of normalization is that of integration—both physical and social. That is, in order to achieve and maintain normative behaviors, appearances, and interpretations of handicapped people, and ultimately their acceptance by society, maximal integration into the Canadian cultural mainstream is essential. Integration is achieved only when the handicapped citizen lives in ordinary community housing, communicates and interacts with other citizens in typical, normative ways, and is able to use typical community resources—recreational, social, occupational, medical, financial, etc.[13]

Concerning the mentally retarded individual, Jerry Spinak states:

> Within normalization there is the belief that the retarded person (as any human being), has the right to dignity in taking risks, choosing with whom to associate, and experiencing choice in leisure time activities, among countless other possibilities. As a basis for action, normalization demands for mentally retarded citizens a life experience which coincides as much as possible with the mainstream of society![14]

Perhaps the most enlightening view of normalization is presented by Jean Edwards in her review of experiences in Scandinavian countries:

> The normalization principle underlies demands for standards, facilities, and programs for the handicapped . . . . Normalization affirms that the retarded and handicapped individual is a human being and citizen as well as a developmental and adaptive organism.
> . . . Very simply, Concept Normalization is making available to the handicapped person, young and old, the same patterns and conditions of everday life that you and I experience. This principle is applied to all handicapped whether mildly or profoundly retarded, physically handicapped or multiply handicapped. It affirms the right of all human beings to live in and experience patterns and conditions of everyday life which are as close as possible to the norms and patterns of the mainstream of society.[15]

Edwards goes on to discuss six essential areas of normalization:

> **1.** A normal daily rhythm must allow for normal, everyday functions, i.e., getting up, dressing, eating, sleeping, going places, having personal respon-

sibilities, playing, being alone, etc. These activities should be paced by the individual rather than staff or agency schedules.

2. Normal routines must allow the handicapped person to be mobile in performing normalizing activities so that eating, playing, working, and sleeping do not all occur in the same space. Handicapped person's routine must vary, and activities must take place as much as possible within the context of the regular routine of society.

3. The rhythm of the year must also be normal. Handicapped persons need to look forward to holiday functions, family get-togethers, hikes, picnics, and special events, just as we all do. Every day of every year must not be the same.

4. Handicapped individuals need the normal developmental experiences of the life cycle, including childhood games (as children), teenage activities (as teenagers), and adult activities (as adults) regardless of mental age. All too often retarded adults continue to be called "boys and girls" and are denied participation in adult activities, i.e., dating, dancing, etc. Likewise, the elderly handicapped should be allowed to live in familiar surroundings with friends and family.

5. Sexual segregation need not exist for handicapped persons. Appropriate social-sexual behavior is only taught by allowing the different sexes to get to know and understand each other.

6. Economic standards should be normal, including payment for work, living environments, allowances, and pensions. [16]

All in all, normalization means living with, playing with, working with, and relating to handicapped individuals just as normally as with other human beings. For some, adaptations and special considerations may be necessary. But for most, segregated programs and facilities tend to enhance rather than overcome disabilities.

integrated versus segregated programs

The concepts of mainstreaming and normalization challenge the separate but equal philosophy that still exists among recreation programmers and facility designers. Mainstreaming and normalization do not mean providing normative experiences created for the handicapped apart from actual, normal ones. The concepts insist on the integration of handicapped and normal populations in all kinds of programs and situations. Rather than having specialized agencies deliver specialized programs to special-interest groups, public and private agencies are asked to provide leisure services for all citizens, whether or not they are handicapped. This does not negate the need for some specialized staff, techniques, or equipment that can be utilized within the framework of total services. It does, however, ask that separate facilities and programs be reduced to a minimum. Some severely handicapped persons will obviously continue to need some specialized services (such as the severely and profoundly retarded). However, most handicapped people do not live and work exclusively with other handicapped people, and there are very many leisure activities that can be enjoyed by handicapped and nonhandicapped simultaneously.

Integrated recreation programming introduces a cost factor for some agencies. All buildings and facilities need to be made accessible for the physically handicapped. The cost of ramps, ground-level entrances, widened doorways, handrails, lowered drinking fountains, hard-top paths and walkways, and directional cues (for the blind) add additional financial burdens to programming budgets. However, these costs are offset by the advantages of integrated programming. Facilities can be shared without the need for duplication. Specialized staff members can work with other staff, teaching them the specific skills necessary to work with handicapped participants, thus reducing the need for two or more separate staffs. Social integration is achieved and special-interest and nonhandicapped groups learn to understand, accept, and help each other. In participating with nonhandicapped persons, handicapped persons are exposed to many more role models than are available in specialized programs. Simultaneously, nonhandicapped persons are exposed to the reality of handicapping conditions and forced to confront and resolve the many myths associated with disability. Integrated programming does not allow the handicapped as many opportunities to avoid the reality of their conditions by escaping to the more sheltered environment of specialized, segregated programs. If handicapped people are to become part of the mainstream of life, integrated environments must exist that are free of barriers—structurally, attitudinally, and financially.

The arduous task of integrating programs to include both the handicapped and the nonhandicapped takes time and perseverance. Spinak suggests the steps shown in figure 4–1 for integrating leisure programs.[17] Each box represents a step toward increased integration and increased independent leisure functioning for handicapped persons. As the handicapped become more willing and better able to risk participation with the nonhandicapped, and as the nonhandicapped begin to appreciate and understand the needs of special groups, the need for segregated programming will diminish (not terminate). As therapeutic recreation programs improve, and handicapped persons grasp the significance of independent leisure functioning, the need for segregated programs will diminish, and integrated programs will be more in demand. The more that integration takes place, the more knowledge and appreciation we will

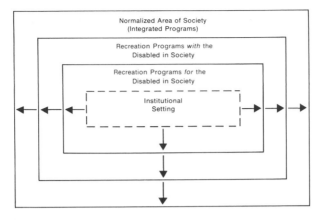

Fig. 4–1

Steps in Integrating Recreation Programs

have of the concepts of mainstreaming and normalization. As we focus more carefully on the individual's uniqueness, we will move away from grouping handicapped people together—not just away from using special facilities and devising special programs, but away from other assumptions about homogeneity that keep us from understanding and appreciating one another.

handicapped versus disabled

Throughout this text, the terms disability and handicap *are used synonymously*. In spite of recent attempts to delineate the meaning of the two terms, much disparity continues to exist. Nesbitt states:

> *Disability is the actual dysfunction or limitation caused by the disease or injury. But, the disability is a "handicap" only to the extent that a person is not able to function normally in employment, education, recreation, homemaking, and so on.*[18]

The disabled person is considered to be someone who has found ways of coping with a dysfunction, while a handicapped person is someone who is blocked from participating. This delineation has met with much disapproval by many handicapped (or is it disabled?) individuals. Perhaps the most forceful opposing argument is presented by Judy Taylor and Eric Gentile, both of whom are handicapped.[19] They want to do away with "disabled" altogether and use instead "handicapped" and "handicapper."

IMAGES, WORDS AND IDENTITY*

Disabled

Handicapped

Handicapper

DIS, N. 1. The Roman God of the Underworld, the dead, identified with the Greek God Pluto. 2. The lower world; Hades.

dis- Prefix indicating 1. negation, lack, invalidation, or deprivation; as distrust, dishonor. 2. Reversal; as disintegrate, disunite. 3. Removal or rejection; as disbar, dismiss. 4. Intensification or completion of negative action; as disable, dismember. *(Old French Des, Latin Dis-Apart, asunder.)*

disabled, Adj. Deprived of ability or power, incapacitated.

impotence, N. Without strength or power; helplessness; . . . Syn. 1. Inability, disability, impuissance, incapacity, inaptness, ineptitude, inefficiency, incompetence, disqualification. 2. Inefficacy (see uselessness), failure, helplessness, prostration, exhaustion, enervation, emasculation, castration.

HANDICAP, N. 1. A race or other competition in which difficulties are imposed on the superior contestants, or advantages given to the poorer ones, so that all have an equal chance at winning. 2. The disadvantage or advantage that is given. 3. The effects of general social or cultural stigmatizing of an individual because of certain physical or mental characteristics which are not recognized or accepted by one's society or cultures as normal, natural, or optimal aspects of humanity. *(See hinder/hindrance.)*

handicapped, Adj. 1. Operating with a handicap, as in a contest. 2. The state of being in which one experiences a social or cultural stigma or devaluation because of a physical or mental characteristic not recognized by one's culture or society as a normal, natural or optimal aspect of humanity.

HANDICAPPER, N. 1. One who determines or assigns handicaps. Usually an official who assigns handicaps to contestants, as in a tournament. 2. A person who tries to predict the winner of a horse race on the basis of past records, track conditions, etc.

Handicapper, N. 1. One who determines the degree to and manner in which one's own definable physical or mental characteristic(s) might direct life's activities. 2. One who may experience a handicap in some specific situation, but who in a specific competition or other activities operates on a par with, or superior to, one who does not experience said handicap. 3. One who rejects the stigma or inactive role in life usually associated with his/her characteristic(s).

*"Images, Words and Identity" is one of a series of articles researched and published by Eric A. Gentile and Judy K. Taylor (copyright pending), Michigan State University/ Handicapper Programs, W-402 Library Building, East Lansing, Michigan 48824.

International symbol of access for "the disabled," those who are *"confined* to a wheelchair"

Handicappers' international symbol of access for wheelchair-*users.*

Symbol of an accessible future through design balance for *all* the public—*ERGONOMICS*

Negative Terms/Phrases/Images	*Positive Terminology*
disability	characteristic (physical, mental, etc.)
defect	handicap (one does not *have* a handi-
chronic illness	cap, one *experiences* a handicap
affliction	*only in certain situations* or as re-
problem	sult of social stigma regarding
tragedy	their characteristics)
	challenge
cripple	Handicapper (only appropriate for
deaf mute	those who reject social stigma,
retard	that is, their characteristics;
victim	those who judge for themselves
	or direct their abilities)
the disabled	Handicappers
the handicapped, crippled	A generic group or class of people
the impaired, infirm, sick, ill	experiencing, but rejecting, so-
invalid, inflicted, deformed	cial stigma and unjust discrim-
the deaf and dumb	ination regarding their charac-
those living in darkness	teristics.
those suffering from . . .	
. . . something wrong with . . .	
confined to a wheelchair	wheelchair user/rider
wheelchair-bound	uses (using) a wheelchair, rides
wheelchair victim	(riding) a 'chair
blanket over legs	works or operates from a 'chair
	chairioteer
walks on crutches	uses crutches/crutch user
Tiny Tim/Tina	Tiger Toni (Tony), Terry (Terri) Ter-
passive poster-child	rific, Speedie (Speedo) "Gettin
home-bound, bed-ridden	it on"
invalid "in" a wheelchair	
The abled-bodied (ABs)	Temporarily or perceived to be able-
	bodied (TAB, PAB or currently
	regarded as AB)
Normal, regular/abnormal, special	Public (for all) transport, education,
(transportation, education, facili-	facilities, services, etc.
ties)	

Negative Terms/Phrases/Images	*Positive Terminology*
Barrier-free design/special facilities separate back-door ramps	Environmental design Ergonomics/design for ALL Equal design consideration/all grade-level exits and entrances
sidewalk, curb cuts (for bicycles)	public way, path ramps (for wheelchair users, baby carriers, seniors, etc.)
"WALK," "DON'T WALK" street crossing signals	"STOP," "GO"—"CROSS," "DON'T CROSS."—"GO," "WAIT"
"WALK IN" door or window welcome signs	"COME IN," "ENTER," "WELCOME"

Identity *is an important factor in how people relate to themselves and others. The identities associated with, or projected by, a person, individually or as a member of a culturally defined group, are to a great degree reflected, reinforced, and shaped by the language and graphics we use in daily communication. Imagery (terminology and graphics), then, is critically important to those who want to understand the basic nature of and to eliminate negative stereotypes and to build positive individual and group identities. Today many groups are struggling with this process, such as Jews, blacks, chicanos, native Americans, and women.*

To understand the implications of terminology and graphics in shaping identity we begin with an analysis of the two most frequently used generic terms, disabled *and* handicapped. *By definition the words* handicap *and* disability *are not synonymous.* Dis *is the Roman and Greek god of the lower world, the kingdom of the dead. When the Romans made* dis *into a prefix, it was to denote something rendered apart or asunder, totally negated. This information gives us some perspective about the negative nature and the social implications of the terms* disabled *and* disability. *Today* dis *as a prefix is defined and used as a simple intensive with a totally negative word-meaning: not; un; lack of; invalid; deprived; caused to be the opposite of; fail; cease; refuse to; the reverse of; the undoing of; the total absence of quality, ability, power, rank, etc.;* completely, thoroughly negated.

When dis *is placed in front of the root word* able, *the meaning of that root word is negated. To disable is to deprive of ability or power; to make useless, cripple thoroughly, to disqualify legally. Disability, likewise, is defined as inability, total lack of ability, a legal disqualification or incapacity. To have or experience a disability is to be considered* completely *crippled, unable, unfit, incapable, useless, ineffective, legally or totally incapacitated. As negative as it is to label someone as having a disability, it compounds the degradation to label that person as disabled. "A disability" may refer to the effects of a specific and total dysfunction of an organ, part, member, appendage, limb, or sector of a person's body. "Disabled," however, can have extremely negative implications about employability and personal and social worth.*

Medical and rehabilitation professionals and government agencies, such as the Social Security Administration, as well as the courts have used the word disabled as an adjective that describes individuals or groups with chronic physical conditions that render them permanently unemployable and unable to be participating, much less productive, elements of society. Lawyers stress the tragedy of physical injury in pleading for huge cash compensation for accident "victims," rather than for comprehensive treatment and retraining. The fund-raising, "tin-cup" activities and "Tiny Tim poster-child" approaches of most "goodwill" agencies and "charitable" organizations also play heavily on the "tragedy" theme without the slightest regard for the dehumanizing effect such propaganda has on society's attitudes toward those being "served." Such approaches have raised huge sums of money, but they also produce attitudes of guilt, pity, and fear and continue to reinforce the negative associations that the public has with the words crippled, and disabled, and to a lesser degree handicapped.

Today such degrading terminology and oppressive attitudes do not take into account that many individuals who experience handicaps are employable, responsible, and productive citizens with positive personal and group identities, rather than negative and medically defined identities. The value judgments implicit in negative terminology reinforce negative attitudes and behavior. Using such terminology is inappropriate for contemporary society in general and especially modern legislative and court experience wherein citizens experiencing handicaps, rather than begging for meager handouts, are securing their God-given, constitutional, and civil rights.

Current dictionaries define handicap much more positively than they do disability. Handicap is defined as a game in which forfeits are drawn from a cap or hat (hand in cap); a race or other competition in which difficulties are imposed on the superior contestant; advantages or disadvantages given to individuals so that each has an equal chance of winning; a disadvantage that makes achievement or success difficult (difficult, a hindrance but not an impossibility as it is in disabled). A characteristic that is labeled a handicap can be an advantage or disadvantage, depending on the situation. Rarely, if ever, is a handicap a disadvantage in every situation. Thus, a handicap is not assumed to be disabling. Also it should not be assumed that experiencing a handicap is the same as having or being a handicap.

The word handicapped is far less negative than the word disabled because handicapped defines a partial limitation of ability in a given situation rather than the total absence of ability in all situations assumed by the word disabled. However, handicapped does have some of the same negative or inaccurate connotations as disabled. Both terms assume an inability or limitation of ability, regardless of the situation.

A "handicapper" is traditionally defined as one who determines or assigns handicaps, who sets the odds, as in a tournament, who tries to predict the winner of a contest on the basis of past records, present conditions, etc. Handicapper is also a term that is increasingly used by persons who experience handicaps to assign to themselves the decision-making power about how their characteristics are to affect their lives. It is an attempt to provide society with the means to positively describe or refer to an individual who happens to be born with, or

51

who acquires at some point in life, a definable physical or mental characteristic that varies from the Greco-Roman obsession with the Adonis/Venus models of physical perfection.

The modern use of the term Handicapper *establishes a positive relationship between this term and human liberty, freedom and self-determination. Categorical terms should be used when such labels are appropriate –such as blind, deaf, paraplegic, and wheelchair user. The term* handicapper is the only noun in current usage that refers to the entire minority group of individuals who experience handicaps *because of the stigmas attached to particular personal characteristics. Handicapped individuals are fully able, as well as determined, to define for themselves the degree to and manner in which their particular characteristics might enhance, direct, or limit their active pursuit of happiness. This attitude is preferable to allowing a hostile physical environment or the prejudices of others to assign individuals totally dependent roles in life. Individuals who experience handicaps are in reality handicappers.* They are the only ones who should determine the direction for and extent of their creative potential and destinies! *Experiencing a handicap is not a* tragedy; *it is a challenge! The manner in which others respond to handicapped individuals' characteristics may well in fact govern the quality of their life if they ever experience a handicap. The manner in which individuals respond to that challenge will largely determine whether they are identified as conditions or persons.*

summary

Programs in therapeutic recreation will be designed and redesigned utilizing both old and new strategies. Model programs and techniques will be conceived of, tested, and revised. Articles and books on program planning and various implementation strategies will be written, marketed, and sold as guiding lights to the profession. Leaders will come and go, and philosophies will change. However, in the final analysis, effective, growth-producing programs will not depend on the strategies, but rather on the attitudes and philosophies held by those who work directly or indirectly with handicapped populations and by society at large. A program philosophy or program design is no better than the values, beliefs, and attitudes each of us hold. If we persist in working for rather than with special populations, if we secretly adhere to an out-of-sight, out-of-mind attitude toward the handicapped, if we remain silent in the face of barrier-ridden environments, and if we prejudice our constituents by our language, we will never have effective, client-centered services. To ignore personal attitudes and philosophies as a part of total program design is to abort before conception meaningful therapeutic recreation programming.

notes

1 A. L. Harney, ed., *Trends* (Arlington, Va.: National Recreation and Park Association, Park Practice Program, 1974), p. 1.

2 Edwin W. Martin, "Planning for the Educational Future of Retarded Children" (speech presented to the New Jersey Mental Retardation Planning Board, Newark, N.J., October 6, 1970).

3 Gerd Jansen and Otto Esser, "Hostility to the Handicapped," *Time*, December 20, 1971, pp. 67–68.

4 John A. Swets, "Introduction," *Psychology and the Handicapped Child* (Washington, D.C.: U.S. Department of Health, Education and Welfare, Publication No., Office of Education, 73–0500), p. 3.

5 (New York: Viking Press, 1968).

6 John A. Nesbitt, "Special Community Education for the Handicapped: A Proposed Model to Meet the Total Life and Leisure Needs of the Handicapped Child and Adult," in *Common-Unity in the Community: A Forward-Looking Program of Recreation and Leisure Services for the Handicapped*, ed. Effie Fairchild and Larry Neal (Eugene, Oreg.: University of Oregon, Center of Leisure Studies, 1975), p. 69.

7 Dennis Edwards, "Activity Dimensions" (unpublished paper, University of Illinois, 1976), pp. 1–3.

8 Edwin W. Martin, "A National Commitment to the Rights of the Individual: 1776–1976" (paper presented at the 54th Annual Council for Exceptional Children's Convention, Chicago, Ill., April 1976), p. 1.

9 ———, "Integration of the Handicapped Child into Regular Schools," *Mainstreaming: Origins and Implications*, 2, no. 2 (Spring 1976), 5.

10 Walter Boyd and Frances Hartnett, "Normalization and Its Implications for Recreation Services," *Leisurability*, 2, no. 1 (January 1975), 23.

11 Martin, "Integration of the Handicapped Child," p. 6.

12 Dr. Wolf Wolfensberger, *The Principle of Normalization in Human Services* (Toronto: National Institute on Mental Retardation, 1972), p. 28.

13 Boyd and Hartnett, "Normalization and Its Implications for Recreation Services," p. 24.

14 Jerry Spinak, "Normalization and Recreation for the Disabled," *Leisurability*, 2, no. 2 (April 1975), 33.

15 Jean P. Edwards, "Concept Normalization," *Common-Unity in the Community*, p. 63.

16 Ibid., pp. 63–65.

17 Spinak, "Normalization for the Disabled," p. 33.

18 Nesbitt, "Introduction," pp. 67–68.

19 Judy Taylor is Coordinator of Programs for Handicappers at Michigan State University. Eric Gentile is Chief of Environmental Design for Handicappers at Michigan State University.

suggested references

AMERICAN ALLIANCE FOR HEALTH, PHYSICAL EDUCATION, AND RECREATION, *Guidelines for the Professional Preparation of Personnel in Adapted Physical Education and Therapeutic Recreation Service*. Washington, D.C.: the author, 1972.

53

ANTHONY, W., "Societal Rehabilitation: Changing Society's Attitudes Toward the Physically and Mentally Disabled," *Rehabilitation Psychology*, 19, no. 3 (1972), 117–26.

AVIRAM, U., AND S. P. SEGAL, "Exclusion of the Mentally Ill," *Archives of General Psychology*, 29, no. 1 (1973), 126–33.

BARKLEY, A. L., AND P. ROBINSON, "Ticket to Re-Integration." *Leisurability*, 2, no. 3 (July 1975), 3.

BIRCH, J. W. *Hearing Impaired Pupils in the Mainstream*. Reston, Va.: The Council for Exceptional Children, 1976.

BIRCH, J., *Mainstreaming: Educable Mentally Retarded Children in Regular Classes*. Reston, Va.: The Council for Exceptional Children, 1974.

BOYD, W., AND F. HARTNETT, "Normalization and Its Implications for Recreation Services," *Leisurability*, 2, no. 1 (January 1975), 22.

BRANNAN, S., "Integrating Education and Recreation for the Handicapped," *Journal of Health, Physical Education, and Recreation*, 44, no. 8 (October 1973), 66.

COHEN, J., AND E. L. STRUENING, "Opinions About Mental Illness: Hospital Social Atmosphere Profiles and Their Relevance to Effectiveness," *Journal of Consulting Psychology*, 28 (1964), 291–98.

COHEN, O. P., "An Integrated Summer Recreation Program," *The Volta Review*, April 1969, pp. 233–37.

DENO, E. N., ed., *Instructional Alternatives for Exceptional Children*. Reston, Va.: The Council for Exceptional Children, 1972.

DUNN, L. M., "Special Education for the Mildly Retarded: Is Much of It Profitable?" *Exceptional Children*, 35 (1968), 5–22.

FAIRCHILD, E., AND L. NEAL, *Common-Unity in the Community*. Eugene, Oreg.: University of Oregon, Center of Leisure Studies, 1975.

FARINA, A., C. H. HOLLAND, AND K. RING, "The Role of Stigma and Set in Interpersonal Interaction," *Journal of Abnormal Psychology*, 71 (1966), 421–28.

FREEMAN, R. D., "Emotional Reactions of Handicapped Children," *Rehabilitation Literature*, 28 (1967), 274–82.

FRIEDSON, E., "Disability as Social Deviance," in M. B. Sussman, ed., *Sociology and Rehabilitation*, 1965, pp. 71–99.

GOODMAN, N., S. A. RICHARDSON, S. M. DORNBUSCH, AND A. H. HASTORF, "Variant Reactions to Physical Disabilities," *American Sociological Review*, 28, no. 3 (1963), 429–35.

GUERIN, G., AND SZATLOCKY, K., "Integration Programs for the Mildly Retarded," *Exceptional Children*, 41 (1974), 173–79.

HARNEY, A. L., ed., *Trends*. Arlington, Va.: National Recreation and Park Association, Park Practice Program, 1974.

HILLMAN, W. AND H. MITCHELL, "The Status and Future of Integration of Handicapped Children into Normal Camping," in *Training Needs and Strategies in Camping for the Handicapped*, ed. J. Nesbitt and others. Eugene, Oreg.: University of Oregon, Center of Leisure Studies, 1972.

JAFFE, J., "What's in a Name: Attitudes Toward Disabled Persons," *Personnel and Guidance Journal*, 45, no. 6 (1967), 557–60.

JONES, R. L., "The Hierarchical Structure of Attitudes Toward the Exceptional," *Exceptional Children*, 40, no. 6 (1974), 430–35.

LAUFMAN, MARJORIE, "Blind Children in Integrated Recreation," *The New Outlook for the Blind*, March 1962, pp. 81–84.

McDANIEL, J. W., "Attitudes and Disability" (chap. 2), in *Physical Disability and Human Behavior*. New York: Pergamon Press, 1969.

MERWIN, J. C., *Mainstreaming: Origins and Implications*, 2, no. 2. Minneapolis, Minn.: University of Minnesota, College of Education, 1976.

MOLLOY, L., "The Handicapped Child in the Everyday Classroom," *Phi Delta Kappan*, January 1975, p. 340.

PILKINGTON, T. L., "Public and Professional Attitudes to Mental Handicaps," *Public Health*, 87, no. 3 (1973), 61–66.

RICHARDSON, S. A., "The Effect of Physical Disability on the Socialization of a Child," in *Handbook of Socialization Theory and Research*, ed. D.A. Goslin. Chicago, Ill.: Rand McNally, 1971.

ROSENHAN, D. L., "On Being Sane in Insane Places," *Science*, 179 (1973), 250–58.

RUESCH, J., AND C. M. BRODSKY, "The Concept of Social Disability," *Archives of General Psychiatry*, 19, no. 4 (1968), 394–493.

SHOTEL, J., R. JANO, AND J. McGETTIGAN, "Teacher Attitudes Associated with the Integration of Handicapped Children," *Exceptional Children*, 38, no. 7 (1972), 677–83.

SIASSI, I., H. R. SPIRO, AND G. CROCETTI, "The Social Acceptance of the Ex-Mental Hospital Patient," *Community Mental Health Journal*, 9, no. 3 (1973), 233–43.

SPINAK, J., "Normalization and Recreation for the Disabled," *Leisurability*, 2, no. 2 (April 1975), 31.

STRAUCH, J. D., "Social Contact as a Variable in the Expressed Attitudes of Normal Adolescents Toward EMR Pupils," *Exceptional Children*, 36, no. 7 (1970), 495–500.

VANCE, E. T., "Social Disability," *American Psychologist*, 28, no. 6 (1973), 498–511.

WEISHAHN, M. W., "Therapeutic Recreation Programming for the Visually Disabled," *Therapeutic Recreation Journal*, 5, no. 2 (1971), 69–71.

WILSON, E. D. AND D. ALCORN, "Disability Simulation and Development of Attitudes Toward the Exceptional," *The Journal of Special Education*, 3, no. 3 (1969), 303–8.

WRIGHT, B. A., "Changes in Attitudes Toward People with Handicaps," *Rehabilitation Literature*, 34, no. 12 (1973), 354–57, 368.

ZIGLER, E. F., AND S. HARTER, "The Socialization of the Mentally Retarded," in *Handbook of Socialization Theory and Research*, ed. D.A. Goslin. Chicago, Ill.: Rand McNally, 1971.

client-centered program planning

a
systems approach
to program planning

PURPOSE: To present an overview of the concept of program planning, levels of programming, a rationale for utilizing a systems approach, and the basic procedures of systems design. Models are presented and described that delineate the various components, content, and relationships to the planning and evaluation process.

Perhaps no topic is talked about more than programming. However, despite the concern for this central issue in the delivery of therapeutic recreation services, little definitive information has been developed related to program-planning techniques and procedures. The absence in the professional literature of defined procedures for program planning leaves us with the hit-or-miss method or, worse yet, the we've-always-done-it-this-way method. In other situations, concerned professionals have developed their own planning methods. This has resulted in unique programming approaches that often cannot be generalized to other populations or settings.

As a profession therapeutic recreation needs to accept some defined procedures for the planning and delivery of services. This mark of a profession—standardized procedures—has been all but absent in the therapeutic recreation field.

It would be naïve to assume that one method of program planning can be determined and implemented across the board. However, program planning guidelines or models can be developed that would be appropriate for all types of settings and populations and for different levels of program involvement. The interdisciplinary tool of systems planning approaches gives us such models.

systems planning approaches

Systems planning models provide developed steps or procedures for program *design, implementation,* and *evaluation.* The models are not designed for one discipline, but rather are procedures that can be used in any field of service.

The flexibility of the systems approach enables diverse program content and structure to exist. The planning, implementation, and evaluation procedures guide the planner systematically through program development without dictating actual content or implementation strategies. However, the method facilitates logical design in interlocking stages, providing continuity and accountability to the program plan.

Simply stated, a systems approach to program planning involves three basic concerns:

1. determining what the program is to accomplish (where you're going),
2. designing a set of procedures to get to those goals (how you're going to get there),
3. developing criteria to determine if the program did what it was designed to do (how you know if you got there).

Many systems planning models have been developed and implemented for various planning needs. Some are very complex and rely on computer technology; others are quite simple and basically outline the major stages of program development. Regardless of the level of sophistication, seven basic components are built into any systems planning model:

1. determining the purpose, goals, and objectives;
2. designing a specific set of procedures and content to accomplish the purpose, goals, and objectives;
3. specifying implementation or delivery strategies;
4. implementing the program;
5. managing and monitoring the program;
6. evaluating the program; and
7. revising the program based on evaluation data.

These steps are presented as a model in figure 5–1. The solid arrows indicate the sequence of steps to be followed. The dotted line is a feedback loop and shows that information acquired during evaluation can be used to improve the program, and that revision may occur at any stage of the planning operation.

Planning is more than just one step. Systems planning approaches are dynamic and cyclical. Planning is always followed by im-

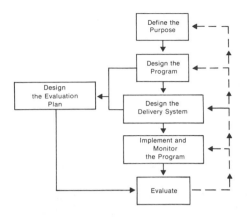

Fig. 5-1
Program Planning Model

plementation, evaluation, and revision. Each cycle should improve the program's ability to come closer to its intended purpose. The term dynamic indicates that programs are always in a state of change. Constant program evaluation and resulting improvements are expected.

rationale for using a systems approach in program planning

The systems approach provides a framework from which programs can be logically planned, conducted, and evaluated. The resulting programs are completely client centered. They are based on an assessment of client needs and proceed from there to the design of program content (activities) and process (method of interacting with clients), which are related to the goals and outcome behaviors. This procedure provides a structure for evaluating how well the program is operating and allows a type of accountability not feasible in traditional program planning approaches. In other words, therapeutic recreators who use systems approaches can determine how well their programs facilitate behavioral improvement. This ability to account to clients, administrators, and taxpayers is particularly important now when all types of human services are being questioned for their value and effectiveness.

Systems approaches to program planning also provide for staff a clear view of program direction. In a systems approach, all aspects of the program are thoroughly designed, including the evaluation plan prior to its implementation. This technique means that staff has thought through all facets of client needs, agency philosophy, and program potential and problems before jumping into the delivery of the service.

A specific plan is like a map, and it is always beneficial in setting up and operating a program. Staff members who have implemented systems-designed programs find that they feel better about themselves because they know what is expected of them. Instead of dealing with the vague notions of the purposes of traditional programs, the specificity of systems designs allows staff realistically to evaluate the outcomes of its efforts.

Most important is how systems-designed programs benefit clients. When client needs and problems are identified and stated as program goals, and then procedures are designed to facilitate the accomplishment of those goals, clients can realistically see good reasons for their participation and have a way of judging their own progress. In the past, this concept of purpose has been in question in therapeutic recreation programs. Clients were often the last to know why their involvement in programs was desired or prescribed. Staff often only gave general reasons for client involvement. Therefore, the benefits of involvement were also nebulous. Clients wondered what improvement was supposed to look like or feel like. The specificity of the systems approach to program planning enables both staff and clients to know the intended outcomes of involvement. Each program has definitely stated purposes and goals, as well as criteria for determining the clients' progress in the program. Usually this information should be shared with the client, although it is not always feasible or desirable to share program goals and outcomes with clients who have certain disabilities or illnesses, e.g., the profoundly retarded.

Systems-designed programs have other distinct advantages. A specific design enables staffing requirements to be determined, including the nature and extent of inservice training (paid and volunteer). Facilities, equipment, and supplies can also be determined more accurately. Budgeting becomes somewhat less confusing, since each program can be budgeted separately. Cost effectiveness can also be determined by comparing the results of the program to the resources (staff, equipment, facilities) used. The advantages of this type of budgeting are numerous; among them, decisions can be made about how best to distribute resources to promote program effectiveness and give priority to client needs.

levels of program planning

Program is a vague term in therapeutic recreation. It sometimes means the entire range of services delivered to clients within an agency, for example, the municipal recreation program for special populations. It also

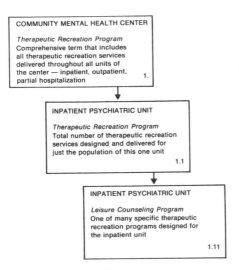

```
┌─────────────────────────────────────┐
│ COMMUNITY MENTAL HEALTH CENTER       │
│                                      │
│ Therapeutic Recreation Program       │
│ Comprehensive term that includes     │
│ all therapeutic recreation services  │
│ delivered throughout all units of    │
│ the center — inpatient, outpatient,  │
│ partial hospitalization         1.   │
└─────────────────────────────────────┘
              │
              ▼
     ┌───────────────────────────────────────┐
     │ INPATIENT PSYCHIATRIC UNIT             │
     │                                        │
     │ Therapeutic Recreation Program         │
     │ Total number of therapeutic recreation │
     │ services designed and delivered for    │
     │ just the population of this one unit    │
     │                                1.1     │
     └───────────────────────────────────────┘
                    │
                    ▼
          ┌───────────────────────────────────────┐
          │ INPATIENT PSYCHIATRIC UNIT             │
          │                                        │
          │ Leisure Counseling Program             │
          │ One of many specific therapeutic       │
          │ recreation programs designed for       │
          │ the inpatient unit                     │
          │                                1.11    │
          └───────────────────────────────────────┘
```

Fig. 5–2
Hierarchy of Program Terminology

describes a specific set of activities and interactions designed for a given group of clients, for example, the leisure counseling program for an inpatient psychiatric unit (fig. 5–2). This multiple use of the term results in confusion when the term program planning is brought into the picture.

The systems approach to program planning can help to conceptualize and design the program of an entire agency or of one program in a given unit. The basic procedure is identical; the only difference is in the number of stages required in the breakdown.

To use the systems approach most effectively, a program must be broken down to the level that is directly related to the delivery of a specific service for a select, identified population, thus making it possible to determine specific outcome behaviors.

In this chapter and the chapters that follow on program planning, program is defined as the activities and interactions designed for a specific purpose related to a defined group of clients.

While different programs may be conducted simultaneously, each program is viewed as a separate entity having its own purpose, goals, procedures, implementation strategies, and evaluation plan. Most agencies would probably have more than one program at a time. Figure 5–3 illustrates this concept, and sets forth the program of a hypothetical unit in a large center.

One patient may be involved in several programs at once. For example, client A may be participating in programs 1.1.1, 1.1.2, and 1.1.5, while client B may be involved in 1.1.3, 1.1.4, and 1.1.5. Each of these programs is still designed and implemented to accomplish specific goals

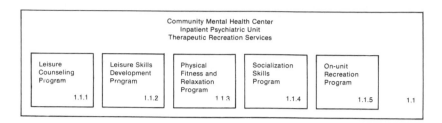

Fig. 5–3
Hypothetical Program

related to overall client needs. Each is evaluated separately and independent judgments are made about their value and effectiveness.

basic program design components

Four basic components are essential in the design of a program. They exist regardless of the nature of the setting or the population served. They are highly interrelated and dependent on each other. They provide the nucleus around which all programs are developed. Figure 5–4 depicts the content and relationships of these components.

clients

All program design starts with an analysis of the clients. The purpose of this analysis is to determine the nature and needs of the clientele so that realistic and appropriate goals can be determined. A variety of factors enter into this analysis. Basic areas are age, sex, marital status, socioeconomic status, education, leisure-skill background, and type and severity of illness or disability. Other information important to realistic program planning is the number of clients, the resources available, the amount of time allocated for the program, the philosophy of the agency, and other administrative concerns. All of this background should lead to a good comprehension of client needs and the abilities and limitations of the delivery system.

goals and objectives

The second major step is to determine program goals. Goals are derived from analyzing the nature and needs of the client. They are written with a realistic perspective on what can be accomplished, given the resources and constraints of the delivery system. Goals are written with the use of behavioral and outcome terminology, although they are not as specific as objectives. Objectives further break down each goal in specific, observable or measurable behaviors and define the criteria for determining whether the objective has been achieved. Simply stated, objectives operationally define a goal's direction. They enable us to know whether the desired behavior or outcome of a program has been achieved.

The shaded area in figure 5–5 illustrates the relationship between goals and client needs. Chapter seven focuses on the procedures for assessing client needs and for determining goals and describes how to derive and state measurable objectives.

activities

The third stage of program design is to select and specify the activities to be used to achieve the goals and objectives. Activities are meant in the broadest sense. In a leisure counseling program, activities could be discussion of or exposure to a variety of existing leisure programs; in an instructional swimming program, obviously the activities would involve swimming. In a program focusing on socialization skills, the activities could be very diverse, such as role playing or traditional recreation activities, as long as they were structured and presented so that they related to the program goals and objectives concerning socialization. A program's content consists of activities. In a systems-designed program they are selected and specified in advance as the best possible choices for attaining the desired goals and objectives. Chapter ten deals with activity analysis, which is a set of procedures and techniques that enables a logical selection of activities based on client characteristics and goals and objectives.

The planning model does not dictate which activities should be

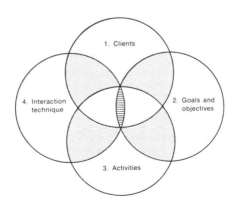

Fig. 5–4
Component Interrelationships

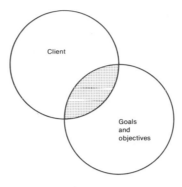

Fig. 5–5
Two Components

included in a program; this decision is left up to the designer. The model does specify that the activities selected must be related to the goals and objectives and must have a high probability of accomplishing them.

In the model, the activities and the clients overlap. It is possible to select an activity in which the client has never engaged (or has no interest!) and still achieve the desired result. However, the activity is more likely to succeed if it is congruent with known interest or skills. It would be foolish to ask a male farm laborer to make potholders with loops when he enjoys woodworking and it is an available activity that would help to accomplish the objective. Whenever feasible, activities should be able to be carried over to future socioleisure life styles. This is true whether it is a new leisure skill or a traditional activity used to improve a behavior or function. The recreator should be aware of each client's past leisure involvement and attitudes and be able reasonably to predict the future potential. Someone recently afflicted with a spinal-cord injury or stroke may require a change in his or her future socioleisure life style. Selecting activities that may develop into future hobbies may necessitate introducing new activities that have little in common with past skills. Even in this situation, an analysis of the client's background is likely to elicit patterns of involvement and general categories of activities that would assist selecting the best activities.

Preparing for a geographical change, such as moving a client from a large state facility to a small community group home, might necessitate choosing different activities that have maximum carry-over value. Most mentally retarded adults do not play volleyball in their new small-group homes or in their community programs! However, other physical activities, such as bowling, dancing, or bicycling, often prepare these clients for the transition to community living.

Activities should relate to characteristics such as age, sex, and ethnic or religious background. Tossing bean bags may be a dehumanizing experience for the alert retired school teacher in an extended-care facility. It is equally ridiculous to ask the Baptist minister's wife in the state facility to play poker.

The significance of all these issues is illustrated in the basic model (fig. 5–6), which shows the relationship and overlap between clients, goals and objectives, and program activities. Using a systems model in program planning takes into account these vital concerns and relationships in the planning stages.

interaction techniques

The fourth component of program design is to select and specify the interaction technique to be used. This aspect of program design has traditionally been given the least attention. Somehow it is assumed that the therapeutic recreation specialist will just know what to do when conducting the program. Equally naïve is the idea that the specialist's dynamic charisma will suffice. Contemporary program design, however, calls for the specification of the *process* to be used in conducting the program. Countless interaction styles exist. There are a variety of techniques, for instruction, therapy, communication, awareness, and leadership from which to select. The systems-designed program describes the interaction method just as thoroughly as it specifies the content of activities. There are several reasons for being this specific. One is that for programs to be evaluated and improvements made based on the information acquired, it is important to analyze the relative success or failure of the interaction style. Improving therapeutic recreation programs is just as often related to changing or improving the interaction style as changing the activity content. As program delivery becomes more sophisticated, outcomes depend more on the appropriate selection of interaction styles.

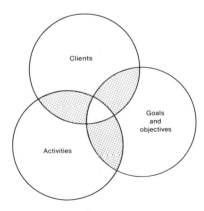

Fig. 5–6
Three Components

This concept has implications for professional preparation programs as well as for inservice training and staff development programs. Currently, most therapeutic recreators have had little or no training in how to use a variety of intervention and interaction techniques. A basic course in recreation leadership hardly equips students to apply advanced interaction techniques such as Gestalt therapy, behavior modification, reality therapy, or transactional analysis.

Specifying interaction skills does not mean that programs should result in rigid, mechanical methods of manipulating people, without room for individual differences. It does mean describing the basic approach used by the staff relative to the program's content and the clients' characteristics. The basic description of the program's process could make explicit that several techniques are to be used simultaneously. Once identified, the program's goals and objectives are expected to be accomplished by using the defined interaction styles in combination with the selected activity content.

Interactions may change as clients gain greater confidence, independence, and higher levels of skill. Identifying such changes in interaction helps the therapeutic recreator to determine why the program achieved, or failed to achieve, its intended outcomes.

The interaction techniques selected relate to the other components of the model. The techniques should be appropriate to client needs, types of illness or disability, client ages, and other client characteristics. Also, the techniques should be in concert with the agency's overall treatment approach. Behavior modification may be appropriate for severely mentally retarded but has questionable value for an alert adult with cerebral palsy. Reality therapy techniques may work well in an activity program with emotionally disturbed teenagers but have limited benefit with autistic children. The issue is not what interaction technique is used, but that at least one is selected and specified as the predominant method of conducting the program.

The interaction techniques selected must be appropriate to the goals and objectives. For example, if a goal deals with facilitating independent leisure behavior, an authoritarian interaction technique may not be appropriate. While goals do not dictate which interaction techniques are selected, the two components must be compatible.

The interaction techniques must also be compatible with the content and activities of the program. A program to develop new leisure skills requires interaction methodologies that focus on exposure and instruction, while a program to facilitate engaging in previously acquired skills may use entirely different interaction techniques.

A well-designed program takes into account clients, goals, activities, and interaction techniques. It is possible to design logical, compatible, and effective programs that consider these components. Further discussion of these concepts in part 2 will provide the necessary detail for

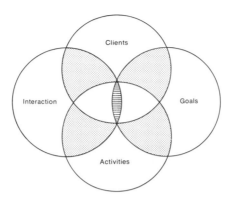

Fig. 5–7
Four Components

designing programs for different populations in various settings. The completed model (fig. 5–7) portrays the basic components of program design.

implementation strategies

Program planning involves more than just the design and development of the basic components. Equally significant is the development of implementation strategies. These strategies involve such concerns as how often the program is delivered (once a week, every day), the length of each session, how long the program will run (six months, ten weeks, continuously), time of day, and other administrative or delivery details. Often these details are taken for granted. Tradition or other influencing factors often determine a program's structure and delivery. A systems-designed program, however, makes no assumption about structure or delivery. Alternative structures and implementation strategies are analyzed before deciding which are the most desirable. The program design and the delivery system must interrelate. There is little value in designing an intricate, comprehensive program if the agency does not have the resources to operate the program. Consequently, in program design, delivery and operational concerns need to be kept in mind during the planning stage.

The design of implementation strategies or delivery systems takes into account a multitude of factors. Not only does the delivery system need to be compatible with the clients, goals, activities, and interaction techniques, it must also be compatible with the other programs and schedules and available resources. For example, a program designed for a specific group of clients might be most effective if it is conducted daily for an hour and a half. However, if this frequency results in other clients receiving no services, the implementation strategy is inappropriate. Or, if a program requires too many staff members to implement its delivery strategy, it is equally inappropriate. Designing reasonable implementation strategies requires a good comprehension of resources, priorities, and other services within an agency. The best-designed programs can turn out to be failures when they are not balanced with other priorities.

Like other components of program planning, implementation strategies must be thoroughly identified and described, since they represent another area vital to evaluation. Often programs are ineffective, not because of their goals, objectives, activities, or interaction techniques, but because the implementation was problematic. Something as minor as increasing the length or frequency of sessions can increase total program effectiveness. Planning for implementation is as important to evaluation as any other aspect of program monitoring.

evaluation

Evaluation is an essential aspect of systematic program design. Systems-designed programs have built-in evaluation potential. By stating goals and objectives in behavioral language, and then logically designing a program to accomplish them, evaluation becomes simple compared to other approaches. It is relatively easy to determine whether goals have been met, or the degree to which the program has succeeded, when data are collected daily and analyzed periodically.

Evaluating a systems-designed program requires that a basic evaluation plan be developed before a program is implemented. The plan indicates what information must be continuously collected and determines the kinds of forms needed to record that information. Most evaluations deal with the same basic questions: Was the program effective? Why did we get the results we did? How can we improve the program? To answer these questions, we need to know a variety of things, many of which are specified in the original program plan: What were the goals and objectives? Were they met? Were the activities appropriate? Were the interaction techniques used appropriate? Was the program implemented as designed? Each of these questions can be relatively easy to answer when information directly related to each is systematically collected throughout the program's operation by the individuals conducting the program.

There are various types and levels of sophistication in program evaluation, but all practitioners should have at least basic skills in evaluation design and procedures. This book emphasizes a basic *discrepancy evaluation* approach that allows the specialist to compare actual program inputs, outputs, processes, and content to the intended (designed) inputs, outputs, processes, and content. The margin of difference, or discrepancy, indicates the degree of program effectiveness and points out areas for possible revision.

Take, for example, a program designed for educable mentally retarded children. They are considered part of the *intended input*. The designer develops goals and objectives appropriate to some area of needed behavioral change or functional improvement, taking into account the characteristics of this group. These goals and objectives are considered to be the *intended output*. Next, the planners select and describe the activities and interactions they believe will achieve these goals and objectives. This step is called the *intended content and process*. The program is then installed and operated. After a while, an evaluation is conducted. Let us say that many of the children did not reach the goals and objectives, indicating a discrepancy between the actual outputs and intended outputs. This information tells us something about the program's effectiveness.

The evaluation, however, does not stop there. The specialists need to know why they got the results they did. Other aspects of the evaluation plan can help to answer that question. Consider the input variables. The program was designed for educable mentally retarded. A review of the clients involved in the program shows that many of the children involved were not in the educable range, but rather in the trainable range. This indicates a discrepancy between the actual inputs (trainable and educable) and the intended inputs (educable). This discrepancy partially explains the results. If the program was designed specifically for the educable retarded, then it is reasonable to assume that children at a trainable level may not perform as well. The discrepancy also points to where a change might improve the program. Either no trainable-level clients will be included in the next program or the goals and objectives and program content and process can be made more appropriate for the learning characteristics of both groups. This brief example gives only one aspect of discrepancy evaluation, but it illustrates the basic concept. Evaluation is discussed in detail in chapter thirteen.

Evaluation is a method for improving program effectivenss and thus improving services to clients. Whether the programs are for treatment, leisure education, or recreation participation, evaluation procedures aid in the accurate reporting of program effectiveness, as well as in indicating areas for revision. Accountability to clients, administrators, sponsoring agencies, and other funding sources is thus established.

summary

Program planning is a total process. It involves the analysis of client needs, agency resources, and philosophical perspectives. The program design specifies goals and objectives, the content (activities), and process (interaction style) selected for obtaining the program's intent. Equally important is the development and description of the delivery strategies. The final stage of planning focuses on the development of an evaluation plan. This planning is essential for the realistic appraisal of the program's worth once it has been implemented.

The concepts presented in this overview are expanded in the other chapters in part 2. The techniques and processes used for this type of systematic planning are detailed for the readers' use.

_____ *suggested references* _____

ARMSTRONG, R. J., T. D. CORNELL, R. E. KRANER, AND E. W. ROBERSON, *The Development and Evaluation of Behavioral Objectives.* Worthington, Ohio: Charles A. Jones Publishing Company, 1970.

BANATHY, B. H., *Instructional Systems.* Palo Alto, Calif.: Fearon Publishers, 1968.

BUCKLEY, W., *Sociology and Modern Systems Theory.* Englewood Cliffs, N.J.: Prentice-Hall, Inc., 1967.

BURNS R. W., *New Approaches to Behavioral Objectives.* Dubuque, Iowa: William C. Brown Company, Publishers, 1972.

CHURCHMAN, C. W., *The Systems Approach.* New York: Dell Publishing Co., Inc., 1968.

COMPTON, D. M., "A Linear Approach for Delivering Individualized Therapeutic Recreation," *Journal of Physical Education and Recreation,* January 1976, pp. 27–28.

COOK, D. L., *Program Evaluation and Review Techniques Applications in Education.* Washington, D.C.: Government Printing Office, 1966.

GAGNE, R. M., *Psychological Principles in System Development,* pp. 1–10. New York: Holt, Rinehart and Winston, 1963.

GRONLUND, N. E., *Stating Behavioral Objectives for Classroom Instruction.* London: The Macmillan Company, 1970.

HARTLEY, H. J., *Educational Planning, Programming, Budgeting: A Systems Approach.* Englewood Cliffs, N.J.: Prentice-Hall, Inc., 1968.

MAGER, R. F., *Preparing Instructional Objectives.* Palo Alto, Calif.: Fearon Publishers, 1962.

PETERSON, C. A., *A Systems Approach to Therapeutic Recreation Program Planning.* Champaign, Ill.: Stipes Publishing Co., 1976.

POPHAM, J., AND E. BAKER, *Systematic Instruction.* Englewood Cliffs, N.J.: Prentice-Hall, Inc., 1970.

CHAPTER SIX

individualized program planning

PURPOSE: To present a systematic approach to individual client assessment that also helps to determine goals and identify specific behavioral objectives. Approaches to determining client needs will be discussed, as well as procedures for deriving and appropriately stating individual program goals and specific objectives. Procedures are then described for developing the individual program plan. Methods of recording progress related to the plan are illustrated.

The concept of individualized program planning has long been neglected in the field of recreation. Historically, recreation program planners have operated from the premise that "what is good and fun for us should be good and fun for you." All too often recreation programs reflect the interests and skills of the staff members rather than the interests and needs of the constituents. If a staff member happens to enjoy throwing pots on a potter's wheel, the program often resembles the local craft shack, with assorted pottery lining every shelf and filling every closet.

Often little consideration is given to the interests of the clients or to the potential carry-over value of activities. After they leave the institutions, most clients involved in various programs have little opportunity to continue the activities they have learned. For example, people who take a pottery or ceramics class while institutionalized may not be able to afford further instruction and may not live close to a studio that has a potter's wheel or kiln. This is not to deny the excellence of some existing ceramics programs, but rather to stress the importance of relying on the assessment of client needs and interests rather than staff interest to mold and shape program content.

Just as staff interests and skills have traditionally molded program content, so have a variety of other factors. The assumption that the recreational needs of specific groups of people are the same (age, sex, and disability groups) has resulted in "canned" programs. Perhaps the most common request made to the recreation consultant is, "What activities are best for five year olds, or blind people, or mentally retarded adults, or old people?" The belief here is that all five year olds enjoy flying kites, all blind people like to bowl, all mentally retarded adults like to dance, and all old people enjoy bingo. Actually, the activity interests of any specific group are as diverse as the individual life experiences and personalities of the group members. Any attempt to conjure up lists of activities for specific groups is an exercise in futility.

Other factors that have traditionally molded program content are the availability of facilities and size of budget. Although facilities and budget are extremely important in finalizing program plans, they should not be the primary or only factors in determining program content. Effective programs must be *client centered*, which implies *individual* client assessment. After client needs are determined, program plans can be formulated within the constraints of budget, facilities, and available staff. It is possible that the limitations of these factors will prohibit some client needs from being addressed, but at least the needs that are addressed will be handled meaningfully.

Many therapeutic recreators feel that individual assessment is not possible because of the large numbers of clients to be served in most settings. Unlike other recreation professionals, however, therapeutic recreators must confront people with eyes that don't see, ears that don't hear, legs that don't walk, and emotions that are damaged. We must acknowledge the needs of our constituents, both individually and collectively. The techniques described for individualized program planning are presented in the purest sense, but may and often must be modified for programs unable logistically to perform comprehensive, individualized planning. However, it should be emphasized that individualized program planning, even minimally, is a moral obligation as members of a helping profession. Also, it is often required by both regulation and legislation in order to receive payment for services. More than ever before, we are asked to be accountable in demonstrating an individual's progress.

There are five basic steps to individualized program planning: (1) individual client assessment, (2) goal determination, (3) specification of individual objectives, (4) writing the individual plan, and (5) evaluation. The material presented in this chapter represents our interpretation of work done by Dr. L. L. Weed.[1] The techniques are adapted to meet the programming needs of therapeutic recreation.

individual client assessment

The term *assessment* is often used interchangeably with the terms *evaluation* and *measurement.* We believe that assessment has a narrower meaning than evaluation, but a broader meaning than measurement. To assess means "to sit beside," "to assist the judge," or "to determine the importance." It therefore seems appropriate in program planning to limit assessment to the process of gathering information and molding it into an interpretable form. Scarvia Anderson and his colleagues state:

> *Assessment, as opposed to simple one-dimensional measurement, is frequently described as multitrait-multimethod; that is, it focuses on a number of variables judged to be important and utilizes a number of techniques to assay them. Its techniques may also be multisource . . . and/or multijudge.* [2]

Programming judgments are based on assessment information. Assessment, then, precedes the final decision-making stages of program determination and delineation of evaluation plans.

Assessment is the process of gathering decision-making information relative to individualized program planning. Assessment information may be objective or subjective. Objective data includes all possible information about the client that can be gathered from sources other than direct client input. Subjective data includes any and all remarks made by the client.

Methods for gathering objective assessment information vary among agencies and depend on factors such as the number of people served, the availability of charts and records, the philosophy about sharing confidential information, the programming approach (community recreation programs may not need the extensive assessment information used in a treatment facility), and the willingness of family and staff members to share information. Although some believe that objective information, which usually dwells on the past, tends to bias the program planner's perceptions, we believe that the more information we have, the better are the chances of obtaining successful outcome behavior.

objective assessment information

Objective assessment information may include

1. Basic demographic information, including name, age, sex, race (if appropriate or important to program planning, i.e., communication barriers), marital status, occupation, city of residence, educational level, date of admission to the program, and referral source.

2. **Historical data**, including appropriate and available information regarding past medical or psychiatric problems and admissions, as well as past social problems or patterns. It is most appropriate, here, for the therapeutic recreator to gather all possible information relative to leisure participation, including activity preferences, activity experiences, participation rates, and problems of participation, i.e., problems with social interaction, emotional stress, and physical failures. A history of the client's current problems should be identified here, which includes a chronological description of the reasons for, and events surrounding, the present admission into the program. This information may include a description of the composition and interpersonal relationships in the family. It may also include information about sexual preferences or adjustment problems. Vocational and educational histories may also be important to note.

3. **Pertinent medical, psychiatric, educational, vocational, and avocational test results** may also be a part of objective assessment if the information is relevant for therapeutic recreation programming. Often it is necessary to identify medical and psychiatric precautions, e.g., diabetic, suicidal, heart conditions. Lists of assessment instruments appear in Appendices A and B.

4. **Initial observations of staff, family, and friends** comprise a fourth area of objective assessment. The behavior of the client as observed by staff, family, and friends before, during, and after admission continues to be a primary source of information both for initial assessment and for evaluation. This form of assessment information is regarded as an opinion or personal observation and is stated as such. Although this type of information appears semantically to be subjective, it is considered to be objective in that it comes from sources other than the client. Objective observations may also be made by direct contact with the clients or by videotapes and tape recordings. It is common to find an observation room available where clients can be observed in participation. Bill Adair, who advocates observation as a useful means of assessing emotionally disturbed children, states, "How a child interacts with his physical environment and others around him in a recreation activity can reveal to the specialist a great deal about personality makeup and behavior patterns."[3]

5. **Reasons for admission to a program and status at the time of admission** should be clearly stated by the referral source (whether parent, teacher, friend, social worker, physician). Most often in medical or psychiatric facilities this information is presented in the form of a diagnostic impression stated in specialized nomenclature. Although traditional diagnostic impressions are often expedient for charting and completing insurance forms, they are of little value to the therapeutic recreator in attempting to design meaningful programs. For example, if the programmer received the following information on a client, it is questionable that a meaningful program could be designed:

Diagnostic impression: The patient is a schizophrenic, paranoid type with auditory hallucinations and compulsive, neurotic behavior; disoriented at times.

To devise an adequate program for this client, the therapeutic recreator would need to know: What or who does the client fear? When does the client seem most fearful? How does the client express his or her fear? Who is around and what is going on in the immediate environment? What does the client hear? When? How often? What sort of behavior is displayed? How often (compulsive)? What other confused (disoriented) behavior is displayed?

Due to the nebulous nature of traditional diagnostic impressions, the therapeutic recreator should request that diagnostic impressions be translated into specific problems: "The patient fears poisoning by family members and therefore washes solid foods before eating and washes dishes and utensils an average of twenty times a day." Specific information about presenting problems leads to meaningful planning.

Most nonspecific assessment information is confusing and often misleading: "The client is having difficulty with family"; or, "the client behaved inappropriately"; or, "the client is senile, disoriented, depressed, uncooperative, manipulative, hostile." Common, nebulous descriptions should be followed by appropriate explanations: "The client is uncooperative in that she or he refuses all invitations to engage in recreational activities." Specificity is a must in stating reasons for program admissions. Whereas concise statements about medical conditions are relatively simple to write, specifying psychosocial conditions requires lengthy description and illustration. Some agencies may not have a formal referral process into the therapeutic recreation program. However, it is still the therapeutic recreator's responsibility to gather the necessary assessment information or to establish a viable referral process.

subjective assessment information

Subjective assessment information is often lacking in the assessment process, or is considered trite. However, the client's direct input into the assessment process is critical and continues to be so throughout program implementation and evaluation. It is presumptuous to assume that we therapeutic recreators, because of our position of leadership, know intuitively or by training the needs, interests, and problems of our constituents. With few exceptions, clients are able and should be allowed to define their status and programming expectations. By developing a trusting relationship between client and therapist, and by negotiating maturely, compatible programming goals can and should be defined.

Traditionally, subjective data include information about: (1) hours of available free time, (2) hobbies, (3) membership in organizations or groups, and (4) possible future interests. Additionally, it is important that constituents be allowed to express (1) what they believe their problems to be, (2) what their limitations are, (3) what their strengths are, and (4) what they hope to gain from participation.

Generally questions such as "What would you like to do?" or "What do you enjoy doing?" are unproductive. All too often the response is, "Oh, I don't know (or care)." Here are some sample questions that can facilitate obtaining useful subjective information:

1. What are you doing when you really like yourself?
2. Imagine yourself feeling really good. Where are you? What are you doing? Who are you with?
3. Imagine the scolding part of you telling the quiet part of you your problems. What are they? How do you tell yourself to deal with these problems?
4. Imagine yourself being free of obligations and very wealthy. Where would you go? Who would you go with? What would you do?
5. Tell me about the nicest vacation you've ever taken.
6. Create in your mind and relate the ideal vacation.
7. Imagine yourself as the leader of your recreation program. How would you program for yourself?
8. Imagine yourself as someone else talking about all of your good traits. What would they be?
9. If the very secret part of you wanted to tell someone else your fears, what would it say?
10. Complete the sentence, "Life would be more fun for me if . . . ."
11. Imagine yourself being very unhappy (or angry, frightened, etc.). What is going on around you? Where are you? Who are you with?
12. Imagine you are your parents (individually). Talk about play.
13. Imagine being a child again. What is a typical play day like for you? What are you enjoying the most? What is missing?
14. As a child, what restrictions were placed on you as a boy or girl?
15. What did your parents do for fun?
16. What does your favorite person do for fun? Describe that person.
17. How did your parents entertain at home? Who did the inviting? Who did they invite? How were you included? How would you like to have been included?
18. Where was your favorite play place as a child? Describe that place.
19. Describe your childhood playmates. Were any of your playmates imaginary? Describe them.
20. Did your size, sex, appearance, or skill level as a child keep you on the sidelines, get you on a team or in a group, or let you be a star performer?
21. In your play behavior were you primarily the leader, follower, referee, or observer?
22. What were your favorite fairy tales? Tell them.
23. What characters did you most identify with? Imagine yourself as your favorite childhood character. Describe yourself.
24. In what way was your play behavior a rehearsal for your present role?
25. What made you laugh as a child? Now?

These types of inquiries are creative and constructively allow for direct client input into assessment. Responses help to clarify the client's personal perceptions of his or her problems, needs, interests, and expectations. Not only are the subjective data essential for effective program planning, but the actual process of obtaining the information can be a therapeutic experience.

The wording and manner of presenting subjective assessment questions will vary with different types and ages of clients. Responses do not always have to be verbal. A child may enjoy drawing her or his favorite activity or person, as well as perceptions of angry or fearful places. Gerald Fain suggests using picture selection to obtain assessment information from clients.[4] Another interesting technique involves having the clients fantasize to music and describe what they are doing, where they are, and with whom they are interacting. When possible, videotaping or tape recording these sessions is useful for later analysis of subjective data. Having gathered as much objective and subjective information about the client as possible, the therapeutic recreator is ready to determine program goals.

determining goals

Individual program goals are broad statements that reflect needs and are directly determined by analyzing assessment data. Unlike objectives, goals are not directly measurable, but rather provide direction in the actual planning of individualized programs. The first step in determining individual program goals is the formation of a problem list.

formulating the problem list

The first draft of the problem list should include all presenting problems that can be derived from the assessment information: all physical, social, and psychological problems. The following items are important in formulating the problem list:

1. State all problems simply and honestly, without presumption. For example, rather than listing typical diagnostic impressions such as "withdrawn, hostile, disoriented, and uncooperative," an effort should be made to present actual problems clearly. For example:

   The client sits in the corner and refuses to participate in any activities.

2. Problems may be stated as observed by staff and others, or as stated by the client:

   The client states that he or she is "afraid of people staring."

3. Problems should be stated in specific terms that can be understood by everyone, avoiding generalized terms and vague diagnostic labels such as,

   The client is "withdrawn" and behaves "inappropriately."

4. Problem lists should be dynamic. New problems should be added as they arise and old problems deleted when they are no longer relevant.

After formulating and reviewing the first draft of the problem list, it should be clearly noted that some problems cannot and should not be the direct responsibility of the therapeutic recreator. Specific medical problems such as the care of a catheter device or administering medications fall into this category. Certain problems may require assistance from other professionals, thus requiring that appropriate counsel be sought or referrals made. For example, a client may be reluctant to participate in therapeutic recreation programming due to concern over financial burdens. In this case, the recreator should seek the assistance of a social worker or other counselor.

The range of available services and the treatment philosophies vary from agency to agency. It is important to delineate those specific problems over which a therapeutic recreation program has control.

The final step in formulating the problem list is to rank problems by priority. It is usually impossible to work on all presenting problems at once. Also, program effectiveness can only be measured in relation to specific problems. The therapeutic recreator should pinpoint the most critical problems to be dealt with first. When priorities have been established, specific client needs can be delineated, from which goals may be determined. Inactive problems—problems existing in the past but not currently problematic—may also be listed. Here is an example of an actual problem list formulated on a client who was referred to a therapeutic recreation program:

Active
1. Does not talk to others.
2. Talks to himself.
3. Does not respond when called.
4. States he is afraid of groups of people.
5. Tends to do nothing unless prodded.
6. Forgets where he is and what he is doing.
7. States he has trouble thinking.
8. Overweight.

Inactive
1. Does not like crowded places.

stating needs

Note in the above example that Sam Spacey "does not talk to others" was given first priority, since programming is difficult without verbal interaction. Sam needs to be able "to communicate verbally with others." This need also relates to problems 2, 3, and 4. In relation to problem 5, Sam needs "to become more self-directed." In relation to problems 6 and 7, Sam may need "to increase his attention span." In relation to problem 8, Sam obviously needs "to lose weight." By asking the question, "What is the need in relation to this particular problem?" the programmer can ascertain the specific information necessary to write individual program goals.

writing individual goals

Again, goals are broad statements of desired terminal behavior rather than specific, measurable criteria. Setting forth individual client needs allows the programmer to ascertain the desired terminal behaviors expected of the client. Appropriate individual programming goals for Sam Spacey are

1. To increase ability to interact verbally with others in social settings.
2. To increase attention span and awareness of realistic surroundings.
3. To increase ability to make decisions regarding leisure participation.
4. To improve body image.

converting problem statements into individual goals

Program goals may be determined by separately analyzing each problem in the following ways:

1. State the problem.
2. Record what the client states about the problem (subjective).
3. Record what others say or observe about the problem (objective).
4. Assess the subjective and objective information about the specific problem.
5. State the need in relation to the problem.
6. State the goal in relation to the specific need.

The next example shows the process through which a problem is converted into a goal statement.

1. Does not talk to others.

Subjective. Client states he is afraid to talk to other people, but wants to get to know others.

Objective. Client seems reluctant to talk during the interview. Sits far away and stares out of the window. Talks only when spoken to and does not seem to talk freely.

Assessment. Seems to be afraid of others and may lack conversational social skills. Also seems to have a short attention span.

Need. To be able to talk to others without being afraid.

Goal. To increase ability to interact verbally with others in social settings.

specifying individual objectives

Having determined individual program goals, the next step is to specify measurable, individual objectives. Since goals are not measurable, they can be activated by formulating behavioral objectives, which are measurable. When a client achieves the behavioral objectives, the individual goals are met. In other words, individual goals must be put into operation by translating them into behavioral objectives. Writing behavioral objectives gives direction to program content and implementation strategies. It also provides the programmer with evaluation criteria.

translating goal statements
into behavioral objectives

Generally speaking, objectives are clear, specific statements that support the main theme of a goal in observable or measurable form. Objectives are derived from goal statements; they indicate behaviors or actions that represent and even clarify the goal in a given context. Objectives are targets that can be realistically achieved within a determined amount of time. Sometimes a goal statement has more than one related objective.

In order to make a goal operational, the programmer must ask, "What behaviors, for this client and in this setting, indicate that this goal has been reached?" The behaviors arrived at are often the result of a brainstorming session with other staff members. Having determined those behaviors that are appropriate for a particular client in a particular setting, the programmer is ready to write the specific behavioral objectives.

Goal Statement. To increase ability to interact verbally with others in social settings.

Representative Behaviors
1. To initiate conversation voluntarily.

2. To sustain appropriate conversation while engaged in an activity.
3. To respond appropriately when spoken to.

The example shows a goal that has been made partially operational by determining appropriate representative behaviors. However, it is still not possible to evaluate the performance of the client. The astute programmer must ask, "How many times must the client initiate conversation?" "How long must the client sustain conversation and what is an appropriate response? Evaluating client progress depends on specific and clear intent. For an effective, individual program to be planned, everyone involved must know precisely what behavior is expected, under what conditions the behavior must occur, and how the behavior will be judged. Behavioral objectives must be specific enough to give direction to program content, process, implementation strategies, and evaluation.

A behavioral objective has three components:

1. The specific *behavior* that is to be demonstrated. A specific behavior is an action or act by the client that can be observed and measured by another person.
2. The *conditions* under which the behavior will be demonstrated. The conditions of behavior clarify where, when, and under what circumstances the behavior will occur.
3. The *standards* to which the behavior must conform (or the *criteria* for judgment). A *standard* of behavior clarifies precisely how a behavior will be judged. A standard often requires that a behavior be repeated a certain number of times or that it be sustained for a certain amount of time.

The behavioral objectives that follow might be appropriate for our hypothetical client, Sam Spacey—the *behavior* is italicized, (the condition is in parentheses), and the standard is without notation:

1. (After three weeks of service involvement,) *the client will voluntarily initiate conversation with other clients or staff,* (while on the unit,) as characterized by these actions and as judged appropriate by the staff:
   a. introduces self to other people and makes appropriate opening statements or comments;
   b. listens to other people's responses, maintaining eye contact and commonly acceptable body positions;
   c. responds with verbal comments related to other people's verbalization;
   d. ends conversations with appropriate salutations.
2. (After four weeks of instruction,) *the client will demonstrate the ability to play a table game of choice with a staff member,* as judged appropriate by the staff and as characterized by:
   a. adherence to all rules,
   b. spontaneous, appropriate verbalization related to the game or related topics,
   c. completion of the game within reasonable time expectations.

For a behavioral objective to be technically acceptable, these questions must be answered positively:

1. Can you readily identify the behavior that is to be demonstrated by the client to show that he or she has acquired the objective?
2. Can you readily identify the conditions under which the behavior will be demonstrated?
3. Can you readily identify the standard to which the behavior of the client must conform?
4. If two of your staff looked at this performance measure and a client's performance, could they agree whether or not the standards and limits had been achieved?

The ability to specify correctly the behavioral objectives that are appropriate to the age and ability level of the client, and to the setting of services, is perhaps the most difficult to acquire of all the programming skills. However, this particular skill is crucial for good evaluation. Practice in brainstorming for the representative behaviors related to individual goals provides good groundwork for learning how to specify behavioral objectives quickly and easily. Once the behavioral objectives are determined, specific individual programs can be planned.

writing the individual plan

The individual program plan is a step-by-step outline of procedures to be followed in assisting the client to achieve the stated behavioral objectives. Program plans vary in complexity and specificity. Generally the program plan will include:

1. activities and programs in which the client will participate,
2. facilitation styles and approaches to be used by staff,
3. hints about working with the client, and
4. schedule for evaluating participation.

Individual program plans should be written with enough detail so that all staff understand the approach and can maintain consistency. The plans must be dynamic rather than static. As the client progresses, the plan needs to change. A well-written individual plan can be an excellent teaching tool for the staff, in that it provides a record of both successful and unsuccessful activities and approaches. Figure 6–1 is an individual program plan for Sam Spacey.

Sam Spacey's initial plan requires a one-to-one relationship with a staff member and does not immediately schedule him into ongoing activity programs. Plans to enroll him in established programs, such as assertive training or music classes, may be implemented when he demon-

Individual Plan	Client Identification: Sam Spacey
Date Plan	Signature

11/3 1. Does not talk to others.

Subjective. Client states he is afraid to talk to other people, but wants to get to know others.

Objective. Client seems reluctant to talk during the interview. Sits far away and stares out of the window. Talks only when spoken to and does not seem to talk freely.

Assessment. Seems to be afraid of others and may lack conversational social skills. Also seems to have a short attention span, which may make it hard to carry on a conversation.

Need. To be able to talk to others without being afraid.

Goal. To increase ability to interact verbally with others in social settings.

Representative Behaviors
   a. To initiate conversation voluntarily.
   b. To sustain appropriate conversation while engaged in an activity.
   c. To respond appropriately when spoken to.

Behavioral Objective. After three weeks of service involvement, the client will voluntarily initiate conversation with other clients or staff, while on the unit, as characterized by these actions and as judged appropriate by the staff:
   a. introduces self to other people and makes appropriate opening statements or comments;
   b. listens to other people's responses, maintaining eye contact and commonly acceptable body positions;
   c. responds with verbal comments related to other people's verbalization;
   d. ends conversation with appropriate salutations.

Plan
   a. Do not schedule into group activities at present.
   b. Work 1:1 (one to one) on individual projects and activities, such as woodworking and table games.
   c. Keep conversation light and nonthreatening. Don't discuss feelings at present. Help build trust.
   d. If client strays off the topic of conversation, remind him what you were talking about.
   e. Don't ask him questions that will put him on the defensive, such as "why" questions.
   f. Gradually and casually begin to explain the assertive training class, but don't push him to join yet.
   g. Record client's progress daily and plan to assess readiness for assertive training and other established programs in one week.
                                                                      Warren Withit, MTRS

Fig. 6–1
Sample Individual Program Plan

strates readiness. Often clients are immediately placed into established programs without having one-to-one staff involvement. This is almost always the case in large, institutional programs where staff is limited, or in community recreation programs where the emphasis is most often on activities skill development. The need for highly individualized programs diminishes when a client's functional and leisure abilities increase. Nevertheless, individual assessment is still encouraged to determine program suitability. This is true even in the community recreation setting, where assessment may be limited to gathering information relative to age, ability level, and interests.

Regardless of where or how they are used, individual plans should be concise and yet contain the essential information for program planning. It should be simple enough to be clearly understood by all. Initially, individual planning may seem laborious, but with practice it can be done quickly and efficiently. Accountable programming, regardless of the level of detail and whether it is for individuals or groups, requires an initial investment of time and energy. However, the end result is well worth the effort. Three actual case studies are presented here, with varying amounts of assessment data, so that students can practice writing individual plans.

Case Study 1
Female
Age 6
I.Q.: 76
Normal Size
Name: Flo

Flo has not yet started school. She is functioning at the prereadiness level. She has poor muscle tone and lacks good physical and emotional experiences with her parents. Her parents are very young and immature. The mother was fifteen years old at Flo's birth.

Flo has a very short attention span and appears to be hyperactive. She often throws tantrums. Flo has been excluded from the public school system due to her inappropriate behaviors.

In a recreational setting, Flo picks up the poor behaviors of others and copies them—gestures, noises, etc. She has problems with hand-eye coordination and static balance.

Case Study 2
Female
Age 28
I.Q.: Normal
Degree Level: BS in Business
Name: Kim

Kim is married to a truck driver and has recently moved to the area. Kim and her husband lived in Chicago where she worked as a buyer for a chain of stores. She has an eight-month old child, which is causing her a hassle in terms of being such a demand on her time. She is accustomed to large cities and seems to be having difficulty adjusting to a smaller town.

Since moving here, Kim has gained twenty pounds, which she feels is unbecoming to her once slim, active body.

Kim's family disliked the man she married and have never really accepted him. They felt he was beneath her and would probably never amount to much.

Last week Kim attempted to kill herself by cutting both wrists badly. She is presently in casts to prevent rotation at the wrist joint, and is a client in a psychiatric facility. She appears to be very depressed, cries a lot, and seeks out several staff members to talk to about the woes of her life.

Kim used to enjoy active types of sports and social recreation, but can't do much now because of the casts.

Case Study 3
Name: Steve
Age 11

The client was admitted to the program about four years ago for nine months in order to assess his functional ability and develop some useful tools to be used by his school in coordination with his educational program.

This was successfully accomplished, and the recommendations we made were, and have been, carried out by the client's teachers. The expectations that were developed four years ago are no longer appropriate. This is the primary reason for the current admission, to reassess his functional academic and social capabilities, develop more appropriate expectations for the client, and develop recommendations for his future educational program and social growth.

The client's father is in his late sixties; his mother passed away since his last discharge. The father seems extremely protective and would rather do everything for the client than teach him how to do things himself. The father is also extremely sensitive to any possible attempts to remove his son from the home. (There have been no attempts in that direction to date.) He is apparently quite content to keep his son totally dependent on him. The client has two brothers and two sisters. The brothers have been reported to tease the client and one seems quite resentful of all the attention given to other siblings. The sisters are very interested in obtaining assistance for the client.

As a result, the client is a very low-functioning child, both academically and socially. He does not initiate verbal interactions, and will usually avoid eye contact. He is afraid of bathrooms and will not go in alone. He is generally compliant when a direct, firm tone of voice is used. He will bite his hand when he is frustrated, and might yell when being noncompliant. He doesn't interact with other children, and, for the most part, keeps to himself. The other children at school are extremely protective of and motherly toward him. Since he will pose no apparent threat to the other boys on the unit, we are likely to witness a similar situation.

The overwhelming consensus of his teachers is concern with his ability to function successfully in his environment. It is clearly their priority to help the client develop the skills necessary to cope with his world, and to increase his ability to function socially.

evaluation

Evaluation leads to program improvement and decisions regarding program effectiveness. It follows assessment and program implementation. Assessment is necessary to determine goals. Assessment is also a prerequisite to determining specific, measurable behavioral objectives, implementation strategies, and evaluation strategies.

Evaluation requires at least two phases—*formative* and *summative*—and follows program implementation. Evaluation takes place while a program takes place and at its completion. Formative evaluation takes place during program implementation and should result in immediate program improvements. In the case of Sam Spacey, daily progress notes and the evaluation at the end of one week exemplifies a type of formative program evaluation. Information obtained from ongoing formative evaluation provides the impetus for continually changing an individual program plan to meet the client's needs. Formative evaluation allows programs to be dynamic. This sample of daily progress notes on Sam Spacey illustrates a simple formative evaluation:

11/4 1. Does not talk to others.

Subjective. Client states that having other clients around makes him uncomfortable, especially when they ask him to talk to them. He said Mrs. K. kept asking him why he was here and he stated it was none of her business.

Objective. Still avoids talking to people. Got up and left his seat when Mrs. K. sat down next to him. He did, however, seem to enjoy our conversation about woodworking tools, and after some prompting he began explaining how he used to be in the contracting business.

Assessment. Still appears scared and threatened and will not talk with other clients, but seemed to come out when he felt he could trust the therapist.

Plan. Continue as scheduled.

11/9 1. Does not talk to others.

Subjective. Client states he really enjoys talking to Mr. S. about baseball and that some of the people here are nicer than he thought now that he has gotten to know them.

Objective. Joined into an informal conversation group today without being asked. Spent forty-five minutes talking with Mr. S. Approached the therapist to talk about a new woodworking project.

Assessment. Becoming less isolated from the group and more comfortable talking with both clients and staff. Could possibly tolerate group activities now.

Plan
1. Encourage client to work on woodworking projects with other clients.
2. Schedule client in assertive training class and music appreciation.

3. Continue with rest of plan.
4. Continue to record progress daily.

Summative evaluation is a summary of formative evaluation data. Summative evaluation data may result in overall changes in any or all phases of the individual's program. Summative evaluation allows for recommendations to be made about continued client involvement or termination.

Summative evaluation for Sam Spacey would state whether or not he achieved the behavioral objectives set forth. Successes and failures would be explained. Summative evaluation for Sam Spacey would also include recommendations for his future involvement in leisure activity programs.

Because, from the early stages of individual program planning, specific behavioral objectives were clearly delineated and daily records kept on his response to program involvement, it is possible to evaluate Sam's continued status in the program and the effectiveness of implementation strategies. Through individualized programming, the needs of constituents are better met and program accountability is ensured.

other approaches to individualized program planning

Despite the efficacy of individualized program planning relative to both program accountability and positive behavior change, few concrete models have been presented in the therapeutic recreation literature. The Linear Model for Individual Treatment designed by David Compton is perhaps the most comprehensive. Using a systems flow chart, he outlines 215 steps that occur within seven phases of individualized program planning:

1. Determining to provide individual therapeutic recreation services,
2. Developing a personal profile of the client,
3. Determining objectives for the unit,
4. Planning activities for the treatment unit and sessions,
5. Implementing the unit treatment plan,
6. Evaluating the results of the completed unit,
7. Determining status of the unit.[5]

Compton states that the LMIT model was designed

to provide the practitioner with a greater degree of accountability for the "purposive intervention" in therapeutic recreation; to utilize the most current and relevant techniques from related areas; to develop precision in the delivery of therapeutic recreation services; to provide the therapist with a step-by-step systems analysis of the delivery of therapeutic recreation services to individuals; for application primarily to those individuals who have accentuated needs, . . . and for application to clients regardless of their age, sex, diagnostic category or severity of dysfunction. [6]

This step-by-step systems analysis of the individualized prescriptive programming process was developed primarily for use in treatment settings and has been successfully tested with severely handicapped individuals.

Anthony Linford offers a criteria-referenced approach as an effective means of program evaluation in therapeutic recreation. The procedure assesses individual behavior and places it on a nonproficiency/proficiency achievement continuum. Normative terminal behaviors are not suggested as criteria references; rather, they are sequentially related to the individual achievement of the clients. [7]

Bill Adair gives special attention to individual assessment and diagnostic planning. He states:

An accurate diagnostic assessment is essential to providing the therapeutic recreation specialist with facts to be used in the setting of relevant and obtainable goals. These goals or behavioral objectives provide the framework from which a continuous assessment process may be established. [8]

Three major techniques are employed in completing a diagnostic assessment: (1) observation of physical behaviors, communication skills, play habits, and social skills; (2) interview with the client; and (3) skill testing. Individual objectives are established relative to assessment data and accurate progress reports are made.

The Comprehensive Evaluation in Recreational Therapy Scale (CERT Scale) was designed for use in short-term, acute-care, psychiatric settings. It identifies and defines behaviors relevant to therapeutic recreation. It seeks to provide an objective means to rate clients on the identified behaviors. [9] Unlike the process of identifying individual problematic behaviors, this scale assesses all clients on the same behaviors, and evaluates their progress in identified problem areas.

summary

Individualization in programming has come of age. No longer can we assume that what is good for one is good for all. Program accountability has become the prerequisite for funding and administrative support. It is no longer enough to report numbers of programs and participants. Accountability is concerned with a specific participant's needs and recorded progress. The need for individual program planning increases with the handicapped because of the number of problems that require handling. Individual program planning is appropriate in institutions, schools, and in community programs.

The procedures outlined in this chapter offer a systematic scheme for individualizing programs. The procedures are flexible enough to be useful in a variety of settings. Unlike many other approaches, the steps outlined make logical and consistent use of all data. Often data that are on file resemble an unassembled jigsaw puzzle. To solve the puzzle, to fit the pieces together appropriately, some organizational scheme is required. Just as organizing the pieces makes a picture, organizing information relevant to identifying and meeting individual needs makes it possible to develop the client's treatment or programming plan and facilitates the implementation process. The payoff is likely to be, above all else, (1) meaningful behavioral change in clients as a direct result of intervention, (2) increased knowledge of the effectiveness of implementation strategies and the utilization of staff time, and (3) improved staff communication.

notes

1 L. L. Weed, M.D., *Medical Records, Medical Education and Patient Care* (Cleveland, Ohio: Case Western Reserve University, 1971).

2 Scarvia B. Anderson, Samuel Ball, and Richard T. Murphy and Associates, *Encyclopedia of Educational Evaluation* (San Francisco, Calif.: Jossey-Bass Publishers, 1975), p. 27.

3 Bill Adair, "The Role of Recreation in Assessing the Needs of Emotionally Disturbed Youth," *Leisurability,* 1, no. 4 (1974), 27.

4 Gerald S. Fain, "Leisure Counseling: Translating Needs into Action," *Therapeutic Recreation Journal,* 7, no. 2, 4–9.

5 David M. Compton and Donna Price, "Individualizing Your Treatment Program: A Case Study Using LMIT," *Therapeutic Recreation Journal,* 9, no. 4 (1975), 127.

6 David M. Compton, "A Linear Model for Individual Treatment in Therapeutic Recreation" (unpublished doctoral dissertation, University of Utah, 1973).

7 Anthony G. Linford, "A Criterion-Referenced Approach to Program Evaluation in Therapeutic Recreation Service," *Therapeutic Recreation Journal,* 5, no. 2 (1971), 54–56, 93.

8 Bill Adair, "The Role of Recreation in Assessing the Needs of Emotionally Disturbed Youth," *Leisurability,* 1, no. 4 (1974), 25–33.

9 Robert A. Parker and others, "The Comprehensive Evaluation in Recreational Therapy Scale: A Tool for Patient Evaluation," *Therapeutic Recreation Journal,* 9, no. 4 (1975), 143–52.

suggested references

ADAIR, B., "The Role of Recreation in Assessing the Need of Emotionally Disturbed Youth," *Leisurability*, 1, no. 4 (1974), 25–33.

AVEDON, E. M., *Therapeutic Recreation Service: An Applied Behavioral Approach*. Englewood Cliffs N.J.: Prentice-Hall, Inc., 1974.

BASHOOK, P. G., W. H. HAMMETT, AND L. J. SANDLOW, *Problem-Oriented Medical Records: Guidelines for Format and Forms*. Chicago, Ill.: Michael Reese Medical Center, 1974.

BECK, H. L., *Social Services to the Mentally Retarded*. Springfield, Ill.: Charles C. Thomas, 1969.

BERRYMAN, D. L., *Recommended Standards with Evaluative Criteria for Recreation Services in Residential Institutions*. New York: New York University Press, 1971.

COHEN, D. H., AND V. STERN, *Observing and Recording the Behavior of Young Children*. New York: Teachers College Press, Columbia University, 1973.

COMPTON, D. M., "Linear Model for Individual Treatment in Therapeutic Recreation" (Unpublished doctoral dissertation, University of Utah, 1973).

CURRIE, K., "Evaluating Function of Mentally Retarded Children Through the Use of Toys and Play Activities," *American Journal of Occupational Therapy*, 23, no. 1 (1969), 35–42.

DINSDALE, S. M., AND P. L. MOSSMAN, "The Problem-Oriented Medical Record in Rehabilitation," *Archives of Physical Medical Journal*, 51 (August 1970), 488–92.

HAMMOND, K., "Improving Patient Records," *Clincial Pediatrics*, 9 (October 1970), 611–16.

HARTLAGE, L. C. AND D. C. PARK, "Criteria for Evaluation of Therapeutic Summer Camping with the Mentally Retarded," *Psychology*, 4, no. 1 (1967), 2–5.

HAWORTH, M. R., AND F. J. MENOLASCINO, "Video-Tape Observations of Disturbed Young Children," *Journal of Clinical Psychology*, 23, no. 1 (1967), 135–40.

HURST, W., "How to Implement the Weed System," *Archives Internal Medicine*, 128 (1971), 456–63.

LINFORD, A. G., "A Criterion-referenced Approach to Program Evaluation in Therapeutic Recreation Service," *Therapeutic Recreation Journal*, 5, no. 2 (1971), 54–56, 93.

MAGER, R. F., *Preparing Instructional Objectives*. Palo Alto, Calif.: Fearon Publishers, 1962.

PETERSON, C. A., *A Systems Approach to Therapeutic Recreation*. Champaign, Ill.: Stipes Publishing Company, 1976.

WEED, L. L., "Medical Records that Guide and Teach: Part I," *New England Journal of Medicine*, 278 (March 14, 1968), 593–600.

———, "Medical Records that Guide and Teach: Part II," *New England Journal of Medicine*, 278 (March 21, 1968), 652–57.

————, *Medical Records, Medical Education and Patient Care.* Cleveland, Ohio: Case Western Reserve University, 1971.

WILLSON, M. A., "Use of Developmental Inventory as a Chart of Progress," *Physical Therapy,* 49, no. 1 (1969), 19–32.

WITT, J. E., AND P. A. WITT, "Planning and Evaluation of Recreational Activities in Therapeutic Settings," *Therapeutic Recreation Journal,* 4, no. 4 (1970), 5–7, 35, 37.

group assessment
and program planning

PURPOSE: To present a rationale for using group assessment techniques and to present simple methods for implementing them. Variables relevant to group assessment will be discussed, as well as suggested ways of translating assessment results into meaningful group programming.

Social interaction in groups has long been regarded as one of the strongest assets in the leisure movement. The enthusiasm about the group experience in therapeutic recreation is not without justification. Many therapeutic interventions take place in the small-group setting. However, our reliance on the group experience can be insidious; we naïvely cast people together and expect them to emerge miraculously as changed individuals. To assume that the mere existence of a group activity will, without careful deliberation and planning, produce measurable, positive changes is as presumptuous as dropping a bottle of milk on the floor and expecting the milk to fall into a map of the United States. Often we seem to chase after the elusive "intrinsic value of a group," convinced of its power but confused by its concept. Never quite sure what the intrinsic value is, we continue to rely on it and acclaim its value in programming.

In reality, there is no one intrinsic value of the group. A group is only as valuable as each of its individual members. Group members are individuals that come together with their own experiences and perceptions. Within the group the *possibility* exists of interacting, sharing, and receiving feedback from each other. Group activities, regardless of content, provide ideal laboratories for learning, provided proper planning has taken place. Participants may "research" their own behavior and "experiment" with new and hopefully growth-producing, goal-directed behavior. This possibility exists in all groups, including groups that play together, work together, talk together, and learn new skills together. In order to measure the value of group activities and experiences, behavior-directed goals must be delineated. The possible outcomes of aggregate or group activities are discussed in chapter ten.

In individual program planning, an attempt is made to look at a person holistically, using the collected information as the basis for an individual plan. In group assessment, the individual is no less important, but the areas of assessment relate to predetermined variables relevant to group interaction. In an effort to make group activities therapeutic for emotionally disturbed youth, Marty Bogan designed a process for diagnosing groups. He believes that group assessment is

> *a diagnostic process in which individual interaction profiles and group-as-a-whole assumptions are examined and formulated into a working diagnostic statement. Criteria are collected from selected observations and assumptions about the group. These data are put together into a logical pattern explaining the nature of what we are dealing with and relating it to what should and can be done.* [1]

In Bogan's design, the group assessment process helps in the selection of appropriate activities. When groups already have previously defined tasks, assessment helps to determine and plan for potential problems or to assign other suitable tasks to group members, such as assigning tasks on a weekend camping trip.

when to use group assessment techniques

Group assessment techniques are appropriate for four basic reasons:

1. The interaction of the group members is the condition under which individual growth is measured. Evidence of change is seen when the members of the group work together. Thus, the ability to perform positively *in a group* is the desired terminal behavior of all group members. The ability of the group to function provides the various criteria for measurement.
2. Aspects of the group process provide the *means* of achieving individual terminal behaviors. The group is an expedient way for members to work on their individual problems. For example, two people will attend the same social dance class for entirely different reasons. One may need the group experience to increase tolerance of closeness, while the other may want to increase a repertoire of leisure skills. In both instances, the group experience is a necessary means to individual ends.
3. In groups that are formed to teach certain skills, assessment and moni-

toring of individual skills within the group determine the level and techniques of instruction. Such is the case in activity or social-skill-development groups, such as photography and music classes and assertive training groups. These groups are formed to address the common needs of group members.

4. Sometimes individuals are forced together due to limited staff, large numbers of participants, or program structure. This is usually the case at camp where groups form as a result of random cabin assignments. This situation is also common in community recreation programs; here, group assessment helps to pinpoint potential problems and deal effectively with them. In large state institutions and community recreation programs, it is often difficult to monitor individual progress. Both group assessment and program planning, then, provide criteria for evaluation. Activities are planned to meet group goals and are measured as such.

constructing individual profiles

Regardless of the setting in which group assessment is conducted, individual profiles on each group member are still a necessity. However, individual assessment does not need to be as comprehensive as the individual assessment necessary for formulating an individual program plan. In group assessment, it is necessary to identify those characteristics of individual group members that are important to the *interaction* of the group. Variables that are important to the functioning of a specific group are first identified, and then an individual profile is compiled on each group member relative to the variables identified. The individual interaction profiles in Bogan's model are the attributes of age, energy level, fight-run, dependency, leadership, and isolation. Based on assessment of these individual profiles, Bogan has found that these group characteristics can be assessed: special or unusual characteristics, the group wish, the group fear, the group mood, and the stage of development. Here is his explanation of these variables:

Energy level. Rank subjectively on a one-to-five point scale. Select one:
1. *No energy available*
2. *Little energy*
3. *Average*
4. *Active*
5. *Hyperactive*

Fight-Run. When the individual is confronted with a problem, does he usually fight or does he run? Withdrawal, denial, and flight are forms of running. Choose either:
   Fight
   Run

Dependency. Choose one:

Independent. The individual behaves in a self-reliant way.

Dependent. The individual behaves as if he or she were dependent on someone else.

Counterdependent. The individual is really dependent but behaves as if she or he were superindependent.

Leadership. Identify positive and negative leaders.

Isolates. Identify isolates.

Special or unusual characteristics. Postulate the group-as-a-whole assumptions.

The group wish. Determine the collective wish shared by most of the group. What would this group like to be or do?

The group fear. Determine the collective fear that is preventing the wish from taking place.

The group mood. Determine the dominant emotion (anger, joy, apathy, etc.).

Stage of development. Determine the stage of group development (beginning, middle, end, etc.). Is there anything significant in the group's history? [2]

The form in figure 7–1 is an example of a group assessment that uses Bogan's format.

GROUP MEMBERS	AGE	ENERGY LEVEL	FIGHT/ RUN	DEPENDENCY	LEADERSHIP ISOLATES
Anthony	46	3	F	CD	
Christy	21	1	R	D	ISO
Judy	30	2	F	D	+L
Mary	16	2	R	D	
Collene	27	5	R	CD	

Group wish: To be taken care of.

Group fear: Afraid of not being able to take care of self.

Group mood: Apathy and anger.

Group stage: Beginning, not working together as a group.

Diagnostic statement: A dependent, angry group unable to take care of itself; no direction.

Objectives: To set goals for oneself and carry them out in a set amount of time.

Activity: Want ads — goal-setting newspaper — each individual sets his goals with help of group and carries them out.

Dependency
  I — Independent
  D — Dependent
CD — Counterdependent

Leadership
ISO — Group isolates
+L — Positive leadership
−L — Negative leadership

Fig. 7–1
Group Assessment Form*

*Marty Bogan, "Diagnosing Groups and Planning from Where They're At," in *Expanding Horizons in Therapeutic Recreation II*, ed. Jerry Kelley (Champaign, Ill.: University of Illinois, Office of Recreation and Park Resources, 1974), p. 75.

Several other characteristics may be important for group interaction, which relate to the nature and functioning ability of the group being assessed. They are

1. *Control level (wanted and expressed).* How much direction and instruction does the individual want from others? How much direction and instruction does the individual give to others?
   a. None
   b. Very little
   c. Average
   d. Much
   e. Total control
2. *Inclusion level (wanted and expressed).* How much does the individual want to be included by other people? How much does the individual include others?
   a. None
   b. Very little
   c. Average
   d. Much
   e. Total inclusion
3. *Affection level (wanted and expressed).* How much affection does the individual want from others? How much affection does the individual give to others?
   a. None
   b. Very little
   c. Average
   d. Much
   e. Total affection
4. *Attention span.*
   a. Like child 0–3
   b. Like child 4–6
   c. Like child 7–10
   d. Like child 10–12
   e. Like teenager
   f. Like adult
5. *Intellectual level.*
   a. Below average
   b. Average
   c. Above average
   d. Superior
6. *Physical limitations.* Identify.
7. *Hygiene problems.* Identify.
8. *Ethnocentricity (if relevant to group interaction).* Identify.
9. *Precautions.* Note any relevant emotional problems, medications, etc.[3]

Other variables that may be important to individual responses in group interaction are identified by the Adjective Check List:

1. **Achievement.** *To strive to be outstanding in pursuits of socially recognized significance.*
2. **Dominance.** *To seek and sustain leadership roles in groups or to be influential and controlling in individual relationships.*
3. **Endurance.** *To persist in any task undertaken.*
4. **Order.** *To place special emphasis on neatness, organization, and planning one's activities.*
5. **Intraception.** *To engage in attempts to understand one's own behavior or the behavior of others.*
6. **Nurturance.** *To engage in behavior that extends material or emotional benefits to others.*
7. **Affiliation.** *To seek and sustain numerous personal friendships.*
8. **Exhibition.** *To behave in such a way as to elicit the immediate attention of others.*
9. **Autonomy.** *To act independently of others or of social values and expectations.*
10. **Aggression.** *To engage in behavior that attacks or hurts others.*
11. **Change.** *To seek novelty of experience and avoid routine.*
12. **Succorance.** *To solicit sympathy, affection, or emotional support from others.*
13. **Abasement.** *To express feelings of inferiority through self-criticism, guilt, or social impotence.*
14. **Deference.** *To seek and sustain subordinate roles in relationships with others.* [4]

When identifying variables to be considered in group assessment, it is important to select only those characteristics that relate to the group being investigated. Ethnocentricity, for example, may be an important consideration for a group that exists in an area of ongoing racial tension. However, most often, this is not a relevant subject to consider. Physical limitations need only be considered for groups with physically handicapped members. When dealing with psychiatric clients, variables such as attention span, inclusion levels, tolerance of authority, abasement levels, deference levels, tolerance for change, and precautions (relative to type of medication and acting-out behavior) may be important variables to consider. When working with mentally impaired clients, variables such as intellectual level, energy levels, attention span, and level of verbalization may be important to consider.

After identifying the variables that are relevant to the individuals in the group, and after constructing the appropriate assessment form (table 7–1), actual individual assessment can be conducted.

individual assessment

Ideally, individuals that are part of a group could be assessed with the use of standardized tests. However, since relevant variables differ among groups being assessed, it is unlikely that one test could be

GROUP ASSESSMENT AND PROGRAM PLANNING FORM

NATURE OF GROUP: <u>SUMMER DAY CAMP</u>

GROUP MEMBERS	AGE	ENERGY LEVEL FIGHT-RUN	DEPENDENCY	LEADERSHIP	WANTED ISOLATES	EXPRESSED CONTROL	WANTED CONTROL	EXPRESSED INCLUSION	WANTED INCLUSION	WANTED AFFECTION	EXPRESSED AFFECTION	ATTENTION SPAN	INTELLECTUAL LEVEL	ETHNOCENTRICITY	PHYSICAL LIMITATIONS	HYGIENE PROBLEMS	PRECAUTIONS
Amy	8	F	CD	-L	2	5	4	4	1	3	3	N/A	N/A	N/A	None	None	Easily agitated May hit others
Ben	9	R	D	I	5	1	3	5	1	2	2	N/A	N/A	N/A	Polio Rt. Leg—Limps	None	Cries a lot
Tommy	8	R	I	I	2	2	1	2	2	2	3	N/A	N/A	N/A	Poor vision without glasses	None	Runs away when angry
Kevin	8	F	D	-L	5	1	3	5	2	2	4	N/A	N/A	N/A	None	Poor oral hygiene —wears braces on teeth	Abusive language when agitated
Andy	7	R	I	+L	3	3	3	3	3	3	3	N/A	N/A	N/A	Epileptic	None	Medication three times per day
Shauna	10	F	I	+L	2	4	4	4	4	3	4	N/A	N/A	N/A	None	None	None
Susan	8	R	D	-L	5	1	1	5	3	4	4	N/A	N/A	N/A	Paraplegic —in chair	Indwelling Catheter—must be kept clean	Transfer weight in chair
Kimberly	9	F	CD	-L	2	5	1	4	4	2	2	N/A	N/A	N/A	None	Sloppy eater	Easily agitated Hits others

(Columns fall under the heading: INTERACTION VARIABLES)

NOTE: I = Independent, D = Dependent, CD = Counterdependent, ISO = Group isolates, +L = Positive leadership, -L = Negative leadership, F = Fight, R = Run, N/A = Not applicable.

Potential Problems (List):

1. Variance of energy level—three are active to hyperactive; three have little energy.
2. Only two are +L; one is youngest in group.
3. Three members of the group are isolates.
4. Group members want more control than they are willing to express to each other.
5. Group members want more affection than they are willing to express.
6. Slight variance in attention span and intellectual level of the group.
7. Two group members have limited ambulation.
8. Three group members need individual help with hygiene problems.

Assessment (Identify strengths as well as weaknesses):

The group is a beginning group, fairly dependent and lacking leaders, with an equal distribution of males and females. The most likely leader is a female (Shauna). Activities for the group should be relatively short in nature with much variety. Initially, the group may need non-threatening types of activities, fairly structured, with no competition. An effort should be made to build the trust of the isolates and help the group members become familiar with the handicapped members. An effort should be made to match the members with those who would best meet their needs (i.e., Amy and Ben are compatible in most areas). The group would also benefit by activities that require physical endurance and concentration.

Group Goals (List):

1. To acquire skills of cooperation and shared responsibility through leisure activities.
2. To acquire positive peer leadership concepts through leisure activities.
3. To acquire new leisure skills that require physical endurance.
4. To acquire new leisure skills that require concentration.

Group Objectives (List):

(For goal 1.) Given a choice of three outdoor group activities appropriate to the program, the group will demonstrate the ability to cooperate and share responsibility to the satisfaction of the leaders, as characterized by the following:

a. Finish the task within a designated period of time.
b. The group divides the task into parts and each child completes his or her part.
c. Individual group members positively reinforce each other with appropriate verbal comments and praise.
d. Group members voluntarily work together or ask for assistance on tasks requiring the skill or strength of more than one person.

Group Plan:

1. Before initiating the project, the group leader may *model* "cooperative behavior" by role playing or creative dramatics.
2. Help the group isolates find a place in the group by asking them to help with various appropriate tasks.
3. Reinforce all cooperative behavior with qualitative praise, e.g., "I like the way you ask for my help. That helps me feel important."
4. Brainstorm various projects with the group and allow each member to express a preference. Assist the group in the decision-making process.
5. Conduct the activity decided on and evaluate as outlined above.

Table 7-1

101

used. The practicality of administering a battery of standardized tests in order to assess a group is questionable in most therapeutic recreation settings due to lack of time, limited staffing, and financial constraints. This, however, does not disallow the practicality and significance of group assessment.

Since standardized testing is usually impractical, we suggest objective assessment by staff. By observing individuals interacting with others and employing the simple rating scales described, it is possible to assess group members objectively relative to the identified variables. These simple measures of group members yield valuable information about the group as a whole.

the problem list

After the profile of each group member is charted, it is possible to "eyeball" the information and isolate probable group problems. Group strengths may also be identified. A potential problem list for the group should be formulated, following the same procedures for individual program planning described in chapter six (see table 7–1).

assessment statement

Based on the data recorded for group members and the subsequent problem list, it is possible to formulate a brief statement summarizing the strengths and weaknesses of the group, the stage of the group's development, and the general status of the group. Suggestions may also be made about how to operate the group (see table 7–1).

group goals

Having assessed individual members and the group as a whole, it is possible to formulate group goals. Group goals depend on the group's purpose. If the group was formed to learn new leisure skills, then the assessment data can be used to identify potential learning problems and to match program participants appropriately with peers and staff members. The data are also useful for deciding on appropriate leadership or instructional styles.

If the group was formed to learn an activity, the group goal might state:

Goal: To acquire leisure skills in outdoor activities.

If the group was formed to allow the group members to experience positive group interaction, the goal might read:

Goal: To acquire skills of cooperation necessary for group activities.

If the group was formed so that its members could work on individual goals concerned with relating to others, the group goal might say:

Goal: To acquire skills of communication and open expression necessary for support groups.

This particular group goal is commonly used in encounter groups where the group structure is necessary for individuals to receive feedback on individual problems. It is also common for leisure counseling groups.

Particularly if the group was formed by rote assignment, the problem list and group assessment will provide a basis for formulating group goals. In most community recreation programs, goals for participation have been previously established, such as "to increase socialization skills" or "to increase leisure skills." These broadly stated goals, however, may be described in detail to suit each group. The group of children discussed in table 7–1 are typically found in a summer day camp for exceptional children. After group assessment was completed, the appropriate group goals were determined (table 7–1).

group objectives

Having identified what appear to be appropriate goals for a given group, the program planner may proceed to write the behavioral objectives. Measurable behavioral objectives should be written for each group goal. However, since it is often difficult to systematically observe and evaluate many behaviors simultaneously, the programmer need not be concerned with more than one goal at a time. Immediate attention should be given to the one group goal that appears to be most related to the functioning of the group. For the children in summer day camp, acquiring skills of cooperation and sharing responsibility through leisure activities appears to be a prerequisite to the other goals (see table 7–1).

Whenever possible, the group should be encouraged to select the activity and the process by which the goal may be achieved. Concerning the formulation of objectives, Bogan states:

> *Ideally people should decide for themselves what they want to do, and then devise their own systematic procedures for achievement. The therapist can help the group to define objectives, i.e., the particular ends it will pursue collectively, or he (or she) can define the objectives for the group. Since the therapist has consid-*

erable control over the group's concrete objectives and what activities it will engage in, he (or she) can attempt to define group purposes so that they are consistent with the goals of the individuals. The establishment of objectives is the heart of this method. Objectives are based upon the working diagnostic statement and they must be attainable, desirable, and controllable.[5]

The process for stating the group's behavioral objectives is identical to the process outlined in chapters six and nine for writing individual behavioral objectives. In order to be evaluated, a behavioral objective must include: (1) a clear statement of the *behavior* to be demonstrated, (2) the *conditions* under which the behavior should occur, and (3) the *criteria* for judgment.

Since the setting for our sample group is a summer day camp and since most of the activities occur outside, the group objective related to goal 1 seemed appropriate (see table 7–1). A number of other objectives could have been selected by the group or its leader, depending on available resources. Having specified a group objective, and when possible having involved the group members in its determination, the group plan may be written.

group plan

The group plan specifies the means by which the group objective is to be achieved. Techniques for writing the group plan are the same as those used for writing individual plans and are also outlined in chapter six. Since volunteers and other staff members may assist in the implementation of the group plan, it is important to keep the items simple and direct. Helpful suggestions may also be included. See table 7–1. The group plan is unique to each group and incorporates the needs of the group, available resources, and programming orientations. After the group plan has been determined, program implementation and evaluation may begin.

evaluation

Evaluation allows for objective decision making related to the revision of the program and to general statements about the program's effectiveness. Basic questions that can be asked are

1. Were the group objectives appropriate to the group goals?
2. Were the activities appropriate to the objectives?

3. Were the activities appropriate to the ages and ability levels of the group members?
4. Were the implementation strategies appropriate to group learning and development?
5. Were there any unexpected outcomes of the program?
6. Were the group objectives achieved?

Evaluations of groups may be based on written observations and comments by staff members as well as forms that note individual and group progress. Methods of evaluation are discussed in chapters six and thirteen.

summary

When individual program planning is not possible or necessary, group assessment and planning make possible quality programming decisions and program accountability. Group assessment begins with a simple assessment of individual group members relative to variables identified as being important to the functioning of the group. By analyzing the individual profiles of the group members, it is possible to formulate a list of potential problems within the group. Summary statements about the strengths and weaknesses of the group are derived from both the individual profiles and the problem list.

This assessment information is helpful in specifying the group goals. One goal is weighted as the most relevant to the functioning of the group, and appropriate group objectives are detailed. The group plan is then determined and the program is implemented, evaluated, and revised. Chapter nine discusses procedures for defining actual program content and processes.

notes

[1] Marty Bogan, "Diagnosing Groups and Planning from Where They're At," in *Expanding Horizons in Therapeutic Recreation II*, ed. Jerry Kelley (Champaign, Ill.: University of Illinois, Office of Recreation and Park Resources, 1974), p. 71.

[2] Ibid., p. 72.

[3] Variables 1, 2, and 3 are tested by the FIRO-B Scale (Fundamental Interpersonal Relationship Orientation Scale); see William C. Schultz, *The Interpersonal Underworld* (Palo Alto, Calif.: Science and Behavior Books, Inc., 1967).

[4] H. G. Gough and A. D. Heilbrun, *Manual for the Adjective Check List* (Palo Alto, Calif.: Consulting Psychologist Press, 1965), pp. 6–9.

[5] Bogan, "Diagnosing Groups," pp. 72–73.

suggested references

BION, W. R., *Experiences in Groups*. New York: Basic Books, 1959.

BOGAN, M., "Diagnosing Groups and Planning from Where They're At," *Expanding Horizons in Therapeutic Recreation II*, ed. Jerry Kelley, Champaign, Ill.: University of Illinois, Office of Recreation and Park Resources, 1974.

BRAMMER, L. M., *The Helping Relationship: Process and Skills*. Englewood Cliffs, N.J.: Prentice-Hall, Inc., 1973.

CARKHUFF, R. R., *The Development of Human Resources*. New York: Holt, Rinehart and Winston, 1971.

———, *Helping and Human Relations*. New York: Holt, Rinehart and Winston, 1969.

———, and B. BERENSON, *Beyond Counseling and Psychotherapy*. New York: Holt, Rinehart and Winston, 1967.

COMBS, A., D. AVILA, AND W. PURKEY, *Helping Relationships Basic Concepts for the Helping Professions*. Boston, Mass.: Allyn and Bacon, 1971.

EGAN, G., *Encounter: Group Processes for Interpersonal Growth*. Monterey, Calif.: Brooks/Cole Publishing Company, 1970.

———, *Face to Face: The Small Group Experience and Interpersonal Growth*. Monterey, Calif.: Brooks/Cole Publishing Company, 1973.

HARPER, R. A., *The New Psychotherapies*. Englewood Cliffs, N. J.: Prentice-Hall, Inc., 1975.

MARTIN, D., *Learning-based Client-centered Therapy*. Monterey, Calif.: Brooks/Cole Publishing Company, 1972.

MATRE, S. V., *Acclimatizing: A Personal and Reflective Approach to a Natural Relationship*. Martinsville, Ind.: American Camping Association, 1974.

MILLS, T., *The Sociology of Small Groups*. Englewood Cliffs, N.J.: Prentice-Hall, Inc., 1967.

SCHUTZ, W. C., *Joy: Expanding Human Awareness*. New York: Grove Press, 1967.

WHITAKER, D. S., AND M. S. LIEBERMAN, *Psychotherapy Through the Group Process*. New York: Atherton, 1964.

determining
program direction

PURPOSE: To provide an overview of program conceptualization, including general client assessment, broad content considerations, and the processes of deriving statements of purpose and developing goals for unit- or agency-level programs. Sample program conceptualization models are included for a variety of agencies.

program levels

One of the most difficult tasks for a program planner is initially to conceptualize program direction. Most often therapeutic recreators inherit programs and continue them because they believe someone somewhere designed them with logic, reason, and good intentions. As a result, many programs continue to operate that were poorly thought out or thrown together in piecemeal fashion. This chapter discusses how to begin a new program. It focuses on a comprehensive level of programming for a unit or agency. Figures 8–1, 8–2, and 8–3 illustrate these program levels.

The word "program" is somewhat confusing, since it is used in so many ways and for so many different levels of services. Generally it indicates a broad range of services offered by an agency or unit. A program also designates a specific set of activities and interactions, e.g., a swimming program that is part of the total therapeutic recreation program of an in-patient unit. The planning procedures presented in chapters nine through thirteen focus on the design, specification, and evaluation of these separate program components. This chapter is concerned with the overall conceptualization of program direction.

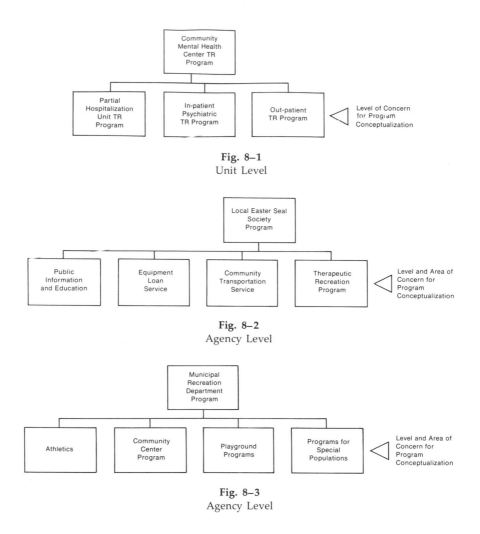

Fig. 8–1
Unit Level

Fig. 8–2
Agency Level

Fig. 8–3
Agency Level

statements of purpose

Well-planned operational program components depend on solid, comprehensive program conceptualization. When appropriate conceptualization does not take place, segmented programs result. New programs are added and old ones discarded without rhyme or reason. An agency or unit using a systems approach starts with a clear picture of its reason to exist. This requires a *statement of purpose.* This statement is broad in nature but gives direction and continuity to all the programs that evolve.

Before developing a statement of purpose for the overall

108

therapeutic recreation program of a unit or agency, certain issues and concerns must be addressed. Tradition should not be the guiding influence in determining program direction. Program planners need to analyze their agency, clients, and community carefully. They also need to assess the possibilities for program content. Objective data and analysis enable good decisions to be made in the later planning stages.

factors to be considered

Clients. Who are the people to be served by the unit or agency? What disabilities do they have? What are the degrees of severity? What is the age range? Is there an equal breakdown of males and females? What is the socioeconomic status of clients? Compiling and analyzing this kind of information have many implications for the development of a sound statement of purpose.

Agency. The nature and type of agency directly affects the content of the statement of purpose. One would expect a psychiatric facility to be involved in treatment or rehabilitation programming. Similarly, one would expect a municipal recreation department to be engaged in instructional and recreation-participation programs.

Although an agency's history is important, the program planner should not be biased by tradition in determining appropriate program direction. Contemporary ideas and new directions in therapeutic recreation services should be reflected in the statement of purpose.

Resources—including staff, facilities, and budget—are factors in any planning effort, although they need not be constraints. The statement of purpose is a general statement and does not specify actual operational components. Thus, an emphasis on resources may limit the perspective of the statement.

Community. Knowledge of the surrounding community is also useful in determining the statement of purpose. The writer should investigate other agencies and the services they deliver. Unnecessary or inappropriate repetition can be avoided in this way; gaps in service can also be discovered.

Identifying available program resources is another benefit of community investigation. Far too often programs tend to reflect an "in-house" orientation. Since a statement of purpose needs to be broad in its scope, an awareness of external community factors may be essential input.

Equally important is an understanding of the socioleisure lifestyles in the community. Programs that emerge out of the statement of purpose need to reflect common community interests and take advantage of the facilities in the area. Clients should be able to move comfortably into community programs after being involved in therapeutic recreation programs. Other factors related to socioleisure lifestyles include rural versus urban characteristics, geographic and seasonal information, ethnic influence, and religious considerations.

content for statements of purpose

Once the essential factors related to the clients, agency, and community have been identified and studied, the planner is ready to develop the statement of purpose. Chapter two presented a comprehensive therapeutic recreation service model. An abbreviated version appears in figure 8–4. Briefly summarized, this model indicates that program direction can be categorized by looking at the primary function or purpose. Three basic areas emerge:

1. *Rehabilitation or treatment*. Programs with this intent focus on the improvement of a client's physical, social, mental, and/or emotional behaviors.
2. *Leisure education*. Programs of this nature focus on assisting the client in learning new leisure skills, acquiring social skills, establishing an awareness of self and leisure, and acquiring knowledge related to leisure resource utilization.
3. *Recreation participation*. Programs in this category provide the individual the opportunity to engage in leisure activities and programs of their choice.

The model can thus be used for conceptualizing the basic content for the statement of purpose. Program direction can focus directly on any one of the three areas or can reflect components or combinations of all three. It is common for a statement of purpose to focus on one or two of these areas.

Selecting the exact content for a purpose statement for a specific agency or unit involves several factors: the type and nature of the agency, the type of clients, and the philosophy of the therapeutic recreation staff.

writing statements of purpose

After the planner has gathered the available information about the clients, the agency, and the community, and has looked at possible program functions related to needs and resources, then basic decisions can be made about program direction. The next step in the process is developing and writing the statement of purpose. The statement should be comprehensive yet brief. It should explain the reason for the program's existence without detail. This statement of intent should provide the nucleus around which all program components can emerge. Two examples are provided below.

Example 1. Therapeutic recreation program in a vocational rehabilitation center.

Statement of purpose: To provide a wide range of recreation and leisure services to enable the acquisition and application of skills, knowledge, and attitudes necessary for successful participation in community socioleisure life.

Example 2. Therapeutic recreation program for a local Easter Seal Society.

Statement of purpose: To provide opportunities for physically handicapped residents of the community to develop recreational skills appropriate to age and limitation and to acquire knowledge of available and accessible community recreational facilities and resources.

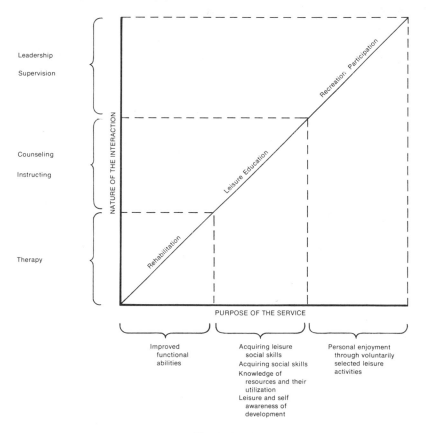

Fig. 8–4
Abbreviated Therapeutic Recreation Service Model

Statements of purpose are the backbone of the planning process. Each successive stage of program development should reflect the direction of the statement. Program components should carry out an aspect of the statement's intent.

Purpose statements will obviously vary in their content, format, and wording. They will reflect the characteristics of the agency and clientele, as well as the writer's philosophy and influence. Regardless of the variations in writing style or content, one central ideal remains: Statements of purpose should be derived carefully, thoughtfully, and with concern.

goals

Once a statement of purpose has been derived for a unit or agency, the next step is to develop goals. Goals describe aspects of the statement of purpose in greater detail. They develop a program's purpose. Usually goals are idealistic, yet they are capable of being put into operation through program components. Goals are not directly measurable; they are statements that show intentions. Possible goal statements for a vocational rehabilitation center (example 1) are:

1. To provide services and resources to enable students to acquire new leisure skills appropriate to their limitations and future lifestyles.
2. To provide the opportunity and structure to facilitate the students' regular participation in previously obtained and newly acquired activity skills and interests.
3. To provide counseling and educational services to assist students in understanding the significance of leisure phenomena and in the acceptance of their personal responsibility for leisure utilization.
4. To provide information related to leisure resources and experiences involving the utilization of resources.
5. To provide information and activity experiences to promote and enable the understanding and acceptance of ongoing health and physical fitness practices.
6. To provide opportunities to improve or increase social interaction abilities that will expand or facilitate the enjoyment of leisure activity participation.

The following are possible goal statements for a local Easter Seal Society (example 2):

1. To establish a resource center for the acquisition and dissemination of information regarding opportunities for recreational participation of physically handicapped community residents.

2. To provide an opportunity for physically handicapped community residents to gain new and well-balanced interests in leisure skills appropriate to age and limitation.
3. To provide the opportunity to participate in recreative activities in order to maintain and expand existing skills and interests.
4. To counsel physically handicapped persons about personal responsibility for meeting their own leisure needs.
5. To provide knowledge and experience to enable the utilization of community recreation resources.
6. To encourage the integration of the physically handicapped into ongoing community recreation programs.

writing goal statements

Goals play a major role in determining program content and direction; consequently they should be developed carefully and with much attention to alternatives, resources, and desired interpretation of the statement of purpose. Content is of vital significance. Equally important are the formating and wording of the statement. The following steps should be useful in deriving and stating goals:

Process for Deriving and Stating Goals
1. Review statement of purpose.
2. Review the characteristics and needs of the population.
3. Review the nature and purpose of the agency, resources, and constraints.
4. Brainstorm possible goal areas.
5. Determine the appropriateness of goal areas for the specific population.
6. Develop goal statements.
7. Analyze goal statements. A criteria list follows that may be used for this final check of goal appropriateness and technical quality.
8. Refine and rewrite goal statements.

Criteria for Judging Goal Statements
1. Statement clearly delineates the goal area:
    a. Statement focuses directly on key concept words.
    b. Surrounding wording does not change possible interpretation of the goal statement.
2. Statement has appropriate level of generality or specificity:
    a. Statement excludes material that would specify exact performance content or measurement.
    b. Statement avoids levels of generality that are too broad to direct reader to specific intent.
3. Statements are parallel in style and general level of content:
    a. Statements are consistent in wording and format.
    b. Statements are consistent in nature of content presented.

4. Statements are both appropriate and feasible for population and agency:
   a. Goals can be substantiated through professional knowledge as appropriate for development or performance expectations.
   b. Goals reflect the philosophy and nature of the agency and are feasible within time, budget, and staffing constraints.
5. Statements reflect the nature and intent of the statement of purpose.

additional content for goal statements

Each agency or unit should develop its own goal statements, reflecting the unique needs of its population, the nature of its setting, and the philosophy of its staff. Generally, however, the content for goal statements reflects the three functions of therapeutic recreation service: treatment, leisure education, or recreation participation. From these three areas, numerous specific goals can be formulated. The following suggestions for goal content are offered merely as a stimulus to the program developer. The areas are generic and not related to specific illnesses, disabilities, or settings. Each is presented as a content area and is not a fully developed goal statement.

Rehabilitation or Treatment Programs
1. To improve physical fitness.
2. To increase physical functioning.
3. To stimulate physical development.
4. To prevent physical deterioration.
5. To maintain current levels of physical functioning.
6. To increase cognitive (mental) functioning.
7. To stimulate cognitive development.
8. To prevent cognitive deterioration.
9. To maintain current levels of cognitive functioning.
10. To improve social and interaction skills.
11. To increase verbalization and self-expression.
12. To stimulate affective responses.
13. To facilitate appropriate expressions of emotion.
14. To assist in the adjustment to a condition of illness or disability.
15. To decrease atypical behaviors or mannerisms.
16. To increase tolerance for authority figures.
17. To decrease avoidance behaviors.
18. To increase independence and the ability to make decisions.
19. To increase awareness of personal feelings.

Leisure Education Programs
1. To develop awareness of leisure and its significance.
2. To develop self-awareness related to play and leisure.
3. To explore personal leisure attitudes and values.
4. To develop leisure problem-solving abilities.

5. To acquire knowledge of leisure resources and their uses.
6. To facilitate integration into community recreation programs.
7. To expand knowledge of leisure opportunities.
8. To stimulate self-directed leisure behavior.
9. To assist in the development of a personal leisure philosophy.
10. To develop social and interactional skills.
11. To acquire new leisure skills.
12. To increase personal repertoire of leisure skills.
13. To provide exposure to new leisure-skill areas.
14. To develop advanced levels of leisure-skill areas.
15. To develop leadership or community-service skills.

Recreation Participation Programs
1. To facilitate participation in previously acquired leisure skills.
2. To facilitate self-expression through diverse activity offerings.
3. To provide opportunities for social interaction through leisure.
4. To encourage ongoing conditions of health and fitness through leisure.
5. To provide an environment for the integration of diverse physical, mental, social, and emotional skills.
6. To provide opportunities for the reinforcement and support of other treatment programs.
7. To provide opportunities for creative and self-directed leisure involvement.
8. To provide opportunities for experiencing enjoyment and contentment.

These suggested goal areas can be made more precise and appropriate once a specific population and setting are focused on. For example, if a population is composed of severely mentally retarded children, a general physical goal might become more definitive, for example: to develop physical coordination and basic body movements. The program planner is urged to make those refinements when selecting and developing goal statements. A vast number of goal areas related to therapeutic recreation programs are not mentioned here because of their uniqueness to a given setting, population, or approach. For example, a goal area for a long-term health-care facility might deal with reduction of disorientation behaviors. The planner can be concerned with the uniqueness of a particular population and at the same time refer to general lists such as the ones provided.

selecting program components

After the statement of purpose and the goals are written, the next stage in comprehensive program planning is to select program components. Program components are the operational units of the overall program conceptualization. Each program component carries out some as-

'pect of the statement of purpose and goals. The number of components depends on the resources available to the therapeutic recreation staff, as well as on the scope of the goals. Regardless of the number and type of components, it is essential that they flow from the goals that have been determined. Each component selected will later be refined and designed in detail. At this point in the planning, the major task is to decide what to do, and how to break this down into operational units.

Basically, a program component is a set of activities and an interactional procedure that is designed for a defined group of clients for some predetermined purpose. Each component can be distinguished by its intended purpose, area of content, and interaction process. Each component is implemented and evaluated separately from the other components.

This stage of program planning is highly creative and calls on the planner's experience and expertise. A wide range of possibilities exist for transforming goals into program components. The planner is free to choose from existing program models or to create new delivery concepts. Familiarity with a large number of other programs and their implementation strategies is obviously useful to the planner, but more essential is the ability to conceptualize the components logically and imaginatively, using the goals of the agency or unit as a basis.

analyzing goals to determine program components

Although the goals refine the intent of the purpose statement, they do not specify exactly what is to be done or how to do it. At this point, creative and imaginative design enters into the picture, along with systematic thinking. The planner looks at the goals, armed with the knowledge of an agency's restraints and resources and the nature and needs of the clients. He or she brainstorms possible ways to achieve the goals through program components, perhaps sketching out alternative ways of achieving goals through the use of different component designs. Attention must be paid to priority goal areas and the dominant client needs. Final decisions are reached through rational and objective decision making based on information, alternatives, priorities, and resources.

Here is a brief example of the conversion of goals into program components.

Vocational Rehabilitation Center, Plainwell, Michigan
Population. Four hundred students, ages seventeen to sixty, male and female, mild to moderate physical disabilities (including visual and hearing impair-

ments), emotional disabilities, substance abusers, legal offenders, and chronic physical conditions (cardiac and respiratory illnesses).

Setting. Residential trade school offering vocational training in many areas. The average program length is one to two years.

Staff. Nine full-time therapeutic recreation staff members: one with master's degree, six with bachelor's degrees, two technicians.

Recreation Facilities. Indoor facilities—swimming pool, bowling alleys, gym, multipurpose rooms, craft rooms, and fitness rooms. Outdoor facilities— tennis and volleyball courts, softball diamond, lake, and wooded area.

Purpose Statement. To provide a wide range of recreation and leisure services to enable the acquisition and application of skills and knowledge necessary for successful participation in community socioleisure life.

Goals

1. To provide services and resources to enable students to acquire new leisure skills appropriate to their limitations and future lifestyles.
2. To provide the opportunity and structure to facilitate students' regular participation in previously obtained and newly acquired activity skills and interests.
3. To provide counseling and educational services to assist students in understanding the significance of the leisure phenomena and in the acceptance of their personal responsibility for leisure utilization.
4. To provide information related to leisure resources and experiences involving the use of resources.
5. To provide information and activity experiences to promote and enable the understanding and acceptance of ongoing health and physical fitness practices.
6. To provide opportunities to improve or increase social interaction abilities that will expand or facilitate the enjoyment of leisure activity participation.

analyzing purpose and goals

The purpose statement for the trade school indicates that the focus is on *acquiring* and *applying* leisure skills and knowledge for continued leisure participation, once the student has completed vocational training. The goals refine this purpose by indicating the need for students to acquire *new* skills that are appropriate to physical, mental, emotional, and social functional levels and that will provide lifelong leisurability. (In fact, many of the vocational students had developed leisure skills, but they were geared to the younger years and with a heavy emphasis on team sports.) The goals also include the need to learn about available leisure resources and how to use them. These goals tie in with the school's concern that many former students, well trained vocationally, were not maintaining jobs, and that a partial explanation was inadequate leisure lifestyles. Inadequate social skills also seemed significant. Ongoing health and fitness is important regardless of types of disability. Since the school is residential and located far away from a large community, the school feels responsible for providing ongoing opportunities for recreational participation.

The result of the analysis of the goals, students, and resources was a decision to plan a program with three major components.

Assessment and Prescriptive Component. In this component each student is first interviewed, with the use of an instrument designed for the program, to determine the current level of leisure skills and frequency of participation. As part of this component, students are introduced to the total program's purpose, content, and process. Included in these counseling sessions is information related to leisure, its implications, and potential. A prescriptive program is then worked out for the student, which takes into account the areas of leisure-skill weakness, social interaction needs, and recreational participation opportunities. Thus this component is directly concerned with goal 3, although the component indirectly relates to all the goals. This component is implemented on an individual basis as new students arrive at the school.

Skill Development Component. The purpose and goals emphasize leisure-skill development. Skill development addresses this issue. Thirty-five courses were developed that fell into eight categories of common, adult leisure activities: (1) individual and dual sports, (2) aquatics, (3) fitness, (4) expressive arts, (5) home and family, (6) community service, (7) mental activities, (8) outdoor activities. Each course was developed with specific behavioral performance objectives. These objectives not only deal with the actual activity skill involved, but also with the *social behaviors* necessary for participation and with learning about the resources involved with the activity. The Skill Development Component thus directly deals with goals 1, 4, 5, and 6. Students are enrolled in courses according to information gained in the assessment process relative to areas of weakness, interest, and leisure lifestyle development.

Recreation Participation Component. The third component deals most directly with goal 2, although it has implications for goals 3, 4, 5, and 6. This component intends to provide a comprehensive set of opportunities in which students can voluntarily engage that simulate experiences available in communities. The component is subdivided into four categories: (1) intramural or athletic competitions, (2) drop-in use of the facilities, (3) clubs and special-interest groups, and (4) special and social events, including entertainment groups, dances, picnics, trips, and sports car rallies. Students are urged to establish an ongoing pattern of leisure involvement through these opportunities. Although they are usually voluntary activities in nature, occasionally some aspect of a program is prescribed so that a student may obtain additional development in social interaction or exposure to other leisure activities not offered in the skill development component.

Before arriving at these three components, the planner discussed and analyzed countless other alternatives. The resulting conceptualization, the planner felt, was the best and most feasible program for this population and setting. It also allows for expansion or revision of the goals and components at a later time.

other agency program conceptualizations

Three agency programs are presented to further the understanding of the conceptualization stage of program development. Each program has a statement of purpose and goals; the components are depicted in the discrepancy evaluation models.

COMMUNITY RECREATION FOR SPECIAL POPULATIONS*
Nancy J. Edwards

Program Statement of Purpose. *To provide opportunities for the physically and mentally handicapped residents of the community to develop leisure and recreational skills appropriate to age and ability level, to acquire knowledge of existing programs and various recreational facilities and resources, and to provide the opportunity for handicapped citizens to engage in self-selected and directed leisure experiences (see fig. 8–5).*

Goals of System

1. *To encourage the integration of the handicapped into the ongoing community recreation program.*
2. *To increase skills of self-expression and provide new options for self-expression through leisure.*
3. *To provide opportunities for enhancing physical fitness and the furthering of physical development.*
4. *To encourage the development of new leisure skills for the purpose of increasing interests and possibilities for development, enjoyment, and fulfillment.*
5. *To provide knowledge and experience to enable the utilization of community resources.*
6. *To counsel the handicapped regarding personal responsibility for meeting their own leisure needs.*
7. *To educate the community concerning the socioleisure needs of the handicapped.*

*Reprinted with permission of the author.

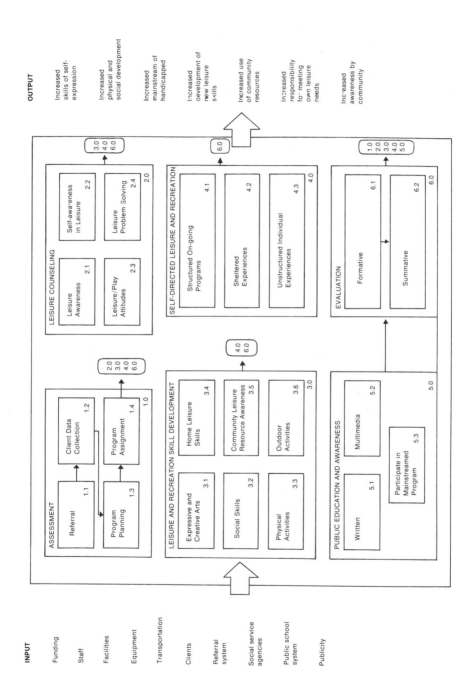

INPUT

Funding

Staff

Facilities

Equipment

Transportation

Clients

Referral system

Social service agencies

Public school system

Publicity

OUTPUT

Increased skills of self-expression

Increased physical and social development

Increased mainstream of handicapped

Increased development of new leisure skills

Increased use of community resources

Increased responsibility for meeting own leisure needs

Increased awareness by community

ASSESSMENT

Referral 1.1

Client Data Collection 1.2

Program Planning 1.3

Program Assignment 1.4

1.0

2.0
3.0
4.0
6.0

LEISURE COUNSELING

Leisure Awareness 2.1

Self-awareness in Leisure 2.2

Leisure/Play Attitudes 2.3

Leisure Problem Solving 2.4

2.0

3.0
4.0
6.0

LEISURE AND RECREATION SKILL DEVELOPMENT

Expressive and Creative Arts 3.1

Home Leisure Skills 3.4

Social Skills 3.2

Community Leisure Resource Awareness 3.5

Physical Activities 3.3

Outdoor Activities 3.6

3.0

4.0
6.0

SELF-DIRECTED LEISURE AND RECREATION

Structured On-going Programs 4.1

Sheltered Experiences 4.2

Unstructured Individual Experiences 4.3

4.0

6.0

PUBLIC EDUCATION AND AWARENESS

Written 5.1

Multimedia 5.2

Participate in Mainstreamed Program 5.3

5.0

EVALUATION

Formative 6.1

Summative 6.2

6.0

1.0
2.0
3.0
4.0
5.0

Fig. 8–5

Systems Approach to Community Recreation for Special Populations

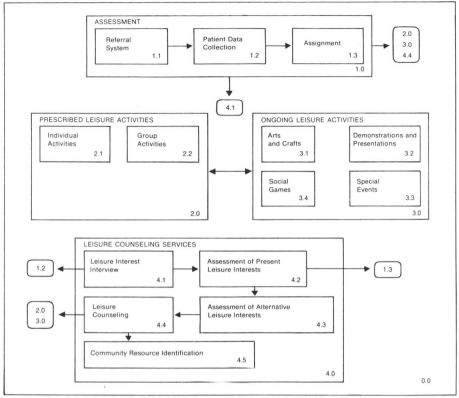

Fig. 8–6
General Hospital Therapeutic Recreation Program Model

GENERAL HOSPITAL THERAPEUTIC RECREATION PROGRAM*
Margaret Connolly

Statement of Purpose. *To provide comprehensive therapeutic recreation services to assist patients in the treatment of and adjustment to illness and disability, and to facilitate the establishment of appropriate socioleisure lifestyles after discharge (see fig. 8–6).*

Goals

1. *To provide assistance for individual patients in adjusting to illness and/or injury and physical limitations related to illness and/or injury.*
2. *To alleviate boredom and/or fear of the hospital setting for patients.*
3. *To teach new leisure activities to patients appropriate to illness and/or injury.*
4. *To encourage socialization and interaction through patient participation in ongoing leisure activities for groups of patients.*
5. *To increase awareness and knowledge of patients' leisure interests and appropriate community leisure resources.*

*Reprinted with permission of the author.

121

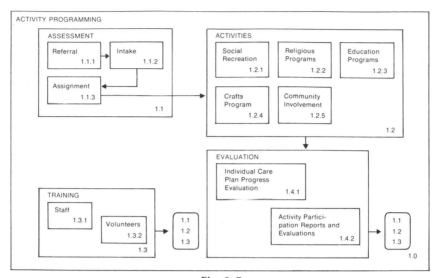

ACTIVITY PROGRAMMING

ASSESSMENT

| Referral 1.1.1 | Intake 1.1.2 |

Assignment 1.1.3

1.1

ACTIVITIES

| Social Recreation 1.2.1 | Religious Programs 1.2.2 | Education Programs 1.2.3 |

| Crafts Program 1.2.4 | Community Involvement 1.2.5 |

1.2

EVALUATION

Individual Care Plan Progress Evaluation 1.4.1

TRAINING

Staff 1.3.1

| Volunteers 1.3.2 | 1.1 1.2 1.3 |

1.3

Activity Partici- pation Reports and Evaluations 1.4.2

| 1.1 1.2 1.3 |

1.0

Fig. 8–7
Long-term Health-care Facility Activity Program

LONG-TERM HEALTH-CARE FACILITY ACTIVITIES PROGRAM
Scout Lee Gunn

Statement of Purpose. *To provide an activity program that supplements treatment, enables participation in ongoing leisure interests, and provides the opportunity to acquire new leisure skills and interests (see fig. 8–7).*

Goals

1. *To provide the opportunity for engaging in previously acquired recreational, religious, and community activities.*
2. *To prevent the deterioration of physical, mental, and emotional functioning.*
3. *To stimulate and encourage the establishment and continuation of social-interaction skills and abilities.*
4. *To provide the opportunity for developing new leisure interests and skills.*
5. *To provide an environment conducive to assisting individuals to adjust to their limitations (illnesses and disabilities) and new living situations.*

summary

Developing a statement of purpose for an agency or unit program, and deriving goals from it, are essential to systematic planning. The process itself allows planners to conceptualize and reach agreement on the fundamental direction and function of the program. With direction clearly established, decisions can be made about the selection of components that will put into operation the program's intent. The next step in the planning process is the design of each program component. Chapter nine focuses on techniques and procedures for the specification and design of program components.

—————————— *suggested references* ——————————

Acuff, S., "Recreation Counseling as an Aspect of Programming for the Short-Term Psychiatric Patient," *Recreation in Treatment Centers*, 5 (1966), 5–7.

Avedon, E. M., "The Function of Recreation Service in the Rehabilitation Process," *Rehabilitation Literature*, 27, 8.

Davis, R. H., L. T. Alexander, and S. L. Yelon, *Learning System Design: An Approach to the Improvement of Instruction*. New York: McGraw Hill Book Company, 1974.

Douglass, J. H., "Realizing Human Potential Through Therapeutic Recreation," *Therapeutic Recreation Journal*, 5, no. 4 (1971), 179–86.

Hitzhusen, G., "Recreation and Leisure Counseling for Adult Psychiatric and Alcoholic Patients," *Therapeutic Recreation Journal*, 7, no. 1 (1973), 16–22.

Humphrey, F., "Recreation Programming in a Psychiatric Setting," *Recreation in Treatment Centers*, 3 (1964), 43–47.

Lefebvre, C., "Sports and Athletics in a 'Sheltered Community Center' Recreation Program for Short-Term Adult, Psychiatric Patients," *Recreation in Treatment Centers*, 5 (1966), 26–29.

Levy, J., "An Intrinsic-Extrinsic Motivational Framework for Therapeutic Recreation," *Therapeutic Recreation Journal*, 5 no. 1 (1971), 32–38.

Mager, R. F., *Goal Analysis*. Belmont, Calif.: Fearon Publishers, 1972.

Malatesta, D., "Body Image and Self-Concept, Implications for Therapeutic Recreation Service," *Therapeutic Recreation Journal*, 5 no. 3, (1971), 130–32.

O'Morrow, G. S., "The Whys of Recreation Activities for Psychiatric Patients," *Therapeutic Recreation Journal*, 5 no. 3 (1971), 97–103.

Post, M. S., "Therapeutic Activities: Objectives and Goals," *Therapeutic Recreation Journal*, 7, no. 2 (1973), 21–25.

Skinner, J., "Recreation Programming for Patients Possessing the Chronic Brain Syndromes Associated with Cerebral Arteriosclerosis," *Recreation in Treatment Centers*, 5 (1966), 33–36.

Stein, T. A., and D. Sessoms, *Recreation and Special Populations*. Boston, Mass.: Holbrook Press, Inc., 1973.

Weishahn, M., and L. J. Neal, "Therapeutic Recreation Programming for the Visually Disabled," *Therapeutic Recreation Journal*, 5, no. 2 (1971), 69–71.

Young, E. G., and I. Hutchison, "Rx Recreation: A Bridge to Community Living for the Narcotics Addict," *Recreation in Treatment Centers*, 3 (1964), 59–63.

specifying program content and process

PURPOSE: To provide information about how to design and specify program content and procedures using a systems approach. Included are procedures for breaking down program goals into behavioral objectives and techniques of task analysis that enable program content to be selected. Sample systems are provided to illustrate applications of the concepts and process.

     After a statement of purpose and goal statements are determined for a unit or agency, the program designer is faced with the task of selecting program components. These components are the operational units that put the goals and purpose into action. Once the components are selected, the program developer is responsible for specifying the exact *content* and *process* of the program. This chapter focuses on techniques of systematically describing each program component. This process includes writing the program's objectives, the performance measures, and the activities that will facilitate the attainment of the objectives. The approach is unique in that it allows for staff to replicate the exact procedures and also allows for valid and reliable evaluation. Specific procedures tend to improve services to clients as well as increase accountability.

     Any program needs to start with a clear understanding of its purpose and *expected outcomes*. In a system's model, this means delineating the expected outcomes in observable and measurable objectives. Following this stage is the specification of the program's activities (content) and method of conducting the program (facilitation or intervention technique). These two strategic descriptions, along with an implementation plan, enable direction, management, and evaluation of the program.

terminal performance objectives

Each program component derived from the goals and selected by the program developer requires a set of terminal performance objectives (TPOs). Terminal performance objectives are not complete behavioral objectives, since they do not identify conditions, behaviors, and criteria per se. These conditions are specified at a later stage of development. Terminal performance objectives identify more global behavioral outcomes that can be considered independent entities for the purpose of program development. For example, in an instructional cross-country skiing program four TPOs emerge as appropriate, measurable, and feasible:

TPO 1. To demonstrate the ability to cross-country ski.
TPO 2. To demonstrate knowledge and ability related to maintenance of equipment.
TPO 3. To demonstrate knowledge of resources related to cross-country skiing opportunities.
TPO 4. To demonstrate knowledge related to the purchase of equipment and clothing.

Terminal performance objectives for trainable mentally retarded individuals who are involved in a program to acquire fundamental motor skills might be:

TPO 1. To demonstrate the ability to run.
TPO 2. To demonstrate the ability to hop.
TPO 3. To demonstrate the ability to catch a ball.
TPO 4. To demonstrate the ability to execute an overhand throw.

Elderly individuals in a long-term health-care facility who are engaged in a program to maintain current levels of functional ability might have these terminal performance objectives:

TPO 1. To demonstrate maintenance of current cognitive skills.
TPO 2. To demonstrate maintenance of current social-interaction skills.
TPO 3. To demonstrate maintenance of current physical abilities.

Individuals with recent spinal-cord injuries who are engaged in a program to establish appropriate socioleisure lifestyles might have TPOs such as:

TPO 1. To demonstrate the ability to modify existing leisure skills for present participation.
TPO 2. To demonstrate awareness and knowledge of new areas of leisure opportunities.
TPO 3. To demonstrate knowledge of resources for developing new leisure involvement.

In all of the illustrations, the terminal performance objectives state the end behavior expected of clients to demonstrate that they have acquired some knowledge, skill, or ability. In other words, TPOs are always written to describe clients' *outcome* behavior.

TPOs are somewhat independent of each other. Breaking down a program component into independent but related TPOs takes experience, skill, and insight. Choosing the appropriate level of ability for a TPO depends on the population and clients' functional abilities, the time allotted for the program, and the nature and intent of the program. For example, it may be appropriate to delineate small units of behavior for the mentally retarded, whereas total activities or groups of activities may be adequate for other populations.

Each TPO requires further breakdown. *A TPO is not directly measurable or observable.* The designer must analyze a TPO's intent and derive from it the *behavioral objectives that indicate its exact interpretation and measurement.*

A terminal performance objective serves as a behavioral statement indicating a broad category of knowledge, skill, or ability that a client is to demonstrate. While a TPO is too broad to be specifically evaluated, it does serve as a behavioral statement of the expected outcomes of the program.

task analysis of a tpo

Each terminal performance objective should be broken down into behavioral units that can be specifically observed and measured. These units are called *enabling objectives* (EOs) and *performance measures* (PMs). Before writing EOs and PMs, the program designer does a task analysis. In this process, the designer studies each TPO to determine what behaviors or actions can be logically broken down. The process results in areas of content that can be converted into the language and format of an enabling objective.

Some TPOs break down easily into logical areas of behavior. They are called *concrete* enabling objectives. Here is an example of a concrete EO taken from a TPO that states, "To demonstrate the ability to play table tennis." A task analysis of this TPO resulted in these areas of content to be used for the enabling objectives: (1) serving, (2) forehand, (3) backhand, (4) drop shot, (5) smash, (6) lob, (7) rules, (8) scoring, (9) etiquette, and (10) strategy. Although there could be some disagreement over the possible number and types of behaviors, skills, and knowledge to be included in the program, most people would agree that these ten areas comprise the essential aspects of playing table tennis. What is essential is to identify the actual areas necessary for the game. Because we are dealing with a specific game and with accepted procedures and rules, the areas of behavior are relatively concrete and direct.

Some TPOs are indirect or *abstract* in nature. A TPO to demonstrate social interaction skills can be considered abstract in that it is subject to multiple interpretations. In this case, the developer must determine the content areas that represent the intent of the TPO for the specific population. Task analysis is still a part of the process. It is used to arrive at the specific content areas that define the meaning or intent of the TPO. The following illustration is of an activity program that intends to establish conversational and verbal interaction skills in five-to-nine-year-old emotionally disturbed children.*

> TPO 1. To demonstrate conversational skills with authority figures.
> EO content areas arrived at through task analysis:
> 1. Making a request.
> 2. Initiating basic conversation.
> 3. Receiving instructions.
> 4. Receiving criticism or correction.

Whether the designer is dealing with an abstract TPO or a concrete TPO, the process of task analysis is essential. The EO behavioral areas that result from task analysis are the designer's interpretation of the meaning or intentions of the TPO. It is critical that the EOs be logical and appropriate for the population being served. For example, the number, nature, and level of EO-content areas would be quite different for a table tennis course designed for trainable mentally retarded and for one designed for spinal-cord-injured individuals. The EO-content areas *operationally define* the TPO for the group under consideration. Those who disagree with the breakdown still cannot refute the fact that the TPO has been operationally defined.

enabling objectives

As discussed, enabling objectives are units of behavior that are essential divisions of a terminal performance objective. An EO is a specific behavioral statement indicating a unit of knowledge or skill that the client is expected to accomplish. Doing a task analysis of the TPO to derive EO-content areas makes the job of writing the actual EOs much easier. Essentially, the planner takes the different EO-content areas and converts them into *behavioral terminology*.

*Material included by permission of the designer, Linda Henrichs.

The EO is written as a client outcome and is stated behaviorally. It differs from a TPO only in that it deals with a smaller unit of behavior. Examples of EO-content areas converted to enabling objectives are:

1. Ping Pong
   EO-content area: Serving.
   Enabling objective: To demonstrate a legal service.
2. Conversational skills for emotionally disturbed children (TPO concerns authority figures)
   EO-content area: Making a request.
   Enabling objective: To demonstrate the ability to make a request.

performance measures

An enabling objective identifies necessary or desired behavior. It is not a complete behavioral objective. A complete behavioral objective contains three parts: the desired behavior, the conditions under which the desired outcome behavior will occur, and the criteria or standards for judging the behavior. See also chapter six. A performance measure includes all three of these parts. A performance measure is, in fact, a complete behavioral objective in the traditional sense of the phrase. The advantage of separating out an EO (only the behavior) from the PM (complete behavioral objective) is clarity in reading. Often a performance measure becomes very lengthy, especially when many behavioral descriptions are used as part of the measure.

Earlier it was stated that enabling objectives provide the operational definition of the terminal performance objective. That concept can be further refined with the addition of performance measures. Each enabling objective has a corresponding performance measure that delineates the standards of behavior that are reasonable representations of the desired outcome. *Thus, when a client has achieved or obtained all of the EOs, as evidenced by his or her ability to demonstrate the actions or behaviors specified in the performance measures, the client has in essence also achieved the terminal performance objective.* A simple way of stating this is, "The sum of the EOs and their performance measures equals the terminal performance objective." Following this line of thought, a client who achieves each of the ten separate EOs on ping pong, as designated by the performance measures, has also demonstrated the intent of the TPO. This is a useful concept, but it also means that the enabling objectives and corresponding performance measures must be complete and logically derived and specified.

The form in figure 9–1 has been developed as a handy tool for writing TPOs, EOs, and PMs. It provides space for the identification of a program, the specific terminal performance objective, and the breakdown of the TPO into enabling objectives with their corresponding performance

PROGRAM SYSTEM:
TERMINAL PERFORMANCE OBJECTIVE:

ENABLING OBJECTIVES	PERFORMANCE MEASURES

Fig. 9-1
TPO, EO, and PM Sheet

measures. This same form is used later in the chapter with samples of developed systems programs.

writing performance measures

The therapeutic recreation specialist works primarily with clients and helps to bring about desired and meaningful behavioral changes and to improve their skills or leisure expression. The program designer needs especially to be sensitive to these concerns while writing performance measures. Performance measures that require too much time to evaluate or are too demanding in the level or amount of behavior to be observed, measured, and recorded will quickly be neglected or totally rejected by the program implementor. Thus, the designer must develop reasonable and valid performance measures. A basic rule of thumb is to look for and select the *least amount of behavior that is still representative of the intent of the objective.* Another principle is to observe and measure the behavior in the *least restrictive environment.* The specialist must set up the most natural environment possible so that evaluation does not interfere with the ongoing program. Evaluating behaviors while a game, activity, or program occurs is much better than evaluating during specific testing periods. In therapeutic recreation, this calls for the creative design of performance measures that provide for necessary measurement while allowing the action and nature of the program to continue. These two concerns (least amount of behavior and most natural testing situation) are central to good program design and measurement as well as acceptance of systems programs by implementors.

three aspects of a performance measure

A performance measure is a complete behavioral objective and as such has three distinct parts: the *conditions*, the *behavior*, and the *criteria*.

conditions

A condition is the situation under which the desired behavior will occur. Phrases that indicate common conditions are:

On request . . .
When given the necessary equipment . . .
After six weeks of instruction . . .
When given a choice of three activities . . .
With an opponent of equal ability . . .
On a written exam . . .

Sometimes conditions are unique to a situation, setting, population, or program. An example is:

> While involved in a trip in the community with the therapeutic recreation specialist and after completing the program of assertive training, the client will . . .

Conditions of a behavioral objective primarily set the stage, identify necessary equipment, activities, time lines, or other events that are essential to the performance of the desired behavior. Normally they occur as the first phrase of the performance measure. Occasionally, the conditions are scattered throughout the performance measure. Conditions are throughout the following PM and are italicized for identification:

> *On request,* the client will play a game of checkers *with an opponent of equal ability,* maintaining contact with reality throughout the activity as evidenced by continuous attention to the game and completion of the game within a reasonable amount of time.

In this example, some conditions are not mentioned but implied. The checker game itself is not specified. Often when a condition is very obvious, it can be eliminated to reduce the length of the complete performance measure.

The behavior identified in the performance measure is the central focus of a behavioral objective. It is the phrase that identifies what the client will be doing to demonstrate the desired knowledge, skill, or ability. The behavior must be observable and measurable in order to meet this requirement. Although measurement is most often dealt with in the criteria section of the PM, the behavior focuses the attention of the reader on the general area of concern. Some examples of the behavioral part of a PM are:

> . . . the client will swim . . .
> . . . the client will verbally interact . . .
> . . . the client will express emotions . . .
> . . . the client will complete the activity . . .
> . . . the client will participate . . .
> . . . the client will run . . .
> . . . the client will demonstrate the ability to bowl . . .

Selecting the behavior aspect of a performance measure is an art. In most cases, the behavior is not the total behavior identified in the enabling objective, but a representative behavior or unit of behavior. The art is in selecting an appropriate, reasonable, and feasible representative behavior.

selecting representative behaviors

Selecting the representative behavior from the enabling objective to be included in the performance measure is a major task in writing performance measures. In a concrete enabling objective, the task is somewhat easier. For example, in demonstrating a proper service in table tennis (EO 1), the client will be asked to show the evaluator that he or she can execute a serve, either on request or while playing a game. It would be ridiculous to ask the client for a written description of a serve in this case. The designer must describe in the criteria how many serves must be executed accurately. In other words, the behavior selected for inclusion in the performance measure for a concrete enabling objective is the stated behavior itself: a simple direct translation from EO to PM, with just the criteria and conditions needing development.

On the other hand, when dealing with an abstract or indirect enabling objective, the designer has a more difficult task in selecting a representative behavior. For example, assume that an enabling objective states, "To demonstrate verbal interaction ability." The population is elderly, ambulatory residents in a long-term health-care facility. Here, the designer must select a *representative* behavior that can be taken as evidence of verbal-interaction ability. Task analysis again comes into the picture, as does brainstorming. The staff and the designer need to agree about what is meant by verbal-interaction ability as well as what behavior would be a reasonable, observable measurement of this action. A possible selection might be:

> While eating an evening meal in the dining room, the resident will demonstrate the ability to interact verbally with others as characterized by:
> 1. initiating conversation with other residents at the table a minimum of one time during the meal;
> 2. responding appropriately to conversation directed at her or him;
> 3. maintaining appropriate eye contact and body position during conversation as judged by the activity director.

In this case, verbal interaction is an ability that occurs in a normal situation involving common and socially expected behavior while eating a meal. It is a much more natural measurement of verbal interaction than would be the case in this example:

> "On request the resident will verbally interact with the activity director during a one-to-one room visitation."

Selecting appropriate representative behavior for abstract enabling objectives is a difficult task and one that requires experience, trial and error, and patience. As the designer's skills improve and observation abilities increase, the task becomes somewhat more comfortable and even challenging.

determining and writing the criteria

The criteria in the performance measure delineate the exact amounts and nature of the behavior that can be taken as evidence that the objective has been met. A criterion is a precise statement or standard that allows individuals to make judgments based on observable, measurable behavior. Good criteria statements are so clear that two or more different evaluators have no problem making the same decision about whether the desired behavior occurred or not.

Writing criteria statements requires that we select representative behaviors and then describe the amounts and nature of those behaviors. Several useful techniques can assist in this process.

Number of Trials. Some behaviors occur by chance and thus the criteria need to be written with a standard of x out of y attempts. For example, hitting a target with darts or catching a ball, or executing a ping-pong serve can occur by chance if just one trial or attempt is called for. In situations such as these, the designer is better off setting a different criterion. An example of this follows:

> On request, the client will demonstrate the ability to execute a legal ping-pong serve three out of five times.

It is unlikely that the client can serve the ball three out of five times by chance. Note also that the word *legal* designates a criterion. There is a standard definition of *legal serve* and thus the criterion does not need to be refined.

Level of Accuracy. Certain behaviors require a criterion of accuracy to be useful. Ability to throw a baseball, putt in golf, or bowl is usually judged by a degree of accuracy in order to be credible. An example of level of accuracy reads:

> Given a putting green with a circle drawn around the hole one yard in radius, the client will putt six out of ten golf balls into the circle from a distance of ten yards.

Note that this performance measure combines accuracy with number of trials.

133

Amount of Time. Other behaviors are credible only if they occur within a specified amount of time. An example of this type of criterion is:

> On request the client can run the hundred-yard dash within twenty seconds.

Note that this behavior may not need a number of trials. Either the client can run that fast or he or she can't. The same can be said for such activities as bike riding or swimming. A client either can or can't do the activity. Thus, increasing the trials only increases the amount of evaluation time required.

Percentage or Fraction of Time. Certain behaviors are only valid if they are maintained over time. The problem is that all activities are not consistent in the amount of time required for action or number of opportunities available. A percentage-of-time criterion allows for such variation. A performance measure of this nature might read:

> While engaged in an activity of her or his choice, the client will refrain from using profane language and obscene gestures 90 percent of the time.
> or
> While engaged in a basketball game, the client will demonstrate the ability to make baskets by hitting one-quarter of the attempted field shots.

Form. Some performance measures require the specification of form in order to be appropriate evaluations. This is most often the case when dealing with motor skills. For example, form is important in executing a forehand shot in tennis, a specific stroke in swimming, or a golf swing. Form in these cases is highly related to success or accuracy within the activity. There are several ways in which this can be described.

1. Relate the performance measure to an existing, known standard that is generally respected and accepted. For example, "On request the client can swim twenty-five yards using the side stroke as described in the *Red Cross WSI Manual.*
2. Judgment of an expert. A good golf instructor knows and can judge form with reliable and valid consistency. In this case, the performance measure might read: "On request the client can drive a golf ball a minimum of 100 yards with acceptable form as judged by the instructor." Note that this PM combines form and distance for a more thorough criterion.

Procedures and Characteristics. In addition to form, some criteria can best be specified that relate to the characteristics of the identified behavior. Countless situations in therapeutic recreation are independent of standardized tests or processes. Thus, they require that the designer specify the criteria. A handy tool for accomplishing this task is to use the phrase, "as characterized by." This enables the designer to set up the

134

unique criteria that are appropriate to the situation and yet are valid and reliable for observation and measurement. Here is an illustration of this technique:

PROGRAM ON CONVERSATIONAL SKILLS FOR EMOTIONALLY DISTURBED CHILDREN WITH AUTHORITY FIGURES.*

After basic instruction and when the situation arises, the client will demonstrate the ability to initiate a basic conversation, as characterized by:

1. *making an appropriate approach to the authority figure,*
2. *assuming an appropriate distance from the person for easy conversation,*
3. *speaking in an acceptable tone and volume,*
4. *maintaining eye contact with the authority figure, and*
5. *completing the conversation in an appropriate manner, as judged by the recreation therapist.*

Most often, when these types of criteria are used, they also require the use of the phrase "as judged by." The phrase indicates that some knowledge and expertise are held by the person making the judgment. In the performance measure above, there are a variety of "appropriate" approaches, distances, tones, volumes, and completions of the conversation. The specialist is expected to make those judgments based on experience, previously discussed acceptable behaviors, and common sense. The criteria in the example are a bit loose, but still serve as adequate guidelines for judging whether the client has acquired the desired behaviors.

multiple performance measures

In the illustrations of performance measure criteria, several techniques were combined to derive a thorough performance measure. For example, form and accuracy are used to evaluate a tennis shot, distance and form are used to evaluate a golf shot, and certain behaviors, occurring over a period of time and in several trials, are used to evaluate emotional control.

Sometimes a given behavior is best evaluated by multiple performance measures. One enabling objective can have two or more performance measures in order to get at different aspects of the same behavioral concern. An example of multiple performance measures is given for scoring related to a skill-development course in tennis.

*Used with permission of the program designer, Linda Henrichs.

135

EO: To demonstrate the ability to keep score.

PM₁: While playing a set of tennis, the client will demonstrate the ability to score by determining points and calling out the correct score before each point and each game, as judged by the opponent who has previously demonstrated scoring ability.

PM₂: On a written test, the client will demonstrate knowledge of scoring by achieving a grade of 85 percent or higher.

In this case, the second performance measure is used, since it is probable that during a game not all issues or situations related to scoring would come up. By giving a written exam in addition to the actual game, the instructor can include situations that are unique or problematic in scoring. Thus, the instructor really tests the student's knowledge of scoring and ability to keep score.

Multiple performance measures are also used when a behavior is of vital concern, yet is abstract. In such situations, approaching the behavior in several ways may yield the most valid and reliable information.

additional comments about performance measures

The purpose of the performance measure is to specify the exact behavior that will provide evidence that the objective has been met. As such, the conditions under which the behavior is expected to be performed and the criteria for judging whether the behavior occurs are extremely relevant. Granted, therapeutic recreators use a range of loose to uptight criteria. Whether or not our criteria are as specific and precise as we desire, we are still accomplishing more than before in accountability and improved services by even attempting behavioral descriptions. The following behavioral objective checklist is provided to assist in the development of technically correct performance measures. In order for a performance measure to be technically acceptable, you must be able to answer each of the questions positively as it relates to the performance measure:

1. Can you readily identify the *behavior* that is to be demonstrated by the client to show that he or she has acquired the objective?

2. Can you readily identify the conditions under which the behavior will be demonstrated?
3. Can you readily identify the standard to which the client's behavior must conform?
4. If two staff members looked at this performance measure and a client's performance, could they agree whether or not the standards and limits had been achieved?

specifying content and process in program design

After terminal performance objectives, enabling objectives, and performance measures have been derived and stated, the program designer moves on to the development of the content and process specification. In systems design, the EO and its corresponding PM are analyzed to determine what needs to be done to accomplish or establish the designated behavior. This step starts again with task analysis. The EO is broken down into concrete tasks, behaviors, and activities that the designer feels are necessary to accomplish the intent of the EO. This breakdown produces the *content* for that EO. Content can be summarized by stating that it is *what is to be done in the program to achieve the EO*. This information is then written out as specifically as possible on a teaching-learning activity (TLA) sheet (see fig. 9–2). (A variety of other titles can be given to this sheet depending on the nature of the program. A few other examples are: leisure counseling activity sheet, program activity form, and activity description sheet.) Several examples of content descriptions appear later in this chapter on the TLA sheets from assorted programs. The information presented in chapter ten on activity analysis is quite helpful in analyzing and selecting activities for the content sections of a TLA sheet. Task analysis is also useful in breaking down specific activities from the TPO level to the EO level in the earlier stages of program development.

After the content has been specified for an EO, the designer develops the *process* for that content. Process refers to the way the content is presented to the clients. Chapter two presented the concept of different intervention styles of the therapeutic recreation specialist, depending on the nature of the program (rehabilitation, leisure education, or recreation participation). Chapter eleven presents a refinement and development of the concept of different intervention techniques (therapy, counseling, instruction, leadership, and supervision) and offers a description of the various types of intervention in each category. When the program designer is developing the process for each EO and its content, she or he further refines and describes how the program is to be conducted within the framework of an established or developed facilitation style. *Process always*

TEACHING-LEARNING ACTIVITIES

TPO _____
EO _____

EQUIPMENT _____

CONTENT	PROCESS

Fig. 9-2
Teaching-Learning Activity Sheet

specifies how the program is to be conducted. Since the content for different EOs varies, the process may also vary. Consequently, it appears best to have a separate process description for each EO and its specified content. A variety of examples of written process descriptions appears in the next section of this chapter, as part of several sample systems.

The program designer proceeds to develop content and process descriptions for each EO in the program. In other words, each EO and its corresponding PM will have at least one TLA sheet with complete descriptions of the content and process designed to bring the desired behavior or outcome into existence. If the program is designed well, the activities or actions should produce the desired results. If not, through the evaluation process, the designer has a more reasonable and systematic way of determining what worked and what didn't. This facilitates the revision and improvement of the system.

sample program systems

Sample program systems are presented on the following pages. None of the systems are complete. For each program, selected TPO sheets including EOs and PMs—and sample TLAs are offered to illustrate concepts discussed in this chapter.*

The systems represent a variety of programs. Different populations and settings are also represented. Included are one leisure-skill instructional system, two social-skill development systems, one group-therapy system, and one leisure-awareness and resource-awareness system.

The first program system is gym hockey for emotionally disturbed, elementary-aged children. The setting is a special education/physical education program. The designer is Marve Ebbens. The second program system is an activity-group therapy class. Kathy Van Houten designed the program for emotionally disturbed adolescents in a private psychiatric hospital. Third is a leisure education program system for mentally retarded adults. Ken Joswiak designed this program for a group home. Linda Henrichs designed the fourth program system, conversation skills, for emotionally disturbed children aged five through nine. The setting is a mental health center in conjunction with a special education district. The fifth program system is a peer-interaction group, designed for developmentally disabled and emotionally disturbed children, ages eight through fifteen. Mary Patricia McCreary designed this program for a residential treatment setting. It is important to note the variation in levels of specificity and style on the TLA sheets.

*We wish to express appreciation to Marve Ebbens, Mary Patricia McCreary, Kathy Van Houten, Ken Joswiak, and Linda Henrichs for allowing us to include their work in this section.

PROGRAM SYSTEM: Gym hockey
POPULATION: Emotionally disturbed elementary-aged children
SETTING: School—special education/physical education program
DESIGNER: Marve Ebbens

SUBJECT: Physical Education   COURSE: Floor Hockey
TERMINAL PERFORMANCE OBJECTIVE 4: To demonstrate the appropriate behaviors required for playing floor hockey

ENABLING OBJECTIVES	PERFORMANCE MEASURES
1. To demonstrate the ability to remain in the entire game.	In a regulation floor hockey game with peers, the student will demonstrate the ability to remain in the entire game, at the assigned position, with these exceptions: a. physical injury, b. physical fatigue, c. legal time out, d. player fouls out or has penalty time.
2. To demonstrate involvement through active play.	In a regulation floor hockey game with peers, the student will demonstrate active involvement throughout the game in a manner characterized by: a. When a puck enters a player's assigned area, he makes an obvious attempt to gain control of it. b. When puck is not in his area, the player remains standing in his own area with stick in hand and follows the play of the puck.

3. To demonstrate the ability to give verbal praise to a teammate.

In a regulation floor hockey game with peers, the student will demonstrate the ability to give verbal praise to a teammate, characterized by one or more of the following during the game:
  a. Congratulate teammate for scoring goal.
  b. Thank teammate for assisting him in scoring a goal.
  c. Congratulate goalie for making a good block in the puck.
  d. Give support to injured or frustrated teammate.

4. To demonstrate good sportsmanship.

In a regulation floor hockey game with peers, the student will demonstrate good sportsmanship by shaking hands with an opposing player at least one or more times after the game.

5. To demonstrate the ability to use appropriate language.

In a regulation floor hockey game with peers, the student will demonstrate the ability to use appropriate language by not using swear words more than two times during the game.

6. To demonstrate the ability to use the hockey stick in an appropriate manner.

In a regulation floor hockey game with peers, the student will demonstrate the ability to use the hockey stick in an appropriate manner, as characterized by all of the following:
  a. refrains from throwing the stick,
  b. refrains from intentionally hitting another player with the stick,
  c. refrains from breaking the stick.

7. To demonstrate the ability to refrain from fighting.

In a regulation floor hockey game with peers, the student will demonstrate the ability to refrain from fighting in a manner characterized by all of the following:
  a. Does not receive more than one misconduct penalty for fighting.
  b. Is not asked to leave the game by the official for fighting.

141

TEACHING-LEARNING ACTIVITIES

TPO: 4   EO: 1   **EQUIPMENT: Posterboard and magic markers**

INSTRUCTIONAL CONTENT	INSTRUCTIONAL PROCESS
EO: To play in the entire game. Remains at position, except for injury, fatigue, time out, or penalty time.	The instructor divides the class into two groups. Each group takes a posterboard and a magic marker and meets in an area of the gym where it won't be disturbed. An instructor accompanies each group. The students then come up with behaviors they feel are appropriate and necessary for playing floor hockey. The group discusses each suggestion and if all agree, the behavior is written on the posterboard. The students meet until they have come up with as many behaviors as they can think of. The two groups then meet together and compare behaviors. The students choose a representative from their group to explain the behaviors they have written down. Each student is given an opportunity to offer additional input. The students are then asked first to name a behavior they themselves need to work on (be aware of) and secondly to name a behavior they feel they do well. This is done until all students have had a chance to respond. If a student is unable to discuss behaviors as they apply to himself, the group can then offer suggestions. However, this should be done in a nonthreatening manner. If the behavior of EO1 has not been listed, the instructor can do so.

PROGRAM SYSTEM: Activity-group therapy class
POPULATION: Emotionally disturbed adolescents
SETTING: Private psychiatric hospital
DESIGNER: Kathy Van Houten

PROGRAM: ACTIVITY-GROUP THERAPY

TERMINAL PERFORMANCE OBJECTIVE 1: To demonstrate the ability to work with and relate positively to the group

ENABLING OBJECTIVES	PERFORMANCE MEASURES
1. To demonstrate appropriate behavior in group activities.	1. While participating in group activities, clients will demonstrate appropriate behaviors, as characterized by: a. being willing to participate in the activity (not refusing to take part, doing their part without having to be pushed);

b. being able to use the activity in the way it was intended, to deal with feelings openly and honestly (not getting their needs met in a roundabout, deceptive manner, now showing obvious manipulation of the activity);

c. staying with the activity physically (not leaving the room or stopping the activity, except to talk about their feelings).

2. To demonstrate attentive behaviors in group "talk-downs."

While participating in group talk-downs, clients will demonstrate attentive behaviors, as characterized by:

a. keeping eye contact with the person talking,

b. not interrupting the person talking,

c. not whispering to someone else,

d. not playing with any objects in the room, and

e. contributing relevant, verbal comments.

3. To demonstrate the ability to confront group members appropriately.

While participating in group activities and in group talk-downs, clients will demonstrate the ability to confront others, as characterized by:

a. using confrontation in relevant situations;

b. telling others when they disagree with their actions, and/or how they are dealing with their feelings;

c. being able to give assistance in helping others to deal with their feelings;

d. not using confrontation time as a chance to get back at others;

e. not becoming unnecessarily judgmental or harsh.

4. To demonstrate the ability to support group members appropriately.

While participating in activities or in group talk-downs, clients will demonstrate support of others, as characterized by:

a. sharing experiences of their own to help others work toward the acceptability of feelings;

b. giving verbal statements that indicate warmth, caring, and acceptance when someone is sharing openly and honestly with the group;

c. showing nonverbal actions or behaviors indicating warmth, caring, and acceptance when someone is sharing openly and honestly with the group.

TEACHING-LEARNING ACTIVITIES

INSTRUCTIONAL CONTENT	INSTRUCTIONAL PROCESS
Appropriate behavior in group activities.	
1. Willingness to participate.	1. a. Use yourself as a model by your own willingness to participate.
	b. Explain to clients the importance of taking part if they or others are going to profit from the sessions.
	c. Request that clients become involved if they still refrain from doing so after the explanation.
	d. Attempt to use the group in getting clients involved. Ask group members how they feel when someone refuses to be a part of the activities.
	e. Ask clients to verbalize why they have difficulty participating (many times they are afraid for some reason; if they can talk about it, it helps them to work through the fear, making it easier for them to become involved).
	f. If clients still continue to refuse to participate, confront them on their lack of involvement, and let them know they can choose to participate, or they can make up the time by some form of discipline after class.
	g. Use positive feedback when they are participating.
2. Using the activity in the way it was intended.	2. a. Use yourself as a model.
	b. Explain the way the activity is to be used and what you see clients doing with the activity.
	c. Request clients to use the activity in the way it was intended.
	d. Attempt to get clients to verbalize why they are misusing the activity.
	e. Elicit the help of the group.
	f. Use confrontation and discipline if they continue to misuse the activity.
	g. Give positive support when they use the activity as intended.
3. Staying with the activity physically.	3. a. Tell clients you would like them to remain with the activity for themselves and because the group needs them.
	b. Ask clients why they feel they need to leave.
	c. Elicit the help of the group in getting them to stay.
	d. Sometimes clients will decide to leave an activity to gain attention; it is better then to let them sit in a corner and not give them the negative attention they are seeking. This, at times, will bother them so much they will want to become involved again.
	e. If clients insist on leaving the room or their presence is disruptive to the continuation of the activity, bring them back to the ward and use discipline.
	f. Positive feedback when clients stay with the activity and don't leave.

PROGRAM SYSTEM: Leisure education
POPULATION: Mentally retarded adults
SETTING: Group home
DESIGNER: Ken Joswiak[1]

TERMINAL PERFORMANCE OBJECTIVE 1: To demonstrate awareness of the meaning of play and leisure

ENABLING OBJECTIVES	PERFORMANCE MEASURES
1. To demonstrate awareness of the concept of play.	1. When asked to "Tell me which pictures (or slides) show people playing," the client will identify a minimum of five out of six photographs (or slides) depicting the client or friends of the client engaged in traditional leisure activities categorized as active leisure phenomena, e.g., playing frisbee, checkers, looking at a magazine, etc. The client will also identify a minimum of five out of six slides depicting the client or friends engaged in obligated activities, e.g., sleeping, washing dishes, etc., as "not play." Performance as observed by the leisure counselor. Note: The client will be shown a total of twelve consecutive slides occuring in no set order. If necessary, before each photograph (or slide) the leisure counselor may ask, "Is this play?"

2. To demonstrate knowledge of the concept of free time.	2. When asked "What is free time?" the client will define free time in his own words, including one of the following three major points:
	   a. It is time in which the individual "is free from doing things that he has to do, like going to school/work, working around the home, eating, sleeping, or washing."
	   b. The individual "is free to do whatever he wants as long as it doesn't break the law or hurt anybody."
	   c. "It's time when we have fun."
	
	 Note: In response to "b," the leisure counselor may ask, if necessary, "Could you do something like break a window or get in a fight?"

145

LEISURE-COUNSELING ACTIVITY

TPO 1: Awareness of the meaning of play and leisure.

EO 1: Awareness of the concept of play.

TIME: 1 hour, 30 minutes (includes the activity but excludes the followup, which occurs at the next session).

PRESENTATION MEDIA: Slide projector, slide screen or sufficient wall space, slides depicting the clients engaged in various leisure activities, leisure resources from around the house, e.g., checker game, "Aggravation" game, frisbee, unpopped popcorn, deck of cards, magazines, etc.

Format:

I. Introduction to the leisure-counseling program.
   A. Ask the clients:
      1. WHO CAN TELL ME WHAT IT FEELS LIKE TO BE BORED? WHAT DOES BORED MEAN?
      2. WHO CAN TELL ME WHAT IT FEELS LIKE TO BE LONESOME? WHAT DOES LONESOME MEAN?
   B. DURING THESE LEISURE-COUNSELING MEETINGS, WE WILL DO SOME DIFFERENT THINGS.
      1. WE WILL TALK AND LEARN ABOUT DIFFERENT THINGS THAT WE CAN DO DURING OUR FREE TIME TO KEEP US FROM GETTING BORED OR LONESOME.
      2. WE WILL LEARN ABOUT HOW IMPORTANT FREE TIME, PLAY, AND FUN ARE IN OUR LIVES.
      3. WE WILL LEARN ABOUT DIFFERENT THINGS WE CAN USE, BOTH HERE, AT HOME, AND IN THE COMMUNITY THAT CAN *HELP US TO HAVE FUN.*
   C. DURING THESE MEETINGS I'M GOING TO ASK EVERYBODY TO DO SOMETHING. IT'LL BE SORT OF AN ASSIGNMENT. CAN SOMEBODY TELL ME WHAT AN ASSIGNMENT IS?
   D. I'M GOING TO ASK EVERYBODY TO DO SOMETHING THAT IS FUN, OR, TO PLAY. BUT I WILL BE ASKING YOU TO DO THINGS THAT ARE FUN IN DIFFERENT WAYS.

II. Discussion concerning the definition of play.
   A. WHO CAN TELL ME WHAT PLAY IS?
   B. Solicit responses from the clients.
   C. Leisure counselor provides a definition of play.
      1. PLAY IS ANYTHING WE DO DURING OUR FREE TIME THAT MAKES US FEEL GOOD. IT CAN HELP US FEEL RELAXED, IT CAN MAKE US LAUGH, OR IT CAN JUST MAKE US FEEL GOOD.
      2. HOW DO WE FEEL WHEN WE ARE RELAXED?
      3. WHAT IS IT LIKE WHEN WE FEEL REALLY GOOD?
      4. SOME PEOPLE CALL THESE THINGS "LEISURE ACTIVITY" OR "ACTIVITY," BUT THEY ARE REALLY PLAY.

III. Examples of play.
   A. THERE ARE A LOT OF DIFFERENT WAYS TO PLAY. LET'S GO AROUND THE GROUP AND EVERYBODY TELL THE REST OF US ONE WAY THAT THEY REALLY LIKE TO PLAY. IF YOU WANT TO TELL THE GROUP ABOUT MORE THAN ONE WAY YOU LIKE TO PLAY YOU CAN. I WILL START. Leisure counselor and staff model the procedure for the clients.

B. If a client responds inappropriately or has difficulty responding, employ the guided-discovery technique to assist them, e.g., WHAT IS IT THAT YOU DO AFTER SUPPER IN THE BACKYARD?

C. AS YOU CAN SEE, THERE ARE MANY DIFFERENT WAYS TO PLAY.

IV. Emphasis on carryover from other programs.

A. WHAT ARE SOME OF THE WAYS THAT YOU LEARN TO PLAY, AND THE PLACES THAT YOU GO FOR FUN AT SCHOOL, WORKSHOP, OR PARKS AND RECREATION PROGRAMS?

 1. Solicit responses from the clients.

 2. Possible answers:

    a. Skills learned in structured programs—bowling, swimming, arts and crafts, croquet, horseshoes, frisbee, table games, dances, etc.

    b. Activities and resources experienced in structured programs—museums, planetarium, movies, plays, library, etc.

B. Emphasize that, WE CAN DO ALL OF THESE THINGS AT HOME, OR WE CAN VISIT THOSE PLACES WITH OUR FRIENDS.

C. Throughout the leisure-counseling program, emphasize that the clients can also participate at the home in activities experienced in other programs or the clients can visit those resources with other people from the home.

V. Slide presentation: "The Clients Having Fun!"

A. Focus of the slides is on the clients engaged in a variety of leisure activities.

B. THESE ARE ALL DIFFERENT WAYS TO PLAY. THEY CAN ALL MAKE US FEEL GOOD.

C. THESE ARE JUST A FEW WAYS TO HAVE FUN. IN THESE MEETINGS, WE WILL BE LEARNING ABOUT OTHER WAYS TO HAVE FUN.

D. If there are any visually impaired clients, ask other clients to describe the activities depicted in the slides.

VI. Activity for the night.

A. I'M GETTING TIRED OF SITTING AND TALKING. I THINK IT IS TIME FOR US TO TAKE A BREAK.

B. LET'S TAKE A TWENTY-MINUTE BREAK. BUT I WANT EVERYBODY TO DO SOMETHING SPECIAL. I WANT EVERYBODY TO DO SOMETHING THAT IS FUN. DO SOMETHING DIFFERENT, SOMETHING YOU USUALLY DON'T DO.

C. I HAVE SOME THINGS HERE THAT WE CAN USE TO HAVE FUN. Refer to the leisure resources, e.g., basketball, sewing materials, paint set.

D. I WOULD LIKE EVERYONE TO PICK OUT SOMETHING AND USE IT TO HAVE FUN.

E. FIRST, WHO CAN TELL ME WHAT ARE ALL THE THINGS WE HAVE HERE THAT WE CAN USE TO HAVE FUN? Allow the clients to identify the resources and describe what they can do with them. Hold each resource up for all to see.

F. LET'S HAVE EVERYONE TELL THE REST OF THE GROUP WHAT HE IS GOING TO DO TO HAVE FUN. I WILL GO FIRST. Leisure counselor and staff model the procedures for the clients.

 1. REMEMBER, PICK SOMETHING THAT YOU USUALLY DON'T USE.

 2. IF YOU WANT TO DO SOMETHING DIFFERENT THAN WHAT IS HERE, THAT IS ALL RIGHT.

 3. If a client responds inappropriately or has difficulty in selecting an activity, employ the guided-discovery technique to assist him or her, e.g., WHAT DID YOU SAY WAS YOUR FAVORITE WAY TO PLAY? COULD YOU DO THAT?

G. Reinforce appropriate responses or approximations.

E. LET'S TAKE A BREAK. EVERYBODY HAVE FUN! WE'LL COME BACK HERE IN TWENTY MINUTES.

F. Allow and encourage the clients to initiate the activity themselves.

LEISURE-COUNSELING ACTIVITY (cont.)

G. Techniques for clients lacking in self-direction or requiring special assistance.
  1. During the break, question the client concerning the activity.
     a. HAVE YOU DONE ANYTHING THAT IS FUN?
     b. WHAT ARE YOU GOING TO DO TO HAVE FUN?
     c. WHEN ARE YOU GOING TO START?
  2. Employ the guided-discovery technique, e.g., WHAT COULD BE SOMETHING FUN TO DO OUTSIDE?
  3. Provide suggestions to the client.
     a. MAYBE YOU COULD DO (name of activity).
     b. WHY DON'T YOU ASK (name of a peer) TO DO THAT WITH YOU?
  4. Provide a strong suggestion to the client. I THINK THAT YOU SHOULD (name of activity).
  5. If necessary, accompany the client during the activity, either participating or observing. Shape independent leisure behaviors.
H. *Reinforce appropriate play behaviors or approximations.*
I. Allow twenty minutes to lapse before calling the group together.

VII. Summary and assignment.
  A. LET'S HAVE EVERYONE TELL THE REST OF THE GROUP WHAT HE DID THAT WAS FUN AND HOW IT MADE HIM FEEL. I WILL GO FIRST. Leisure counselor and staff model the procedure for the clients.
  B. Possible questions to ask the clients:
     1. HOW DID YOU PLAY?
     2. HOW DID YOU FEEL AFTER YOU DID THAT?
     3. WERE YOU GLAD THAT YOU DID THAT?
  C. *Reinforce descriptions of appropriate play behaviors or approximations.*
  D. Emphasize that PLAYING WELL CAN MAKE US FEEL GOOD.
  E. Assignment.
     1. NOW I AM GOING TO ASK EVERYONE TO DO SOMETHING BEFORE OUR NEXT MEETING. EVERYONE DO SOMETHING THAT IS *FUN* BEFORE OUR NEXT MEETING. MAKE IT SOMETHING *DIFFERENT* THAN WHAT YOU USUALLY DO.
     2. LET'S HAVE EVERYONE TELL THE REST OF THE GROUP WHAT HE IS GOING TO DO TO HAVE FUN. WHO WOULD LIKE TO GO FIRST? Allow a client to model the procedure.
     3. Leisure counselor and staff also share their plans for fun.

4. If a client responds inappropriately or has difficulty selecting an activity, use the guided-discovery technique as previously described.
5. Reinforce appropriate responses or approximations.
F. Optional: If using an assignment chart, remind the clients to check their names off or ask a staff member to help them.
G. Techniques for clients lacking in self-direction or requiring special assistance.
  1. Before the next session, question the client concerning the activity.
     a. HAVE YOU DONE ANYTHING THAT'S FUN?
     b. WHAT ARE YOU GOING TO DO TO HAVE FUN?
     c. WHEN ARE YOU GOING TO START?
  2. Employ the guided-discovery technique, e.g., WHAT WOULD BE SOMETHING YOU COULD DO IN THE BASEMENT THAT WOULD BE FUN?
  3. Provide suggestions to the client.
     a. MAYBE YOU COULD DO (name of an activity)
     b. WHY DON'T YOU ASK (name of a peer) TO DO THAT WITH YOU?
  4. Provide a strong suggestion to the client. I THINK THAT YOU SHOULD (name of an activity).
  5. If necessary, accompany the client during the activity, either participating or observing. Shape independent leisure behaviors.
H. *Reinforce appropriate play behaviors or approximations.*
VIII. Followup at the next session. Time: 15 minutes.
  A. WHO CAN TELL ME WHAT I ASKED EVERYBODY TO DO AT OUR LAST MEETING?
  B. LET'S HAVE EVERYONE TELL THE REST OF THE GROUP WHAT HE DID THAT WAS FUN AND HOW IT MADE HIM FEEL. WHO WOULD LIKE TO GO FIRST? Allow a client to model the procedure.
  C. Possible questions to ask the clients.
     1. HOW DID YOU PLAY?
     2. HOW DID YOU FEEL AFTER YOU DID IT?
     3. WERE YOU GLAD THAT YOU DID IT?
     4. WHY WERE YOU GLAD THAT YOU DID IT?
  D. Leisure counselor and staff also share their experiences with the group.
  E. *Reinforce descriptions of appropriate play behaviors or approximations.*
  F. Emphasize that PLAYING WELL CAN MAKE US FEEL GOOD.
  G. ALSO, EVERYONE ASK EACH OTHER WHAT YOU HAVE DONE FOR FUN. THIS CAN BE A WAY TO HELP EACH OTHER GET IDEAS FOR FUN THINGS TO DO.

PROGRAM SYSTEM: Conversation skills
POPULATION: Emotionally disturbed children, ages five through nine
SETTING: Mental health center in conjunction with a special education district
DESIGNER: Linda Henrichs

PROGRAM SYSTEM: Conversational skills
TERMINAL PERFORMANCE OBJECTIVE 1: To improve conversational skills with authority figure

ENABLING OBJECTIVES	PERFORMANCE MEASURES
1. To demonstrate the ability to make a request.	1. During the recreation therapy program, the client will demonstrate the ability to make a request of the recreation therapist, as characterized by: a. making an appropriate approach to the authority figure, b. assuming an appropriate distance from the person for easy conversation, c. speaking in acceptable tone and volume, d. maintaining eye contact with the authority figure, e. standing and waiting attentively for the reply, as judged by the recreation therapist.
2. To demonstrate the ability to initiate a basic conversation.	2. After basic instruction and when the situation arises, the client will demonstrate the ability to initiate a basic conversation with the recreation therapist, as characterized by: a. making an appropriate approach to the authority figure,

3. To demonstrate the ability to receive instructions.

4. To demonstrate the ability to receive criticism or correction.

---

    b. assuming an appropriate distance from the person for easy conversation,
    c. speaking in acceptable tone and volume,
    d. maintaining eye contact with the authority figure,
    e. completing the conversation in an appropriate manner,
    as judged by the recreation therapist.

3. During the recreation therapy program, the client will demonstrate the ability to receive instructions from the recreation therapist as characterized by:
    a. attending to the instruction—
        (1). no talking during instruction,
        (2). no inappropriate moving around during instruction;
    b. following the instructions—
        (1). acknowledging the instruction was heard,
        (2). doing what is necessary to follow the instructions;
    as judged by the recreation therapist.

4. When the appropriate situation arises, the client will demonstrate the ability to receive criticism or correction from the recreation therapist, as characterized by:
    a. not trying to put the blame on someone else,
    b. not calling the authority figure names,
    c. not threatening the authority figure,
    d. not walking away from the authority figure,
    e. attending to the criticism or correction and acknowledging the intention,
    as judged by the recreation therapist.

PROGRAM SYSTEM: Peer-interaction group
POPULATION: Developmentally disabled and emotionally disturbed children, ages eight through fifteen
SETTING: Residential treatment
DESIGNER: Mary Patricia McCreary

LEARNING SYSTEM: Peer-interaction group   MODULE: Social Skills
TERMINAL PERFORMANCE OBJECTIVE 1: To interact in a structured activity with assistance

ENABLING OBJECTIVES	PERFORMANCE MEASURES
1. To play games according to the rules, using external cues.	1. While engaged in two of the selected games taught in the regulated sessions, the child will demonstrate the ability to play by the rules, using external cues, as characterized by:* a. completing the game, b. complying with the rules, and c. attending throughout the session to the extent that the ongoing activity is not disrupted.
2. To interact with verbal or nonverbal communication, using external cues.	2. During a designated evaluation session, the child will demonstrate the ability to communicate verbally or nonverbally with an adult or child, using external cues, as characterized by:* a. making statements about the activity; b. asking questions about the activity; c. initiating appropriate physical contact, such as handshake, light touch, hug, pat on the back (inappropriate physical contact would be hitting, slapping, pushing, kicking, pulling); d. responding to verbal or nonverbal communication, verbally or nonverbally, within five seconds.
3. To demonstrate the ability to choose to play with children in games, with assistance.	3. During a designated evaluation session and in a game requiring the tagging or selecting of another person, the child will select another child (rather than an adult) using external cues, for two out of three turns.* *As judged by staff.

TEACHING-LEARNING ACTIVITIES

TPO 1, EO 1, PM 1

INSTRUCTIONAL CONTENT	INSTRUCTIONAL PROCESS
1. Completes the game.	The instructional process is the same for all three PMs.
2. Complies with the rules.	1. Shaping. A child is put through an activity by holding on to him physically so that staff can move him through the specific steps. This gives the child the kinesthetic input of an activity—the feeling of the activity. For example, in the game "Good Morning," staff may need to hold on to the arms of a child and pick him up to a standing position after he's been tapped on the head. The staff will then move him in the direction of the tapper to help the child try to tag the tapper.
3. Attends throughout the session to the extent that the ongoing activity is not disrupted.	2. Positive Reinforcement. The staff gives the child verbal and physical praise, such as hugs, pats on the back, "That's a good job," or "You are sitting nicely." This reinforcement is given for the behaviors in EO 1 and PM 1.
	3. Modeling. The child observes the staff or other children playing the game or parts of a specific game. The child then plays the part of the game he observed. He tries to imitate the person he observed. This performance determines whether or not he has correctly modeled the action he observed.
	4. Coaching. The child himself performs a game or part of a game. Then the child gets feedback from another person on his performance. (Coaching may also include modeling.) For example, the child could touch another's head and run around the circle in the game "Duck, Duck, Goose." He could sit down before being tagged. The feedback could be, "Good job. You ran very fast and sat down quickly." The child would then know he had played the game correctly and would probably repeat his performance the next time. If the child got tagged, the coaching would be, "You need to run faster. You must sit down before he tags you." Then the child will begin to realize that he indeed does need to run faster and if he sits down before he's tagged, he gets another turn. He has played the game correctly. Part of the learning process here may also include shaping the child so that he gets the feeling immediately and will have a better chance of behaving correctly the next time.

summary

Determining and writing terminal performance objectives, enabling objectives, and performance measures start the design procedure for a program component. This is followed by specifying the content and process for each EO. When completed, the designer has a well-developed and logical program description that should be appropriate for the designated population, feasible within the agency's constraints and resources, and compatible with other agency programs and services. However, the program design is not complete at this stage. Two other aspects need to be developed: the implementation plan and the evaluation plan. These two other parts of the comprehensive program plan are presented in chapters twelve and thirteen. Chapters ten and eleven present additional material that is useful in the development of the content and process sections of a program plan.

note

[1] Ken Joswiak, *Leisure Counseling Program Materials for the Mentally Impaired* (Washington, D.C.: Hawkins and Associates, Inc., 1976). Note the detail in the leisure-counseling activity sheet. A system of this type enables a recreator to implement the program fully, independent of the designer.

suggested references

ARMSTRONG, R. J., T. D. CORNELL, R. E. KRANER, AND E. ROBERSON, *The Development and Evaluation of Behavioral Objectives.* Worthington, Ohio: Charles A. Jones Publishing Company, 1970.

EBEL, R. L., "Behavioral Objectives: A Close Look," *Phi Delta Kappan*, 52, no. 3 (1970), 171–73.

EISNER, E. W., "Educational Objectives: Help or Hindrance," *The School Review*, 75 (1967), 250–60.

GAGNE, R. M., *The Conditions of Learning.* New York: Holt, Rinehart and Winston, 1965

———, "Educational Objectives and Human Performance," in *Learning and the Educational Process*, ed. J. D. Krumboltz. Chicago, Ill.: Rand McNally, 1965.

GRONLUND, N. E., *Stating Behavioral Objectives for Classroom Instruction.* London: The Macmillan Company, 1970.

HITCH, C. J., "On the Choice of Objectives in Systems Studies," in *Systems Research and Design*, ed. Donald P. Eckman. New York: John Wiley and Sons, Inc., 1961.

KRATHWOHL, D. R., "Stating Objectives Appropriately for Program, for Curriculum, and for Instructional Materials Developed," *Journal of Teacher Education*, 16 (1965), 83–92.

———, *Taxonomy of Educational Objectives, Handbook II: Affective Domain*. New York: David McKay, 1964.

MAGER, R. F., *Preparing Instructional Objectives*. Palo Alto, Calif.: Fearon Publishers, 1962.

MAGUIRE, T. O., "Decisions and Curriculum Objectives: A Methodology for Evaluation," *Alberta Journal of Educational Research*, 15 (1969), 17–30.

PETERSON, C. A., *A Systems Approach to Therapeutic Recreation Program Planning*. Champaign, Ill.: Stipes Publishing Company, 1976.

SIMPSON, E. J., "The Classifications of Educational Objectives: Psychomotor Domain," *Illinois Teacher of Home Economics*, 10 (1966–67), 110–44.

TYLER, R. W., "Some Persistent Questions on the Defining of Objectives," in *Defining Educational Objectives*, ed. C. M. Lindvall. Pittsburgh, Pa.: University of Pittsburgh Press, 1964.

activity analysis and its applications

PURPOSE: To present a definition, rationale, and procedures for activity analysis. Discussed are the therapeutic use of activities based on inherent characteristics and techniques of activity modification.

Once program goals are determined and behavioral objectives are specified, the designer has the task of selecting content (activities) for the program. This process is often taken for granted and traditional activities are selected blindly, based on staff skills or interests, available facilities and limitations of budget. In systems-designed programs, however, activities should be carefully selected according to their ability to contribute to the achievement of the behavioral objectives.

If the program is an instructional one, then the task is somewhat simplified. The activities must relate to the recreational skills being taught. However, choices are more difficult when the objectives are oriented to treatment or behavioral change. For example, an objective dealing with self-confidence or increasing social skills does not directly indicate that a particular activity should be chosen. The designer is thus free to select from a wide range of possibilities. A variety of factors must be considered, such as age, sex, carry-over value, feasibility, budget, facility constraints, and staffing concerns. The real trick, however, is in picking activities that have *inherent* characteristics that contribute to the objectives.

Activity analysis is a procedure for breaking down and examining an activity to find inherent characteristics that contribute to program objectives. It is a process that allows the therapeutic recreator to understand an activity and its potential contributions to behavioral outcomes. Activity analysis provides a more exact method of selecting activities in that activity components are analyzed before utilization for their behavior and interaction requirements. In activity analysis, different activities and their therapeutic value can be compared so that better programming decisions can be made.

Breaking down activities into components makes the designer aware of what skills are required to be able to participate in the activities. Thus, the specialist can determine exactly where modifications are needed for clients to become involved in certain activities. Activity analysis makes it possible to make the fewest possible modifications.

Activity analysis occurs independently of clients. The specialist can take an activity and analyze it for its basic requirements and demands in terms of actual participation factors. Of basic concern are the physical, cognitive, affective (emotional), and social components of the activity as it is traditionally engaged in. Such an analysis considers just the activity itself. The goal is simply to understand the activity and its inherent characteristics. The process, however, has many applications in therapeutic recreation programming. If the program is instructional in nature, the process of activity analysis, combined with the functional assessment of a person with a disability, allows the instructor to know exactly what modifications of the activity are needed to accommodate that person. For example, an analysis of the physical requirements of the front crawl in swimming compared to the functional ability of an individual with cerebral palsy would indicate the exact areas needing adaptation, i.e., the kick, or the coordination of arms and breathing.

On the other hand, if the program is rehabilitation-oriented, an analysis of a selected activity, compared with the stated treatment goal, would allow the therapist to ascertain whether that activity would contribute to the desired behavioral- or functional-improvement objective. Bingo, for example, has no inherent social-interaction requirements. The players merely listen for numbers, search their cards for those numbers, and cover them with tokens. Through analysis, an activity that is commonly billed as a social activity is discovered to possess none of the essential components of human interaction. Therefore, it is not an appropriate selection for a treatment goal dealing with social skills. It would, however, be a good activity for increasing concentration.

Admittedly, analysis is much more difficult for some activities than for others. Structured activities, such as games and sports, can, because of their exact rules and procedures, be more easily and more accurately analyzed and understood than unstructured activities, such as crafts, wilderness camping, or spontaneous play. Unstructured activities vary in their analysis outcomes based on the context and situation surrounding the participation experiences. Nonetheless, the attempt at systematic analysis of activity components is beneficial for comprehending participation requirements and possible outcome behaviors, regardless of the limitations imposed by the nature or structure of the activities.

Activities also vary considerably in their participation requirements and demands. A casual evaluation of an activity can often be misleading. The complexity of many activities is frequently hidden because of an assumed familiarity. Thus, an activity like checkers is considered simple because it is so well known, whereas, in fact, the game requires advanced cognitive skills, including evaluation and decision making (strategy) as well as the recall of countless rules governing the play. It is this type of information that is gleaned from employing a systematic and comprehensive activity analysis.

A variety of methods exist for analyzing activities. Although there are many established processes of activity analysis, the following definition appears to explain its basic aim while also encompassing the multiplicity of concerns and procedures:

Activity analysis is a process which involves the systematic application of selected sets of constructs and variables to break down and examine a given activity to determine the behavioral requirements inherent for successful participation. [1]

Activity analysis leads to a deeper understanding of activity components and participation requirements. Activity analysis provides:

1. a better comprehension of the expected outcomes of participation;
2. a greater understanding of the complexity of activity components, which can then be compared to the functional level of an individual or group to determine the appropriateness of the activity;
3. information about whether the activity will contribute to the desired behavioral outcome when specific behavioral goals or objectives are being used;
4. direction for the modification or adaptation of that activity for individuals with limitations;
5. useful information for selecting an intervention, instructional, or leadership technique;
6. a rationale or explanation for the therapeutic benefits of activity involvement.

overview of activity analysis

When an individual engages in an activity, action is required in three behavioral areas: physical (psychomotor), cognitive, and affective behaviors are all involved, regardless of the type of activity. For example, when playing ping-pong the *physical* actions are obvious. The player must be able to grasp and hold a paddle, have sufficient elbow, shoulder, and wrist movement to hit the ball, enough mobility to move quickly, and hand-eye coordination. *Cognitive* skills are also required. There are rules to remember, there is continuous scoring, and there are strategies to plan. These cognitive or mental requirements add to the totality of the involvement. *Affective* requirements for controlling or expressing emotions are also part of the action. An activity analysis of ping-pong, or any activity for that matter, examines each behavioral area.

A game, such as checkers, that is normally considered a mental game, has demands in all three behavioral areas. Cognitive requirements include knowledge of rules and strategy and concentration. Physically, the game requires sight as well as the ability to grasp and move pieces. Affectively, checkers demands control of emotions when pieces are jumped and removed.

When analyzing activities for use in therapeutic recreation programs, it is important to understand the demands in each behavioral area. The more we know about how the activity pertains to each area, the better able we will be to select appropriate activities for treatment or to know how to modify them for successful participation.

Besides the behavioral areas of involvement, we should also look at the social or *interactional* skills needed. Far too often clients have problems with an activity (or refuse to play) because the interactional skills required are too demanding or just not part of their current functional ability. For example, a client may know the activity skills necessary to play basketball but avoids the game because he or she cannot handle the verbal interactions needed to be a team member. The analysis of interactional requirements is thus critical for total comprehension of participation demands.

The therapeutic recreator must understand the demands in all four areas, realizing that they are complex and interrelated. Failure to be concerned with any one area could easily result in inappropriate program content. An example of this is selecting an activity for a group of mentally retarded teenagers and only looking at the physical demands of the activity. While conducting the activity, the leader becomes embarrassingly aware that the mental requirements or social demands are beyond the group's functional level. An analysis ahead of time might have saved the situation, either by allowing the leader to plan for modifications, or by selecting a more suitable activity.

The following pages present some major considerations in each area of concern. The information is far from complete. Additional factors can be identified for specific populations. The attempt here is to provide general material that cuts across all groups. Therapeutic recreators are encouraged to design their own activity-analysis checklist, including items that are of specific concern to their clientele. Our own general checklist is presented only as an example; it appears at the end of this section.

physical requirements

All recreational activity requires some physical action. Often it is difficult to distinguish what action is *required* to participate from what action may be associated with an activity. Some activities do not require specific actions. There are many ways to fly a kite, whereas other activities, such as gymnastics, have definite ways of moving. The problem is to identify only the actual demands of the activity.

One can begin analyzing the physical requirements of an activity by noting the basic body position, then determining the body parts involved. Each involved body part must be identified—separately, such as fingers, hand, wrist, and elbow, or by grouping parts into larger categories, such as arm or upper torso. The amount of detail needed usually relates to the population that is receiving recreational services. For example, more detailed information is required when analyzing activities for the physically handicapped than with the mentally ill.

The types of movement must also be determined. Common body actions are bending, stretching, twisting, reaching, grasping, and rotating. These actions are usually part of a movement pattern that can be identified in such broad terms as catching, throwing, kicking, striking, running, and hopping. Pinpointing the fundamental movement patterns in an activity helps to determine the complexity of an activity and also what skills need to be taught. When more detail is needed, the therapist can isolate the exact motions involved in each body part. An excellent example of this is found in Elliott M. Avedon's book *Therapeutic Recreation Service: An Applied Behavioral Approach*. This illustration identifies each body part and its position and describes in detail the movements required for archery. Such specific analysis, however, is rarely needed in most therapeutic recreation program situations.

It is also important to know the number and nature of the movements involved. For example, softball is extremely complex; it requires running, throwing, catching, and striking (batting), all with a fair degree of accuracy. Bowling, on the other hand, has just one basic movement pattern. This type of information is crucial when it comes to the selection of activities for certain populations.

Coordination of body parts is another major factor to consider. Many activities require a high degree of coordination. Golf is a good example. It is a simple game by one standard, in that the entire game consists of one basic movement pattern, a swing of a golf club. However, coordination is critical, to which any frustrated, amateur duffer can attest. Activities that require little body-parts coordination are easier to participate in—an insight that has obvious implications for special populations. Scheduling activities that continuously frustrate a client because too much coordination is needed certainly blocks the therapeutic intent or the enjoyment in participation. Most special populations, whether mentally retarded, mentally ill, emotionally disturbed, cerebral palsied, blind, deaf, or elderly, all have difficulty with activities requiring high levels of body coordination.

Hand-eye coordination is another critical area. Unfortunately, many basic recreational activities require some form of hand-eye coordination, whether the activity is a sport, a craft, or a table game. Again the issue is determining how much coordination is required for successful participation. An awareness that the level and amount of hand-eye coordination is extremely high in a certain activity may result in the selection of another activity to comply with the limitation of a person or group.

A variety of other physical factors can be analyzed. Among these are strength, speed, endurance, energy, flexibility, agility, joint stress, and cardiovascular activity. Determining how much or how little of these elements are involved in a given activity is equally important when selecting and modifying program content.

The different senses should also be considered as part of the physical requirements of activity participation. Sight is vital to successful participation in many activities, as is hearing. Rarely do we stop to analyze an activity for these two essential areas. The inability of a client to hear clearly in and of itself could make participation in many activities extremely frustrating, if not impossible. Smell and taste are not as often required for most activities, but touch is inherent in most sports and crafts.

Understanding the various physical demands of an activity is complex. Indeed, the variety of factors to consider and their diversity makes the task tedious. However, the result of such a process enables appropriate selection of activities for clinical or community programs. Knowing where and how to modify an activity is also a result of the process.

cognitive requirements

Cognition may be the most important requirement of activity participation since the mind regulates body movement as well as other behavioral aspects of playing. Several aspects of cognition are important considerations in activity analysis.

The number and complexity of rules need to be determined. Chess and bridge have many rules, whereas creative dramatics has no inherent rules. The leader may impose some, but the activity itself is rule free. These rules not only must be remembered, but also the players must regulate their behavior according to them. Many individuals—mentally retarded, emotionally disturbed, stroke-disabled, psychotic, neurotic, and elderly—have much difficulty in playing games that have complex rules.

Memory retention is another vital area of cognition. It pertains not only to rules but also to new information that needs to be processed, stored, and used continuously during the activity. Both the amount and nature of long- and short-term memory retention need to be analyzed before recommending the use of a certain activity.

Concentration needs should also be noted. Some activities require intense, continuous concentration. Ping-pong is a good example. Bowling, however, requires intermittent concentration. The specialist must be aware of the level of concentration required to perform an activity, as well as its frequency.

Does the activity require verbalization or a command of language? The act of speaking is actually physical, but generally language usage is considered to be a cognitive function. Activities have differing degrees of selecting, organizing, and using words. Bingo requires little verbalization, whereas planning and putting on a skit require a lot.

Strategy is another cognitive skill inherent in many recreational activities. It requires an ability to analyze alternatives and make decisions. There is a big difference between the amount of strategy required in Chinese checkers and a game of Old Maid, just as there is between tennis and horseshoes.

The requirements of intellectual skill versus chance can also be considered in activity analysis. Some activities involve mental functioning, but the outcomes are pretty much chance-related. For example, Parcheesi, poker, or blackjack depend more on the luck of the deal or the roll of the dice than they do on mental functioning.

The academic skills of reading, writing, and math should be analyzed in relation to most activities. For example, countless activities require the ability to keep score, which are mathematical calculations. Frequently we take this ability for granted or overlook its complexity because an activity is primarily physical in nature.

Other cognitive concerns are basic factors, such as directionality; spacial awareness; and object, person, part, and symbol identification and discrimination. Activities differ immensely in their utilization of these concepts. Although the normal individual acquires these abilities early, many adults (an acute psychotic, for example) may temporarily be unable to function in one or more of these areas.

The analysis of activities for an understanding of their cognitive demands is essential. More often than not, some cognitive inability makes a client's participation difficult, frustrating, or impossible. Cognitive requirements are as equally complex as physical requirements, but by nature are more difficult to detect and are thus more likely to be overlooked by the therapeutic recreator.

interaction and social requirements

Activities have different physical and cognitive requirements; they also demand interactional skills. In many activities it is necessary to relate to others. The nature of the interaction may be cooperative or competitive and there may be any number of people involved. An analysis of these inherent interaction patterns within activities is significant to select activities appropriately and to help clients develop social skills.

interaction patterns inherent
in recreational activities

Elliott Avedon has developed a classification system of interaction patterns found in activities that quickly enables the therapeutic recreation specialist to understand some of the dynamics of participation. Once an activity has been analyzed to determine which of the eight interaction patterns are inherent, the specialist can make a variety of judgments about the complexity, demands, or appropriateness of that activity for a specific individual or group. In addition, interaction analysis facilitates the selection and sequencing of activities for building social and interactional skills. Since many therapeutic recreation programs focus on social factors, it is advantageous to comprehend as much as possible about an activity's contribution in this area. The eight interaction patterns follow.[2]

Intraindividual. "Action taking place within the mind of a person or action involving the mind and a part of the body, but requiring no contact with another person or external object." Activities in this category are few and are seldom used in therapeutic recreation programming. Twiddling thumbs or daydreaming fall into this category. Intraindividual actions are, however, frequently engaged in by individuals, although they are rarely discussed in professional literature or presented in programs. "Head trips" are a form of recreation, although they have not previously been recognized as such. Needless to say, it is not a type of activity that can be programmed, but it is one that should be given permission to exist and be enjoyed.

Extraindividual. "Action directed by a person toward an object in the environment, requiring no contact with another person." Countless activities fall into this category. Anything done alone that involves an object fits the requirements. Watching television, engaging in a craft project, working in a garden, playing solitaire, and reading—all can be considered extraindividual activities.

Everyone engages in individual activities. However, this category of activities is seldom dealt with in therapeutic recreation programs. The reasons are usually time and resources. Because we are faced with providing programs for numbers of people, we tend to rely on group activities. Ironically, however, in the process of helping people prepare for leisure living, we frequently overlook the fact that many ill and handicapped people spend a large amount of time alone and thus need leisure skills that can be engaged in while alone. Extraindividual activities are therefore a must for program consideration. The ability to enjoy oneself while alone should be a basic concern of the therapeutic recreator who realistically confronts the needs of ill or handicapped people.

Extraindividual activities can also serve another major function: they can be stepping stones to learning social abilities. It is often easier for a client to engage in a social experience when an activity is the focus, as opposed to an emphasis on interacting with others. Assisting clients to engage in individual activity involvement is therefore an important step in acquiring interactional skills. When a person is comfortable engaging in an activity alone, and is receiving some degree of satisfaction from that involvement, it may then be possible for him or her to begin to interact comfortably with others.

Aggregate. "Action directed by a person toward an object in the environment while in the company of other persons who are also directing action toward objects in the environment. Action is not directed toward one another, and no interaction between participants is required or necessary." Many activities that can be done alone (extraindividual) can also be done in groups. In therapeutic recreation, this is indeed common. Crafts programs, entertainment, and hobby groups are all examples of aggregate activities, as is the infamous game of bingo. Aggregate activities *require* no interaction between participants. This quality, however, has several inherent therapeutic characteristics and applications.

First is physical proximity. When a group of individuals are together, all engaging in their own projects, they have the opportunity to warm up to each other without any pressure to interact. Each individual focuses on her or his own activity, but spontaneous interaction stimulated by the action often results. Borrowing a piece of equipment, sharing a success, or asking a question, all are social responses that are natural and easy to make. In a program geared to develop social and verbal interactional skills, aggregate activities are ideal in the early stages when nonthreatening interactions are essential. Aggregate activities are frequently used to begin a sequenced program of socialization.

Aggregate activities, as well as extraindividual activities, can be either competitive or cooperative. Solitaire, a crossword puzzle, or a pinball game are competitive. The individual can learn competitive action without the reality or threat of another person as the opponent. Testing one's abilities against the game or task has a variety of therapeutic benefits. The ability to compete in many areas of life appears to be an essential ingredient of survival in our culture. Competitive aggregate activities provide a simulated experience for acquiring this skill in a safe or supervised situation.

Cooperative aggregate activities, such as crafts, woodworking, writing, reading, and gardening, allow the clients to gain internal motivation and stimulation without competitive demands. Increasing one's ability to enjoy an activity without feeling the pressure of competition can be a meaningful lesson. When actions are initiated by the individuals themselves, and conducted without external expectations or demands, a feeling of self-sufficiency and independence results.

Aggregate activities provide opportunities for those involved to master activities independent of others. Since many ill or handicapped people spend time alone, they should have a repertoire of activities in which they can engage without others. The aggregate pattern enables the therapeutic recreation specialist to facilitate the acquisition of such skills while still working in a group situation.

Interindividual. "Action of a competitive nature directed by one person toward another." This interaction pattern is basic for many mental and physical activities. Chess, checkers, honeymoon bridge, singles tennis, badminton, and racketball are all examples. The pattern requires the ability to interact continuously with one's opponent and to apply the necessary skills with the intention of winning or at least enjoying the attempt. This competition simulates many interpersonal encounters in daily living in which individuals need to stand up for themselves against other persons.

Interindividual activities vary in the amount and degree of necessary interaction. A game of checkers requires very little, if any, verbal exchange; other games require calling out scores, requesting information, or responding verbally in other ways. Interindividual activities can be selected and sequenced to produce a progression of verbalization and other social responses.

Another therapeutic application of this pattern relates to the frequency of the interaction. A game like ping-pong requires continuous attention and response as the ball quickly moves from one side of the table to the other. In games like chess, however, there is no pressure to act immediately. Changes in frequency allow the specialist to provide a sequence of more and more challenging interactional activities.

Since the pattern is always competitive, it has the therapeutic quality of assisting people deal with stress, pressure, and concepts of winning and losing. The therapeutic recreation specialist must focus on this aspect in order for it to be beneficial. Continuous losing can be destructive, as can be the overwhelming need always to win. Because interindividual activities are competitive, they always have rules. A characteristic of these activities is playing by the rules and regulating one's behavior according to the rules in order to participate successfully. The players agree to interact and behave in certain ways, to their mutual benefit. The value of such agreement extends beyond the game into many life situations. In interindividual activities, clients can experience appropriate role modeling for many interactions.

Unilateral. "Action of a competitive nature among three or more persons, one of whom is an antagonist or *it.*" Many children's games have a unilateral pattern. Tag games, hide-and-seek games, and chase games are in this category. Fewer adult games fit it. Nonetheless, some characteristics of the unilateral pattern apply to interactional skills. Unilateral activities provide opportunities for role differentiation. In these kinds of games, all players except one have the same roles. It is the beginning stage of letting different players have different functions, a concept that develops to the complex roles found in games like basketball or softball. When just one person is "it," the concept of different roles is quickly learned and understood.

Several other benefits occur from unilateral activities. When working with mentally retarded individuals, it is often easier to teach beginning concepts of competition with unilateral activities. With other populations, unilateral activities put one person in the limelight. The competitive pressure also shifts from one player to another, thus removing the continuous, competitive pressure in other types of activities.

Multilateral. "Action of a competitive nature among three or more persons, with no one person as an antagonist." In multilateral activities, every player is against every other player. Games like Scrabble, poker, and Monopoly are examples of activities that have this pattern. (Some social activities like cocktail parties often appear to have this pattern also!) Multilateral activities have several characteristics that can be used for therapeutic outcomes.

Multilateral activities require each person to initiate competitive action with the others. For the individual who cannot tolerate sustained, competitive action with just one person, activities of this type allow for a diffusion of effort. In multilateral activities, the individual is often pressured to perform by a number of people simultaneously. This simulated life experience has value for other real-life situations when the individual has to face pressures that come from a variety of people at the same time.

Multilateral activities place the responsibility for control directly on each individual since each is an independent agent within the game. Decision making, strategy, and action are not shared by team members. The result is a feeling of self-sufficiency—for the individual who is ready for it. Obviously, many clients need to work up to this type of interaction pattern, since it places high demands on internal strength and independence.

Intragroup. "Action of a cooperative nature by two or more persons intent upon reaching a mutual goal. Action requires positive verbal and non-verbal interaction." Examples of activities requiring this pattern include such things as musical groups (bands and choirs), dramatic plays, service projects, and tandem-bike riding. Learning how to cooperate and function successfully as a group member is a difficult task, but one that most clients need. Unfortunately, without the motivation of competition, it is often hard to build the concepts of cooperation. *Recreational activities of the intragroup type do not inherently create cooperative action.* Sensitive and astute leadership is needed to maximize the benefits of intragroup activities. Activities in this category are essential in helping to establish social skills, since so many interactions in life require compromise and cooperation. Family life, most social situations, and work are everyday examples that require intragroup abilities of interaction. Programming activities in this category are overwhelmingly important if we wish to assist clients in the development of positive and cooperative interactional skills.

Many professionals feel that competitive activities are overemphasized in therapeutic recreation programs and in the world of leisure at large. The concept that fun has to involve doing someone else in or beating the other guy is indeed narrow. Enjoyment should be fostered through cooperative action as well.

Finding or creating good activities that utilize the intragroup pattern is a challenge for the therapeutic recreator. It is often difficult to establish a mutual goal that is attractive enough to the participants to facilitate positive interactions. Nevertheless, the benefits resulting from successful participation in intragroup activities make the effort well worthwhile.

Intergroup. "Action of a competitive nature between two or more intragroups." All team sports and games fall into this category. Softball, kickball, doubles tennis, and bridge are examples. These activities are the most difficult to perform, since participants must cooperate with other team members as well as compete against their opponents. Far too often, clients are put into intergroup activities long before they are ready to handle the advanced interactional skills required. This often results in mass confusion, not to mention negative reactions. Therapeutic recreators should avoid introducing intergroup activities until they are sure the participants are functionally and developmentally able to handle the diverse interactions involved. Unfortunately, many traditional and familiar activities are of this type; we overlook their complexity because of their popularity.

Intergroup activities have many rather obvious therapeutic benefits. Learning to be a good team member is one. This interaction pattern represents many realistic life situations of working with one group against another group. The give and take needed to mount an effective attack can be experienced through games, with carry-over to other work and social situations.

An advantage of intergroup activities is that they often produce peer pressure among team members, which can effectively result in significant behavior changes in participants. This outcome, however, has both positive and negative implications. Good leadership is needed to effect the peer pressure desired. Deep understanding of group dynamics is needed to produce therapeutic peer pressure.

The fact that intergroup activities have the element of competition is another benefit, if handled wisely. The pressure to cooperate in order to win often brings a group together that otherwise could not or would not function as a unit. In this case, competition is a positive influence. Through the process, individuals frequently gain greater respect and liking for each other, which opens up other avenues of positive interaction.

Another therapeutic benefit of the intergroup pattern is the concept of a support system. To be a member of the team, to sense belonging, and to experience unity within a group are all important and positive experiences. Many times these experiences are missing in the lives of handicapped individuals. Intergroup activities may facilitate the feeling of belonging and give individuals a base from which to develop other group ties.

Understanding the inherent interaction patterns found in activities contributes a great deal to our comprehension of the dynamics of involvement as well as to the therapeutic possibilities in the selection and sequencing process. Analyzing activities with the use of interaction patterns provides a valuable tool for the development of social-interaction skills by enabling us to focus on the critical issues surrounding activity participation.

other social factors

In addition to the interaction patterns inherent in activities, a variety of other social factors can be identified and used in the analysis process. Since the word social encompasses such broad categories of behavior in our culture, the list of factors could be extremely lengthy. Some of the more generic and useful items are presented below.

1. Does the activity provide opportunity for interaction with the opposite sex? No activity can be categorized as male or female, but traditionally certain activities are participated in by one sex or the other or in segregated programs. If meeting and enjoying members of the opposite sex is a client need, therapeutic recreation programs should present activities in which both sexes can engage mutually. Likewise, if sex-role identification is an issue, perhaps it is best to select traditionally male or female activities.

2. Does the activity facilitate social interaction by proximity? Often our goal is to increase social or verbal interaction, yet we erroneously select an activity like softball where the players are spread out all over the field with little opportunity to communicate easily, thus eliminating any opportunity for either spontaneous or structured interaction.

3. How much physical contact does the activity require? Facilitating human warmth and contact may be a controversial subject, but there are times when assisting individuals to touch and be touched could be important. The issue is more of knowing whether an activity requires physical contact or whether it promotes spontaneous contact. Square dancing requires touch, whereas volleyball does not. The latter, however, may call for a pat on the back or a hug after winning or losing. Being able to cope with physical contact is a problem area for some psychiatric and emotionally disturbed patients. In such cases, it could be very inappropriate to select activities requiring too much contact before the individual is ready for it.

4. How much verbal communication is required in the activity? Although interaction is comprised of nonverbal as well as verbal communication, more often program goals deal with increasing or improving verbal-interaction skills. Analyzing activities for the amount and type of verbalization is therefore vital. Bingo requires no verbal interaction between clients, even though it is usually considered a social activity. Monopoly requires a lot of verbalization as the players buy and sell or share "chance" and "community chest" cards.

5. How many participants does the activity require? Some activities have a set minimum and maximum number of participants. Checkers or chess are two-people games. Other activities have set numbers of players by the official rules, but the number can be expanded or decreased. Volleyball is an example of such an activity. Other activities have no required numbers and thus can accommodate as many or as few participants as the resources, leadership, or facility can handle. Modern dance or creative dramatics fit this category. The activity selected must coincide with program goals and client needs. A two-person activity is appropriate for encouraging comfortableness in a sustained interaction. A large-group activity is appropriate for promoting interactions among many people.

Other social or interactional items can be included in activity analysis depending on the population served and its unique needs. Additional examples are included in figure 10–1.

emotional (affective) factors

Of all the behavioral areas of functioning, the affective domain causes the greatest difficulty in activity analysis. One problem is that of definition. Affective behaviors are often difficult to deal with and as a result are often just skipped over. They are, however, a vital part of activity involvement and therefore cannot be excluded from examination. Therapeutic recreators are naturally concerned with how to recognize various emotional responses, since so much of therapeutic recreation programming focuses on developing, stimulating, and otherwise facilitating the appropriate expressions of feelings.

Activities do not have set, inherent, affective requirements that can be identified the way physical or cognitive requirements can be. Each client brings to an activity a lifetime of experience with a variety of ways of responding emotionally. An activity that causes excitement in one person fosters fear in someone else. Thus, there is no simple way to categorize the emotional responses or requirements of activities.

basic emotions

Six emotions are generally accepted as basic to the human experience. These six can therefore be generalized in relation to activity participation. The following descriptions are offered as guidelines for understanding possible emotional responses and are in no way intended to be absolute. Individuals should be expected to vary in their responses. The therapeutic recreator can, however, be aware of possible outcomes and thus become a bit more prepared to cope with emotional reactions. Predominantly, we are concerned with what emotions are *likely* to be evoked or stimulated by the type of activity used.

Joy. We want people to feel good about themselves, to experience enjoyment, or at least to feel contentment. One thing that seems to produce this feeling in most cultures is winning. Any activity that involves competition and in which the participants have a fairly equal amount of skill should produce a sense of enjoyment for the winner. The opposite, unfortunately, is also true for the loser, who will probably not sense the same amount of happiness. Very few people have really mastered the ability to feel good because of performing well even if they lose, or just feeling good for having participated. Our egos are too tied up with being the best and that is quickly determined in any competitive activity.

Normally, enjoyment results from good interaction with another person. Activities, therefore, that have a high possibility of creating social interactions are likely to produce some emotions of joy and contentment.

Completing a task is another event that seems to bring good feelings to many people. Note the frustration level when individuals cannot complete a craft project because the time is up, or when tennis players have to get off the court in the middle of a set because the court was reserved by someone else. Contentment seems to be tied up with a sense of closure.

Guilt. Guilt is a very destructive emotion. It produces feelings of shame and inadequacy, and often results in counterresponses of resentment and hostility. Individuals feel guilty when they let someone else down. This happens frequently in competitive team situations. Players feel they are not good enough or other team members convince a player that this is true. To be lousy at something and then to be forced to play and to have the outcomes affect others—this situation sets up a guilty response. People generally feel guilty when they hurt someone else. Any activity that has much combative contact has a high probability of producing guilt, whether the act of hurting was intentional or accidental.

Pain. Pain or hurt can be experienced through physical, mental, or emotional occurrences. We feel pain when we lose a game or when we have to acknowledge that we aren't as good as someone else. Competitive activities produce this response. There can only be one winner; someone always loses. We feel pain when we are rejected or eliminated. Activities that send an individual away to the sidelines or outside the circle can produce hurt. Musical chairs or a simple elimination dodgeball game selectively exclude more and more people as the activity continues.

Physical pain is easily understood. Lots of activities have a high risk of physical pain and should be carefully considered. Emotional or social pain is hard to predict since it deals more with an individual's personality and previous experience.

Anger. Anger can be expected in a variety of situations. Any activity that requires physical restraint will normally produce anger in the person being held down or held back. King of the Mountain and wrestling are good examples of this.

Being struck by a person or object also produces anger (as well as the possibility of physical pain). Many activities require striking, directly or indirectly, and thus have a high potential for this emotional response. Obvious activities are boxing and fencing, but other activities such as tag, volleyball, floor hockey, and dodgeball have the potential of producing this response.

If someone needs to express anger, the activity can be analyzed similarly. It is often useful to select activities in which striking is a requirement of the action. However, the striking is best done through an object and toward an object. Softball, tennis, golf, and bowling allow for appropriate hitting within the rules and without danger to others.

Anger needs to be understood as well in terms of symbolic attacks. Capturing the pieces on a chess or checkers board or sending a piece home in Parcheesi can produce the same response of anger as a direct physical blow.

Activities and situations that create a great deal of dependency on others can also result in anger and hostility. Although dependency is inherent in some activities, this condition is more often created by the therapeutic recreator.

An individual can become angry over a vast array of events or circumstances that the therapeutic recreator cannot know about and that are unrelated to an activity. Anger can result from defeat, frustration, or from not meeting one's own standards of performance. In these examples, the response is obviously not inherent in the nature of the activity.

Fear. Fear is a strange emotion. In most cases it is perceptual and usually unrealistic, but the felt response of the individual is real. Fear often results when individuals are insecure about their abilities to perform, or when they are concerned about the judgments of others concerning their abilities. People are afraid of not succeeding or of not measuring up to expectations. These psychological fears often keep people from participating in order to protect themselves from perceived humiliation. Most often therapeutic recreators do not initially know what fears people have relative to activity involvement and thus cannot make many judgments about them ahead of time.

Some fears are easier to identify and understand, like the fear of physical injury or the fear of social rejection. An activity can be analyzed to anticipate fear reactions to certain of its aspects.

Frustration. This emotional response is a common one and is frequently expressed during activity involvement. It is not inherent in activities, but is again a factor that the individual brings to a situation based on personality makeup and past experience. Frustration commonly occurs when one's abilities do not match the requirements of the task. A highly physical activity is likely to produce frustration because of the exact coordination of body parts required. Golf is a good example. Activities requiring a great deal of accuracy, such as archery or riflery, are likely to create frustration because the feedback is immediate. Other activities that do not have a well-defined outcome are less likely to be frustrating, such as crafts, or camping, or watching a television show.

Frustration is an expected response when two or more people are unequally matched in any competitive activity. It is also a common response when individuals are not performing at the level at which they know they are capable. Frustration is frequently seen when chance factors over which the individual has no control affect the outcome. It also occurs when individuals perceive that they are not meeting the expectations of others, particularly the leader.

Frustration levels vary a great deal. Some individuals are easygoing and are not easily frustrated. Others have high standards of performance and suffer a great deal of frustration in any activity. The therapeutic recreator has the task, regardless of individual personality factors, of selecting activities that can be performed realistically by clients.

Much more needs to be known about affective behaviors before activity analysis in this area can claim any real sophistication or accuracy. Awareness, observation, and common sense for the moment appear to be essential when considering this aspect of activity selection. The limited material presented here perhaps raises more questions than it gives answers. Hopefully, we are moving in the direction of being more concerned about affective stimuli and responses related to activity involvement. Predicting responses and being aware of possible outcomes appear to be important jumping-off points, as long as generalizations are not carried too far.

activity analysis rating form

The rating form (fig. 10–1) provides an example of a variety of items that have proven useful for analyzing a given activity. It also demonstrates different ways of rating activities, such as the absence or presence of characteristics, frequency ratings, simple checklists, and the use of Likert scales. It is not comprehensive; many other items could be added and others presented could be deleted.

The reader is encouraged to select an activity and analyze it with the use of the form. Focus on the activity and its inherent requirements as it is traditionally engaged in. While doing this, try to keep your attention away from a specific disability or person. *Analyze just the activity itself*.

A therapeutic recreation specialist would not use a form such as this to analyze each activity under consideration for a program. It serves basically as a learning tool. Most therapeutic recreators find themselves automatically doing an analysis in their heads after becoming familiar with the items that are critical to the populations that they are concerned with.

ACTIVITY ANALYSIS RATING FORM

ACTIVITY: _____

Physical Aspects

1. What is the primary body position required?

   prone   kneeling   sitting   (standing)   other

2. What types of movement does the activity require?

bending ✓		catching ____
stretching ✓		throwing ____
standing ✓		hitting ____
walking ✓		skipping ____
reaching ✓		hopping ____
grasping ✓		running ____
punching ____		

3. What are the primary senses required for the activity?

   Rate: 0 = not at all; 1 = rarely; 2 = occasionally; 3 = often

   touch ✓ 3 _____
   taste 0 _____
   sight ✓ 3 _____
   sound 3 _____
   smell 0 _____

4. Strength:

   Much strength   1   2   3   4   (5)   Little strength

5. Speed:

   Much speed   1   2   3   (4)   5   No speed

6. Endurance:

   Much endurance   1   2   3   4   (5)   Little endurance

7. Energy:

   Much energy   1   2   3   4   (5)   Little energy

8. Muscle Coordination:

   Much coordination   1   (2)   3   4   5   Little coordination

9. Hand-eye Coordination:

   Much hand-eye coordination   (1)   2   3   4   5   Little hand-eye coordination

Fig. 10–1

10. Flexibility:

Much flexibility   1   2   ③   4   5   Little flexibility

11. Agility:

Much agility   1   2   3   ④   5   Little agility

12. How much of the body is involved?

_✓_ top half   _✓_ arms   _✓_ hands   _✓_ ears
_✓_ bottom half   _✓_ legs   _✓_ feet   ____ neck
   ____ torso   _✓_ eyes
   ____ head   ____ mouth

13. How much coordination of these parts is necessary?

Much   1   2   3   4   5   Little

Explain:

14. Rate degree of cardiovascular activity required.

Much activity   1   2   3   ④   ⑤   Little activity

15. Rate the degree of joint stress.

Much stress   1   2   3   4   ⑤   Little stress

Social Aspects

1. Interaction Pattern

intraindividual _____
extraindividual _____
aggregate _____
interindividual _____
unilateral _____
multilateral _____
intragroup X_____
intergroup _____

2. How many primary participants does the activity demand? _____

3. Does the activity promote sexual homogeneity or heterogeneity?

Explain:

Fig. 10–1 *(cont.)*

4. Can everyone communicate with everyone else by nature of the activity?

Yes   No

5. What is the primary communication network?

_____ 1 to 1
_____ 1 to group
_____ groups of 2-5
_____ groups of 5-10
_____ groups larger than 10

6. Does the activity demand that there be a leader in the group (does one person get most of the group focus)?

Yes   No   Occasionally

7. Does the activity require cooperation or competition?

Explain:

8. How much physical contact does the activity demand?

| Much physical contact | 1 | 2 | 3 | 4 | (5) | Little physical contact |

9. How closely spaced are the participants?

| Close together | (1) | 2 | 3 | 4 | 5 | Far apart |

10. What level of social relationship does the activity promote?

| Intimate relationship | 1 | 2 | 3 | (4) | 5 | Distant relationship |

11. How structured is the activity?

| Highly structured | 1 | 2 | 3 | 4 | (5) | Freely structured |

12. Type of interaction:

| Verbal communication | 1 | 2 | 3 | 4 | (5) | Nonverbal communication |

13. Inclusion-Exclusion

| Inclusion | 1 | 2 | (3) | 4 | 5 | Exclusion |

14. Noise Level

| High | 1 | (2) | 3 | 4 | 5 | Low |

15. Independence-Mimicry

| Independence | 1 | 2 | 3 | 4 | (5) | Mimicry |

Fig. 10–1 (*cont.*)

16. Independence

Independent   1   2   3   4   (5)   Dependent

17. Innerdirected

Innerdirected   1   2   3   4   (5)   Outerdirected

18. Rewards

Immediate   (1)   2   3   4   5   Delayed

19. Maturity

Adult   1   2   3   4   (5)   Childish

Cognitive Aspects

1. How complex are the rules which must be adhered to?

Complex   1   2   3   4   (5)   Simple

2. How much memory retention is necessary?

Much memory   1   2   3   4   (5)   Little memory

3. How much strategy does the activity require?

Much strategy   1   2   3   (4)   5   Little strategy

4. How much verbalization is required?

Much verbalization   1   2   3   4   (5)   Little verbalization

5. How much concentration is required?

Much concentration   1   (2)   3   4   5   Little concentration

6. How often are the following skills used?

0 = never; 1 = rarely; 2 = occasionally; 3 = often

Reading _____

Writing _____

Math _____

Spelling _____

7. Skill required

Much skill   1   2   3   4   5   Chance

8. Rate the demands for the following identifications:

	Often				*Never*
Form and Shape	1	2	3	4	5
Colors	1	2	3	4	5
Size	1	2	3	4	5
Tactile	1	2	3	4	5
Objects	1	2	3	4	5

Fig. 10–1 *(cont.)*

	Often				Never
Classes	1	2	3	4	5
Numbers	1	2	3	4	5
Nonverbal Questions	1	2	3	4	5
Auditory Symbols	1	2	3	4	5
Visual Symbols	1	2	3	4	5
Concrete Thinking	1	2	3	4	5
Abstract Thinking	1	2	3	4	5
Body Parts	1	2	3	4	5

9. Check directionality required:

Left/right _____

Up/down _____

Around _____

Over/under _____

Person/object _____

Person/person _____

Object/object _____

10. Complexity of scoring

Very Complex	1	2	3	4	5	Not complex

Emotional Demands

1. Rate the opportunities for the expression of the following emotions during this activity.

	Often				Never
Joy	1	2	3	4	5
Guilt	1	2	3	4	5
Pain	1	2	3	4	5
Anger	1	2	3	4	5
Fear	1	2	3	4	5
Frustration	1	2	3	4	5

2. Rate the likely responses.

Success	1	2	3	4	5	Failure
Satisfaction	1	2	3	4	5	Dissatisfaction
Intrinsic reward	1	2	3	4	5	Extrinsic reward
Acceptance	1	2	3	4	5	Rejection

Fig. 10–1 (cont.)

	Often				*Never*	
Confidence	1	2	3	4	5	Inferiority
Excitement	1	2	3	4	5	Apathy
Cooperation	1	2	3	4	5	Defiance
Patience	1	2	3	4	5	Impatience
Manipulation	1	2	3	4	5	Nonmanipulation
Awareness of others	1	2	3	4	5	Awareness of self

Administrative Aspects

LEADERSHIP: Minimum _____ Maximum _____

EQUIPMENT: None _____ Required _____

DURATION: Set Time _____ Natural End _____

Continuous _____

FACILITIES: None _____ Required _____

PARTICIPANTS: Fixed Number or Multiple _____

Any Number _____

COMMENTS:

Fig. 10–1 *(cont.)*

selection factors

The ability to analyze an activity thoroughly in all four behavioral areas enables the therapeutic recreator more accurately to select appropriate activities for predetermined therapeutic or educational outcomes. Assessing client needs and specifying objectives have previously been discussed. Once objectives have been stated, the task is undertaken of selecting the most appropriate activities for a program. It is obviously valuable to use activities that have *inherent in their structure* the qualities that relate most directly to the objectives. *This information is only ascertained by activity analysis.* The process also allows several activities to be compared so that the best ones can be selected and used.

Some professionals have found that the process of activity analysis has expanded their repertoire of assessment categories as well. For example, by realizing the many aspects of cognitive action involved in activity participation, practitioners have added these dimensions to their assessment of client needs, and as a result may end up with different or expanded objectives dealing with these areas.

The process of selecting activities for program content must also include a concern for a variety of other factors. These are briefly identified as:

1. *Age.* Although we cannot categorize activities specifically by age groups, certain activities are more appropriate at different stages of life. A common violation of this factor occurs when we program children's activities for adults. This situation is dehumanizing and humiliating. It occurs frequently, however, when working with mentally retarded adults and older people in extended-care facilities. Occasionally the opposite situation occurs. Children are asked to participate in activities that are above their physical, social, emotional, or mental development. For example, elementary-school-aged children may be pushed into team competition or learning social-dance skills too soon. Successful programming considers the appropriateness of age for an activity.

2. *Number of clients.* The sheer number of people to be served influences the selection process. Square dancing cannot successfully be done with less than eight people; likewise, individual leisure skills are difficult to schedule when the client population is large. Staff-client ratios, as well as budget considerations, enter into this critical area. However, program content should never be solely determined by expediency.

3. *Facilities available.* A certain activity may be advantageous for an identified client need, but the absence of the required facility may render it inappropriate.

4. *Equipment and supplies.* Many activities require much equipment or many supplies; limited budgets often hinder buying them. In this situation, the therapeutic recreator must find a similar activity, with the same characteristics and dynamics, but without the heavy emphasis on paraphernalia.

5. *Staff skills.* Selecting an activity that the staff member does not have the skills to conduct is obviously inappropriate or even dangerous (an unqualified person taking clients swimming). However, program content does not need to be limited just to activities that the staff likes to do or can do. Staff should acquire skills through inservice training or professional development opportunities. In some situations, volunteers can supplement existing staff abilities. In either case, program content related to client needs should not be dictated by staff skills.

6. *Carry-over value.* Whenever possible, activities should have the greatest possible amount of carry-over value. Selection procedures can be based on knowledge of a client's future lifestyle and environment. The narrow focus on the immediate setting and its resources defeats the long-range goals of therapeutic recreation services. Carry-over considerations should also include awareness of ethnocentricity and socioeconomic factors.

The selection process requires the sorting out, and attention to, a vast number of variables. Assessment of client needs and determination of objectives precede the process. Activity analysis and the review of agency constraints follow. Based on all the issues and resources, activities can be selected and programs developed that more systematically and appropriately meet the needs of clients.

activity modification

Activity analysis allows us to determine the appropriateness of selected activities for specific treatment or educational objectives. It also serves a second basic function. It enables us to modify activities realistically and appropriately when needed.

Two major conditions require activity modification. The first occurs when working with handicapped individuals in recreational participation, leisure-activity skill development, or instructional programs. The analysis of the activity indicates the *actual participation requirements* for the physical, mental, social, and emotional areas. The individual is then assessed relative to these standard requirements. When certain functional abilities are absent or impaired, this indicates where a modification needs to take place. Sometimes the regulation of the activity is modified, e.g., a rule is eliminated or simplified. Sometimes a procedure is changed, e.g., rolling a bowling ball from a stationary position. Sometimes a change is made in the equipment or the way it is used, e.g., adapting a pistol so that it can be triggered by mouth. Regardless of the type of modification, several factors should be considered:

1. Keep the activity and action as close to the original or traditional activity as possible. It's not much fun for the handicapped to engage in a common activity when their version is so far removed from the traditional version.
2. Modify only the aspects of the activity that need adapting. A mentally retarded individual may need the rules of a game to be simplified but is fully capable of performing the physical actions as expected.
3. Individualize the modification. No two people with the same handicap have the exact same adaptation needs.

The second major condition that requires activity modification occurs most often in treatment or rehabilitation settings, where client needs have been assessed and objectives written. An activity analysis determines the appropriateness or contribution of an activity to the treatment goal. The activity checks out and is selected based on the variety of factors previously described. A quick second assessment is made concerning the group members who will engage in the activity. This assessment reveals that some individuals may have difficulty with certain aspects of the activity. Minor modifications are then made for those individuals or for the group so that the therapeutic benefits can be obtained.

Here is an example of this process. The treatment goal for a group of psychiatric patients is to increase contact with reality. The game of Parcheesi is selected and analyzed. It meets all of the physical, social, and mental requirements. It contributes to focusing attention and to staying in contact with reality. The individuals know how to play it and have the necessary control and skills. Therefore, Parcheesi is chosen as the activity. A quick assessment of the actual clients on the unit who would play the game reveals that one client cannot grasp and move the pieces or roll the dice because he has attempted to cut his wrists, resulting in heavy bandages on both arms. The activity is modified for this person by assigning a partner to do the physical actions while the client makes all the decisions. Further client assessment reveals that several have trouble sustaining attention. The game is modified by decreasing the pieces from four to two, also decreasing the length of the game and thus increasing the possibility of all clients being able to "stay with it" throughout the game.

In this case, the modifications were made to enable the therapeutic outcome of the activity; often these minor modifications are necessary and beneficial in the treatment context. Whether modifications are made to enable participation by a handicapped person or for therapeutic purposes, activity analysis and client functional assessment are required. This process ensures that just the necessary adaptations are made.

The flow chart (fig. 10–2) serves as a helpful tool in learning activity modification procedures. It deals with administrative or operational concerns as well as with participation requirements. It can be used as a final check of an activity's appropriateness in the selection process or as a guide to where modification needs to occur. It summarizes the many aspects of activity analysis and thus initially should be used in conjunction with an activity analysis rating form. A worksheet (fig. 10–3) provides the opportunity to examine the modified activity.

other activity-analysis models

The literature in therapeutic recreation contains countless descriptions of methods for activity classification. Many of them seem to be geared more for defining play or recreation than for establishing models for activity analysis.

Classification or descriptive models are somewhat useful in understanding the nature of activities, but appear to have limited use for therapeutic applications. Several existing models have limitations because their categories are not mutually exclusive or because they deal with only one type of activity (much work has been done with physical activities and sports). Several models focus more on the situation surrounding the participation, such as social or motivational factors, than with inherent characteristics of the activity itself. Other models of analysis have been designed as components of larger programming projects or service efforts. The following models are presented to expose the reader to alternative approaches and viewpoints.

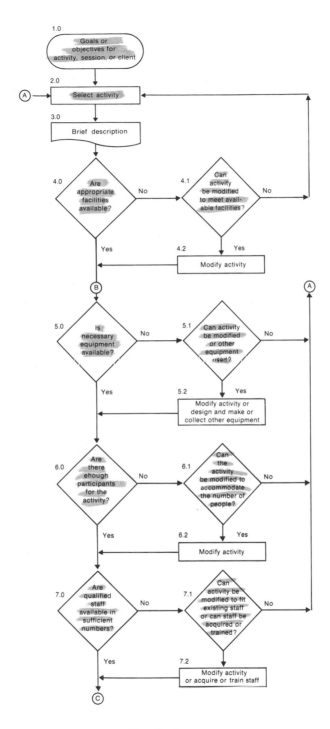

Fig. 10–2
Selection of Activity and Modification Model

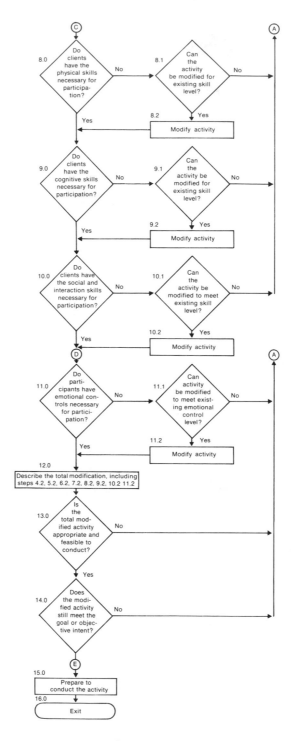

Fig. 10-2 *(cont.)*

Goal or objective:

Selected Activity: _____

Description:

Modifications from Step 4.2
(facilities)

Modifications from Step 8.2
(physical skills)

Modifications from Step 5.2
(equipment)

Modifications from Step 9.2
(cognitive skills)

Modifications from Step 6.2
(participants)

Modifications from Step 10.2
(social-interactional)

Modifications from Step 7.2 (staff)

Modifications from Step 11.2
(emotional control)

Description of completed modified activity

Decisions based on feasibility and appropriateness of the modified activity still to meet the intent of the goal or objective:

☐ Accept   ☐ Reject

Fig. 10–3
SAMM Worksheet

roger caillois's model

This model is a "description and system of classification of games"; however, its content seems also to apply to other recreational or leisure activities. Four basic headings are:

1. *agon* —competition is dominant,
2. *alea* —chance or luck is paramount,
3. *mimicry* —focus on simulation,
4. *ilinx* —pursuit of vertigo (disequilibrium) is the dominant factor.

Another dimension is referred to as the paidia-ludus continuum and can be applied to any of the four areas.

> *Paidia* refers to activities that are unstructured —free of control, full of improvisation and exuberance.
>
> *Ludus* refers to activities that are characterized by discipline, control, and rigid rules and regulations.[3]

This model primarily characterizes the nature of a given activity when it falls into the appropriate classification where the six variables are useful. Although it enables some prediction of participation outcomes, it appears limited in providing information about the requirements and demands of involvement.

peter mcintosh's model

This model focuses on sports, but can also deal with noncompetitive activities. The model depends more on motive and the nature of the satisfaction that the sport gives than it does on the activity itself. It has four categories.

1. games and sports that enable an individual or team to demonstrate superiority over an opponent or other team, based on some exercise of skill;
2. activities that involve personal or group combat and physical contact directly or indirectly through a weapon;
3. activities that are based on the conquest of some element of the natural environment; and
4. activities that enable expression of beauty through human movement.[4]

This model is severely limited in that countless recreational activities do not fall into any of the four categories, i.e., crafts or music.

gerald kenyon's model

This model is designed only for physical activities, regardless of the absence or presence of competition. The six categories are

1. physical activities whose primary purpose is to provide a medium for social intercourse;
2. physical activities for health and fitness;
3. physical activities for the pursuit of vertigo (thrill through speed, acceleration, sudden change of direction, danger, etc.);
4. physical activity for release of tension; and
5. physical activity for an ascetic experience (long, strenuous, tough, demanding delayed gratification).[5]

This model gives some indication of the nature and outcomes of participation. Its major flaw is that almost any activity could fall into any of the six categories, depending on the individual involved.

brian petrie's model

This model combines elements of the previous four models. Its focus is also on classifying physical activity. It classifies physical activity as:

1. a way of pursuing personal risk, thrills, or danger;
2. a way of meeting people in social situations;
3. a way of matching skill in using a weapon against a target or quarry;
4. a way of improving health or body fitness;
5. a way of involving the individual against chance or luck in an attempt to win an object or money;
6. a way of of having fun and for pure enjoyment;
7. a way of expressing ideas and feelings in movement;
8. competition involving skill as the predominant part of performance;
9. competition involving combat as the predominant part of the performance; and
10. competition against part of the natural environment.[6]

Petrie's model concentrates on the participants' perceptions of involvement rather than analyzing the activities themselves. As a result, categories are not mutually exclusive. One activity could easily fall into more than one category, thus limiting the value of the model for activity-analysis purposes. In addition, the model only purports to deal with physical activity.

elliott avedon's model

This model presents a method of ~~determining the various ele-ments of games~~. The ten categories are further broken down into the components of a game:

1. *Purpose of the game; aim or goal, intent, the raison d'etre. Example: Checkmate one's opponent (chess). Bid and make a contract (bridge). Complete the course in as few strokes as possible (golf).*
2. *Procedure for action; specific operations, required courses of action, method of play. Example: Roll dice, move counter in clockwise direction around board, the number of spaces indicated on dice. Act in manner indicated by last space on which counter lands, i.e., take a chance, pay rent, go to jail, etc. (Monopoly). Stand in box, toss two successive shoes at far stake, travel to that stake with opponent, tally score, pitch back to first stake (horseshoes).*
3. *Rules governing action; fixed principles that determine conduct and standards for behavior. Example: Go back where you were, you didn't say, "May I?" (giant steps). [Note:] Some games have very few rules; others have such elaborate sets of rules as to require a nonparticipant to keep track of infringement of the rules or to enforce the rules. Example: Regulations regarding weight and types of blows that may be employed. Panel of judges and referee determine infringement of rules, and have responsibility for enforcing rules (boxing).*
4. *Number of required participants; stated minimum or maximum number of persons needed for action to take place. Example: Minimum of two required, no stated maximum (hide-and-go seek). Eleven men required for each team, minimum and maximum of twenty-two (football). [Note:] Sometimes minimum and maximum are identical.*
5. *Roles of participants; indicated functions and status. Example: Goalkeeper, center, others. Each player has a different role (hockey). Each player has no more or less power than the others, and each functions in the same way (backgammon).*
6. *Results or pay-off; values assigned to the outcome of the action. Example: Money (blackjack). A kiss (spin-the-bottle). A gold medal (relay race).*
7. *Abilities and skills required for action, aspects of the three behavioral domains utilized in a given activity.*
8. *Interaction patterns. [This material is presented earlier in this chapter.]*
9. *Physical setting and environmental requirements: a. Physical setting: Man-made or natural facility in which action takes place. Example: Four-walled court (squash). No special setting (charades). b. Environmental requirements: Natural circumstances that are indispensable or obligatory. Example: Pool (water polo). [Note:] This element may not always be present. Example: No special environment (dominoes).*
10. *Required equipment; man-made or natural artifacts employed in the course of action. Example: Rackets, bird, net (badminton). [Note:] This element may not always be present. Example: No equipment necessary (twenty questions).* [7]

This model appears to be most useful in activity analysis because of its comprehensive nature. Although it is limited to games, which implies structure and competition, many categories have implications for activities other than games. This model focuses on the activity itself and therefore provides a greater opportunity for accurate analysis.

robert overs's model

This model classifies activities by type. Major categories, such as games; sports; nature; collection; homemaking and homecraft; art and music; education, entertainment, and culture; volunteer, organizational, and social, were first selected and numbered. Subcategories were determined under games such as active and inactive. Individual activities were then sorted into each category and numbered. Eight hundred and ninety-nine activities are categorized in this way.[8]

This classification model is basically used in interest-finding surveys and in the process of determining an individual's existing leisure skills. One of its major contributions is its identification of a large number of activities by type.

doris berryman's model

Doris Berryman developed a method of activity analysis at New York University for a research project entitled "Systems Utilization for Comprehensive Modular Planning of Therapeutic Recreation Services for Disabled Children and Youth." Two project objectives relate to activity analysis:

1. *Develop a conceptual model for comprehensive analysis of play and recreational activities to determine the sensory-motor, cognitive, and social dimensions inherent in the activities.*
2. *Using the model, analyze a large number and variety of activities, match selected dimensions of the activities to specific behavioral objectives, and develop an information storage and retrieval system for the data gatherer.*[9]

This project, which focuses on systematic, computer-based, prescriptive programming, analyzes activities in a comprehensive manner. The significant kinesiological and physiological; conceptual and intellectual; social, structural, organizational, and implementation requirements of various activities are analyzed and stored in the computer. The following material identifies the major activity descriptors and prescriptors used in the analysis process:

General Category

Collecting
Games of low organization
Music and rhythm
Card, table, paper-and-pencil games
Social mixers
Individual sports
Duo-sports
Team sports
Drama/literary/linguistics
Nature orientation and outdoor
     recreation
Dancing and movement expression
Art: painting and dying
Art: drawing
Art: cutting and carving
Art: printing and photography
Art: gluing
Art: molding and sculpting
Art: stitching and weaving
Aquatics

Facilities

No specific environment
Specific environment
Modicum of space
Unlimited space

Equipment and Supplies

Requires little or no equipment
Equipment a major factor
Equipment normally at hand
Equipment not necessarily at hand

Participants (Minimum Number)

One
Two to five
Six to ten
Eleven to fifteen
No specific number required

Activity Structure

Formal
Informal
Active

Activity Structure (cont.)

Inactive
Single skill
Multiple skill
Simple rules
Complex rules
Scoring
Time limits
Self-sufficient locomotion
Manipulative locomotion
Competition
Chance
Skill and chance
Simulation (mimicry)
Pursuit of vertigo
Sociability
Skill void of competition
Excursion
Creative expression
Immediate reward
Penalties
Dependence
Cooperation
Independence
Inclusion
Exclusion

Sensory Facilities Required

Auditory
Visual
Verbal
Tactual
Taste
Smell

Physical Contact

None
Infrequent
Frequent

Physical Factors

Stationary balance
Moving balance
Unilateral
Bilateral

190

Single Physical Movements

Head (mouth)
  Oral motor manipulation
  Chewing
Neck
  Bending (flexion)
  Stretching (extension)
  Twisting (rotation)
  Shaking
Shoulder and upper arm
  Shrugging (elevation)
  Bending (flexion)
  Stretching (extension)
  Twisting (rotation)
  Shaking
Arm (elbow)
  Bending (flexion)
  Stretching (extension)
  Twisting (pronation and
    supination)
  Shaking
Wrist, hand, fingers
  Bending (flexion)
  Stretching (extension)
  Twisting (pronation and
    supination)
  Shaking
Spine
  Bending (flexion)
  Stretching (extension)
  Twisting (rotation)
Hip and upper leg
  Bending (flexion)
  Stretching (extension)
  Twisting (rotation)
Leg (knee)
  Bending (flexion)
  Stretching (extension)
  Twisting (rotation)
  Shaking
Ankle, foot, toes
  Bending (flexion)
  Stretching (extension)
  Twisting (pronation and
    supination)
  Shaking

Multiple Physical Movements

Walking
Running
Kicking
Jumping
Leaping
Hopping
Skipping
Throwing
Hanging
Crawling
Sliding
Swaying
Hitting
Galloping
Pushing
Tagging
Stooping
Crouching
Reaching
Seizing
Squeezing
Stepping
Catching
Rolling
Climbing
Creeping
Swinging
Clapping
Pinching
Grasping
Pulling
Turning
Whole body movement

Movement Attributes

Speed
Agility
Endurance
Rhythm
Strength
Coordination

Body Awareness

Crossing the midline
Cross-patterning

Body Awareness (cont.)

Laterality
Directionality
Body-part identification

Perceptual Factors

Manual dexterity
Visual figure-ground
    discrimination
Auditory figure-ground
    discrimination
Spatial relationships
Visual pursuit
Eye-hand coordination
Eye-foot coordination
Reaction time

Language and Communication Factors

Visual symbols
Auditory symbols
Letter identifications
Writing comprehension
Auditory comprehension
Writing (expressive)

Language and Communication Factors (cont.)

Verbal: phonation
Verbal: limited
Verbal: moderate
Verbal: extensive
Verbal: structured
Verbal: unstructured
Required to respond to directions
Required to give directions

Cognitive Factors

Ranking
Matching
Number concepts
Arithmetic: addition
Arithmetic: subtraction
Arithmetic process: multiplication
Arithmetic process: division
Abstract thinking
Memorization
Whole-part concepts
Decision making
Planning/strategy
Discrimination[10]

This comprehensive project that uses activity analysis, individual assessment, development of behavioral objectives, and computer-assisted, individual, prescriptive programming, shows dynamically a major application of the activity-analysis process.

summary

Activity analysis is a practical and necessary tool of the therapeutic recreator in the program-planning stage. In its purest form, activity analysis focuses on determining the inherent characteristics of activities. It enables a greater comprehension of participation requirements and gives insight into the dynamics of activity involvement. Practically applied, activity analysis makes it possible to select appropriate activities for therapeutic outcomes and facilitates sequencing and modification of instructional and recreation programs. Activity analysis gives more accuracy and accountability to program-design efforts.

notes

[1] Carol Ann Peterson, "State of the Art: Activity Analysis," in *Leisure Activity Participation and Handicapped Populations: Assessment of Research Needs* (Arlington, Va.: National Recreation and Park Association and Bureau of Education for the Handicapped, United States Office of Education, April 1976), p. 82.

[2] Elliott M. Avedon, *Therapeutic Recreation Service: An Applied Behavioral Science Approach,* © 1974, pp. 162–70. Adapted by permission of Prentice-Hall, Inc.

[3] Roger Caillois, "The Structure and Classification of Games," *Diogenes*, 12 (1955), 62–75.

[4] Peter McIntosh, *Sport and Society.* (London: C. A. Watts and Company, Ltd., 1963).

[5] Gerald S. Kenyon, "A Conceptual Model for Characterizing Physical Activity" (unpublished research paper, University of Wisconsin, Department of Physical Education for Men, 1966).

[6] Brian Malcolm Petrie, "Physical Activity, Games and Sports: A System of Classification and an Investigation of Social Influences Among Students of Michigan State University" (unpublished doctoral dissertation, Michigan State University, Department of Health, Physical Education and Recreation, 1970).

[7] Elliott M. Avedon, "The Structural Elements of Games," in *The Study of Games*, ed. E. M. Avedon and B. Sutton-Smith (New York: John Wiley and Sons, 1971), pp. 419–26.

[8] Robert P. Overs and Ann R. Trotter, *Guide to Avocational Activities*, Vols. 1, 2, 3 (Milwaukee, Wis.: Curative Workshop of Milwaukee, 1972).

[9] Doris Berryman, "Systems Utilization for Comprehensive Modular Planning of Therapeutic Recreation Services for Disabled Children and Youth" (Final Progress Report, BEH Project OEG 0-73-5171, New York University, May 1974), p. 1.

[10] Ibid., p. 33–38.

suggested references

ADAMS, R. C., A. DANIEL, AND L. RULLMAN, *Games, Sports, and Exercises for the Physically Handicapped.* Philadelphia, Pa: Lea and Febiger, 1972.

AVEDON, E. M., "The Structural Elements of Games," in *The Study of Games*, ed. E. M. Avedon and B. Sutton-Smith, pp. 419–26. New York: John Wiley and Sons, Inc., 1971.

———, *Therapeutic Recreation Service: An Applied Behavioral Science Approach.* Englewood Cliffs, N.J.: Prentice-Hall, Inc., 1974.

BERRYMAN, D., "Systems Utilization for Comprehensive Modular Planning of Therapeutic Recreation Services for Disabled Children and Youth." Final Progress Report, BEH Grant OEG-0-73-5171, New York University, May 1974.

BLOOM, B. S., ed., *Taxonomy of Educational Objectives Handbook I: Cognitive Domain.* New York: David McKay Company, Inc., 1956.

BROER, M., *Efficiency of Human Movement.* Philadelphia, Pa.: W. B. Saunders Company, 1973.

BROWN, R. C., AND B. J. CRATTY, *New Perspectives of Man in Action.* Englewood Cliffs, N.J.: Prentice-Hall, Inc., 1969.

CAILLOIS, R., *Man, Play and Games.* London: Thames and Hudson, 1962.

——, "The Structure and Classification of Games," *Diogenes,* 12 (1955), 62–75.

CAMMERON, W., AND P. PLEASANCE, *Education in Movement.* London: Basil Blackwell Company, 1965.

CRATTY, B. J., *Movement Behavior and Motor Learning.* Philadelphia, Pa.: Lea and Febiger, 1967.

——, *Movement Perception and Thought.* Springfield, Ill.: Charles C. Thomas, Publisher, 1969.

——, *Social Dimensions of Physical Activity.* Englewood Cliffs, N. J.: Prentice-Hall, Inc., 1967.

FAIT, H. F., *Special Physical Education: Adapted, Corrective, Developmental.* Philadelphia, Pa.: W. B. Saunders Company, 1966.

FRANDSEN, A. N., *How Children Learn: An Educational Psychology.* New York: McGraw-Hill Book Company, Inc., 1957.

FRETZ, B. R., W. R. JOHNSON, AND J. A. JOHNSON, "Intellectual and Perceptual Motor Development as a Function of Therapeutic Play," *The Research Quarterly,* 40 (1969), 687–91.

GARRISON, M., ed., *Cognitive Models and Development in Mental Retardation.* Monograph supplement to the *American Journal of Mental Deficiency,* 70, no. 4 (1966).

GODFREY, B. B., AND N. C. KEPHART, *Movement Patterns and Motor Education.* New York: Appleton-Century-Crofts, 1969.

GUILFORD, J. P., *The Nature of Human Intelligence.* Toronto: McGraw-Hill Book Company, 1967.

GUILFORD, J. P., AND R. HOEPFNER, *The Analysis of Intelligence.* Toronto: McGraw-Hill Book Company, 1971.

HARROW, A. J., *A Taxonomy of the Psychomotor Domain.* New York: David McKay Company, Inc., 1972.

HIRST, C. C., AND E. MICHAELIS, *Developmental Activities for Children in Special Education.* Springfield, Ill.: Charles C. Thomas, Publisher, 1972

HOLLANDER, C., "The Social Dynamics of Therapeutic Recreation," *Hospital and Community Psychiatry,* 18, no. 8 (August 1967).

HUIZINGA, J., *Homo Ludens, A Study of the Play Element in Culture.* Boston, Mass.: Beacon Press, 1950.

JOKL, E., AND E. SIMON, eds., *International Research in Sport and Physical Education.* Springfield, Ill.: Charles C. Thomas, 1964.

JOHNSON, W. R., B. R. FRETZ, AND J. A. JOHNSON, "Changes in Self-Concepts During a Physical Development Program," *The Research Quarterly,* 39

JONES, R. O., *A Theory of Thought Processes.* New York: Philosophical Library, Inc.. 1969.

KRATHWAHL, D. R., B. S. BLOOM, AND B. B. MARIA, *Taxonomy of Educational Objectives, Handbook II: Affective Domain.* New York: David McKay Company, Inc., 1956.

Loy, J. W., and G. S. Kenyon, *Sport, Culture and Society.* New York: Macmillan Publishing Company, 1969.

McIntosh, P. C., *Sport and Society.* London: C. A. Watts and Company, Ltd., 1963.

Meeker, M. N., *The Structure of Intellect: Its Interpretation and Uses.* Columbus, Ohio: Charles E. Merrill Publishing Company, 1969.

Mundy, J., *The Mundy Recreation Inventory for the Trainable Mentally Retarded.* Tallahasee, Fl.: Florida State University, 1966.

"Need Help with Activities? Ask a Computer," *Modern Nursing Home,* 27, no. 5 (November 1971), 39–41.

Overs, R. P., E. O. O'Connor, and B. Demarco, *Avocational Activities for the Handicapped.* Springfield, Ill.: Charles C. Thomas, 1974.

Overs, R. P., and A. R. Trotter, *Guide to Avocational Activities,* Vols. 1, 2, 3. Milwaukee, Wis.: Curative Workshop of Milwaukee, 1972.

Peterson, C. A., "State of the Art: Activity Analysis," in *Leisure Activity Participation and Handicapped Populations: Assessment of Research Needs.* Arlington, Va.: National Recreation and Park Association and Bureau of Education for the Handicapped, United States Office of Education, April 1976.

Petrie, B. M., "Physical Activity, Games and Sport: A System of Classification and an Investigation of Social Influences Among Students of Michigan State University." Unpublished doctoral dissertation, Michigan State University, Department of Health, Physical Education and Recreation, 1970.

Piers, M. W., ed., *Play and Development.* New York: Norton, 1972.

Pinderhughes, C. A., and J. P. Pederson, "The Psychodynamics of Recreation and Basis for Its Use as Therapy," *Recreation in Treatment Centers,* 4, (September 1965), 34–37.

Phillips, J. L., Jr., *The Origins of Intellect: Piaget's Theory.* San Francisco, Calif.: W. H. Freeman and Company, 1969.

Scott, M. G., *Analysis of Human Motion.* New York: Appleton-Century-Crofts, 1963.

Singer, R. N., *Motor Learning and Human Performance.* New York: Association for Brain Injured Children, 1968.

Ulrich, C., *The Social Matrix of Physical Education.* Englewood Cliffs, N.J.: Prentice-Hall, Inc., 1968.

Wadsworth, B. J., *Piaget's Theory of Cognitive Development.* New York: David McKay Company, Inc., 1971.

Weertz, D. J., J. R. Healy, and R. P. Overs, *Avocational Activities Inventory.* Milwaukee, Wis.: Milwaukee Median for Rehabilitation Research, Report 5, 1968.

Wickwire, G., "Activity Analysis for Rehabilitation," *The Archives of Physical Medicine and Rehabilitation,* September 1955, pp. 578–86.

CHAPTER ELEVEN

facilitation techniques

PURPOSE: To present various interactional techniques useful in removing blocks to play behavior. Techniques of counseling, leisure counseling, instruction, supervision, and leadership are discussed. Criteria are presented for appropriate utilization of specific facilitation techniques with various populations and suggestions are offered for their implementation.

Chapters five and ten introduced the concept that in systems program planning it is not sufficient just to delineate and describe the activities to be used. It is equally important to specify the interactional or facilitation technique to be employed while conducting the program. The interface between the facilitation style and the activities selected is critical, not only for the achievement of the program objectives, but also for evaluation.

Countless facilitation styles can be used in designing therapeutic recreation programs. We rely heavily on other fields and borrow their techniques. Sometimes a technique is not modified at all; at other times the uniqueness of involvement in an activity requires adaptation of the selected method of facilitation.

Appropriate intervention techniques must be chosen for each population and each type of program. In systems program planning, this technique must be described as thoroughly as any other aspect of the program's content.

This chapter identifies various facilitation techniques and discusses their usefulness. Techniques are chosen according to the purposes of the therapeutic recreation services. Various facilitation techniques are presented for each of the three major areas in therapeutic recreation—rehabilitation or treatment, leisure education, and recreational participation. The program planner should decide which techniques are best suited to a program. Different facilitation techniques may be required at various stages of the continuum of services made available to ill and handicapped clients.

play behavior: the goal of facilitation

The concept of leisure has been lifted out of the constraints of "time blocks" and "activity skills" and is now considered "a state of mind,"[1] "a struggle for significance,"[2] and "a state where one fulfills oneself and feels fulfilled."[3] Someone who achieves leisure may be characterized as exhibiting behavior that is freed from imposed societal and environmental constraints or expectations to elicit specific responses. In achieving a state of leisure, the player is allowed optimum exploration of the unknown and is free to respond in his or her own way. Individual freedom and self-regulation is maximized. Play behavior while at leisure is spontaneous and allows for a pure expression of oneself, and is therefore not capable of being encapsulated by definition and sold as a product to be consumed during specific time constraints or even in defined leisure activities.

For years we have been "selling" the benefits of activity involvement for the ill and the handicapped. We have justified therapeutic recreation programs in terms of physical, emotional, social, and mental values. We have defended our services according to a medical model and our contribution to the amelioration of pathology. Now we have a new concept that is somewhat different from earlier ideas about the human experience and far different from the traditional concepts of health-related processes: *facilitating play behavior.*

Play is a basic human behavior. It is a developmental need for the young, a self-expressive need for adults. Yet it is a significant behavior that has not been recognized. Although play is a meaningful and basic human experience, unlike other basic behaviors, such as eating, sleeping, and mating, it is often considered frivolous, nonutilitarian, and useless, in line with the Protestant work ethic. Yet, ironically, play has a dominant role in contemporary culture, motivating and satisfying individuals despite criticism. The play element of human behavior exists and slowly we are recognizing and accepting it as part of the totality of existence. It can be rationalized in terms of physical, mental, and emotional release and relaxation, or used as a method for developing and mastering these capabilities, but it does not need to be defended as such. Play exists as a *basic behavior,* part of the human repertoire, requiring no further justification or explanation. As such, then, its existence needs only to be facilitated.

Until recently the relevant questions about leisure and play behavior were "What is play?" and "Where do people play?" and "When do people play?" But perhaps an even more important question is "What *keeps people from* playing?" What keeps people from feeling significant and self-fulfilled? What *blocks* the ability to experience a state of leisure in which personal freedom is personified and social constraints minimized?

blocks to play behavior

For most of us, the spontaneous expression of ourselves in play is blocked in a variety of ways. Authority messages quickly inhibit play behavior. As children we are told, "Clean up your room and get your homework done, then you can play"; "Don't spend your money on such foolishness" (meaning playthings); "Don't be a sissy" (to boys); "Don't be such a tomboy" (to girls); "Be responsible, work hard, be strong, don't feel." These are messages that subtly, but ever so surely, teach us to feel guilty about playing and ask us to be something other than ourselves. Conflicting authority messages compound the problem and make it even less likely that we will achieve a leisurely state of mind. As young adults, we sit baffled before our high-school English assignment that asks us to answer the question "Who am I?" Conflicting advice comes to mind. "Be nice to other people, even if you don't like them" versus "Don't tell lies. Be honest." "To think about yourself is to be egotistical" versus "Stand up for your rights because no one else will." "Don't talk to strangers" versus "Trust other people." And so it goes. This barrage of authority messages can set us up to fail in our struggle for significance, self-awareness, and self-fulfillment.

Imposed structure, such as organized games, may also block play behavior. Whenever we are told how to play, who to play with, and how long to play, our naturally playful responses are hindered. Structure implies right and wrong ways of responding and interacting, which heightens the possibility of making mistakes. Perhaps in its purest form, play means not having to make mistakes. If we can reduce the possibility of players making mistakes (including *faux pas*), we increase their chances of finding significance and self-fulfillment through play.

In many religions, worship is considered serious business; play is perceived as idleness and idleness as evil. Closely related to this concept is the Protestant work ethic, which defines work as the most significant characteristic of a worthwhile human being. Because play is nonessential, it is also unacceptable. However, play is often used as a reward for work accomplished by children.

Parents often teach children to covet play by withholding it to punish perceived inappropriate behavior and by using it to reinforce perceived desired behavior. Young children's spontaneous play is often noisy, messy, and dirty. These play characteristics are often antithetical to parental expectations of quiet, clean, well-behaved children. Consequently, creative play is discouraged.

Just as frequently, parents do not model spontaneous play behavior themselves and do not even talk about the importance of play. This becomes a negative reinforcement to children, because they believe that adults only do and talk about things that are important. Therefore, the lack of permission to be spontaneous in play becomes a block to experiencing feelings of being significant through play.

additional blocks for the handicapped

The problem of blocked play behavior is even more complex for handicapped individuals. They are asked to guard against situations in which they may be ridiculed, to suppress sexual energies, to limit social contacts, and to avoid situations in which they may be physically injured. These sometimes overprotective warnings add to the already existing environmental blocks to self-fulfillment: narrow doorways, myriads of stairs, and inaccessible bathrooms. It also seems that the parents of handicapped children either play less or in more constricted ways with their children, i.e., not tussling with a cerebral-palsied child for fear of stimulating spastic contractures.

Removing blocks to play behavior requires far more than merely a repertoire of activity skills. Utilizing activities purposefully may require additional skills in counseling or therapy. Teaching activities requires instructional skills, while facilitating leisure awareness requires the therapeutic recreator to be skilled in leisure counseling. In still other situations, leadership and supervisory skills may help interaction. The following section discusses interaction patterns within the spectrum of therapeutic recreation services.

context of facilitation techniques

The simplified version of the therapeutic recreation service model, discussed in chapter two (fig. 2–1) portrays three basic components of therapeutic recreation services and five categories of facilitation or interactional skills (fig. 11–1). This model places the roles of the various interaction styles in the broad context of therapeutic recreation services.

rehabilitation

The first component in the model is therapy or rehabilitation, which is concerned with improving or bringing into existence basic, *functional* living behaviors through activity involvement. As with the mentally retarded individual who learns how to run, the psychiatric patient who acquires the ability to stay reality-based through structured game involvement, and the individual with cerebral palsy who works on relaxation and coordination through swimming, the treatment goals are to improve basic physical, social, emotional, or mental functioning. The long-range, highly functional goal in rehabilitation services is for clients to be able to have self-directed, socioleisure lifestyles. The basic mode of interaction generally requires skills in counseling and therapy.

leisure education

The second component of the leisure service model focuses on leisure education. A leisure education model was developed to show its various content aspects (fig. 11–2). The assumption in leisure education is that learning to engage in meaningful leisure activities requires that the individual acquire diverse knowledge and skills as well as positive attitudes and self-understanding. The intervention techniques used to facilitate the acquisition of these various abilities differ with each of the areas. The purpose of leisure education is to enable the individual to acquire meaningful leisure skills and attitudes. These four major content areas are inherent in the leisure-education process:

1. developing awareness of leisure values and attitudes,
2. developing social-interaction skills,
3. developing leisure-activity skills, and
4. developing knowledge of leisure resources.

Developing Awareness of Leisure Attitudes and Values. Before successfully engaging in meaningful leisure pursuits, an individual must first develop an understanding of the concept of leisure and an awareness of personal attitudes and values about leisure and play behavior. The person must become aware of her or his own play behavior and the process of making decisions about leisure.

These questions are pertinent to becoming more aware of attitudes about leisure: "What is leisure? What is the significance of leisure? How does leisure relate to me—to my health and functioning? How do I

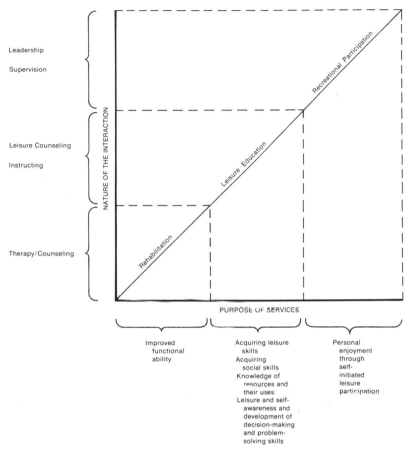

Fig. 11–1
Therapeutic Recreation Service Model

feel about play? How do I keep myself from playing? What do I value most about play and leisure? How do I feel when I'm playing? What abilities and skills do I have? What limitations do I have? How can I acquire playfulness—leisure abilities and skills? What problems do I have in play?"

Provoking consciousness about how one feels about leisure is primarily a cognitive process and uses *leisure counseling* skills. Leisure counseling is a process that uses verbal facilitation techniques to promote self-awareness, awareness of leisure attitudes, values, and feelings, and to develop decision-making and problem-solving skills related to leisure participation.

Two assumptions are central to the leisure education component. The first is that meaningful leisure involvement requires more than just

201

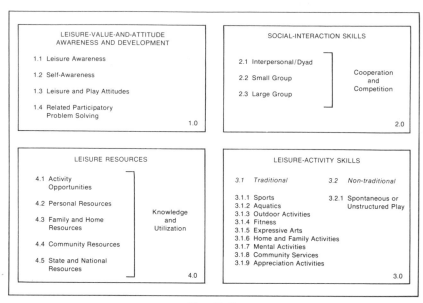

Fig. 11–2
Leisure Education Model

activity skills per se. Leisure values, attitudes, and awareness are equally important. The second is that leisure counseling techniques can effectively clarify and develop these aspects of leisurability. Leisure counseling is a process, not a program. Leisure counseling techniques are among the many tools used to deliver leisure services. With increased awareness comes increased ability to make decisions and have experiences that facilitate play behavior.

Developing Social-interaction Skills. People play in a social context with relatives, friends, lovers, and peers. Meaningful leisure involvement therefore requires that players learn social-interaction skills. We often overlook the importance of teaching people how to interact in dyads, small groups, and large groups, either cooperatively or competitively. Social-interaction skills can be acquired through activity involvement. Inherent in activity participation is the immediate opportunity for feedback and the availability of positive role models. Socially appropriate behavior can be immediately reinforced and problematic behavior can be dealt with on the spot. Again, leisure-counseling techniques can be helpful in dealing with problematic behaviors, attitudes, and feelings. In addition to counseling techniques, social-interaction skills can be taught through the use of established instructional methods.

Developing Leisure-activity Skills. Teaching specific activity skills appropriate to the interests, ages, needs, and limitations of participants has long been a function of the therapeutic recreator. Unfortunately, it

202

has sometimes been done in isolation, ignoring the need for the other major components of leisure education. Only as participants understand themselves at play and feel confident in the resulting social interactions can they truly enjoy leisure activities. Good instructional strategies are essential for teaching leisure-activity skills. Again there is the relationship of process to content and purpose. Self-awareness, or confronting leisure problem behavior, is an area in which leisure-counseling strategies have proven effective. One can provide counseling relative to leisure interests, values, or attitudes, but the act of acquiring specific recreational skills requires a different intervention technique, i.e., a teaching strategy.

Any attempt to categorize successfully the multiplicity of activities available to participants results in argument. This list is therefore offered only as a guide to developing leisure-activity categories: sports, aquatics, outdoor activities, fitness, expressive arts, home and family activities, mental activities, community-service activities, appreciation activities, and spontaneous-play activities.

Developing Knowledge of Leisure Resources. This component of leisure education is predominantly cognitive and purports to teach participants to locate, then use available resources and leisure opportunities. "When can I play?" "How do I get there?" "What's available to me once I arrive?" "What are my other alternatives?" These are all questions asked of participants. Assisting the handicapped individual in developing awareness of leisure attitudes and values, social-interaction skills, and activity skills is not enough. In the leisure education process, we must direct the individual to available resources that he or she can use independent of our programs. These include knowledge of activity opportunities available to them, personal resources, family and home resources, community resources, and state and national resources.

When individuals have developed meaningful awareness of leisure attitudes and values, social-interaction skills, leisure-activity skills, and knowledge of leisure resources, they are equipped to exercise independent choices in ongoing leisure pursuits. For some, independent leisure involvement may continue to require a protective environment, offering assistance, supervision, and adaptations. For others, the world of leisure opportunities will be totally open to them. In either event, the leisure education process will have assisted individuals in determining their own leisure behavior and evaluating the outcomes in relation to personal goals for self-fulfillment.

recreational participation

The third component of a comprehensive leisure services model includes those opportunities provided by agencies that enable individuals to select and participate in the activities of their choice for their own enjoyment. The intervention style for recreational participation is *leadership* or *supervision*. No attempt is made at instruction or specific behavior change (theory). The individual is functioning as an independent agent, using the available resources, programs, and facilities to meet his or her own needs, express his or her own individuality, expand his or her potential for enjoyment, and claim his or her right to the play behavior.

Thus, the three components of a comprehensive therapeutic recreation service model can be presented and described relative to their purpose (rehabilitation, education, or recreational participation). They can also be further described by the type of facilitation or interactional technique utilized (therapy and counseling techniques, leisure-counseling techniques, instructional strategies, and leadership techniques or supervision). The remainder of the chapter addresses these five categories of interaction strategies.

basic counseling

Counseling is one of the oldest helping professions known, and it currently pervades not only the established circles of health and allied health agencies but also school, judicial, industrial, and religious systems. The disparity between philosophies, practices, and techniques permeates all counseling circles and provokes numerous arguments about authentic versus superficial counseling services. To date, no single professional has been able to convince the world successfully of her or his unique position as "the authentic counselor."

counseling defined

Counseling is an adjustive process designed to assist in the growth and development of clients. It is not a casual happening that results in the client's adjustment. Nor is it a natural by-product of relationships between facilitators and their constituents. Counseling is a well-thought-out professional service rendered by trained individuals who adhere to specific philosophies and beliefs concerning human nature. Buford Stefflre views counseling as

> a professional relationship . . . designed to help the client understand and clarify his view of his life space so that he may make meaningful and informed choices consonant with his essential nature and his particular circumstances. . . .
> [c]ounseling is a learning-teaching process, for the client learns about his life space . . . . If he is to make meaningful and informed choices, he must know himself, the facts of his present situation, and the possibilities . . . as well as the most likely consequences of the various choices . . . . [4]

C. G. Wrenn further reiterates the importance of self-understanding and responsible decision making as an integral part of the counseling process:

> *A large emphasis of modern counselors in any setting is to aid in the process of self-identification, in helping a person answer the questions of "Who am I and what am I here for?" . . . A counselor aids in decision-making, in expanding his client's range of alternatives or options open to him, in modifying his behavior patterns in desired directions.* [5]

John Pietrofesa and William Van Hoose define counseling as

> *the process through which a person professionally prepared to counsel attempts to help another person in matters of self-understanding, decision-making, and problem-solving.* [6]

Counseling deals with a client's problems with (1) understanding of self, (2) understanding of self in relation to others, and (3) understanding of environmental influences. It is conceivable, then, that on a continuum, counseling could range from teaching to psychotherapeutic intervention. Regardless of the degree of complexity inherent in the counseling relationship, specific training in counseling is clearly necessary in order to effect positive behavioral changes.

selected counseling theories

Counseling theories are as diverse as the people involved in the process. A theory is most often a conjecture put forth as a possible explanation of a phenomenon, practice, or technique. A theory is useful in that it enables one to describe and explain what is being done in the helping relationship. It is an intellectual tool that helps us simply and systematically to make observations and explain techniques. If the theory stresses the significance of feeling, we focus on the clarification of feelings. If the theory stresses appropriate behavior, we use techniques to teach adaptive behaviors. If the theory focuses on realistic problem solving, we apply various forms of rational analysis in the helping process.

For the sake of understanding the basic theoretical differences between counseling theories, three general categories of theories are presented, along with several combined theories. Within and between these categories, basic beliefs concerning human nature and the counseling relationship are discussed. The techniques inherent in each facilitation style are also discussed.

All counseling theories can be understood by their relationship to three dominant philosophical domains: (1) an affective domain, (2) a behavioral domain, and (3) a cognitive domain. The model (fig. 11–3) portrays the selected counseling theories according to their dominant orientation.

affective approach

Affective counseling theorists contend that awareness and acceptance of feelings are primary prerequisites to growth and positive behavioral change. When people claim and express feelings appropriately, it is believed that feelings, thoughts, and behavior change toward self, others, and environment. Counselors who focus on feelings, above thought and behavior, ask the basic question "How?" They ask, "How are you feeling?" and "How are you keeping yourself from your feelings?" A counselor does not predict changes in behavior or thought patterns when a client acknowledges certain feelings. However, the counselor expects some behavior and thought to change with new feeling awareness. The counselor who uses an affective approach must believe that human behavior is healthy if not blocked and distorted by unexpressed feelings. Feelings are the signals through which the human organism recognizes needs. Feelings that are recognized, accepted, and expressed when they first present themselves are appropriate to growth and produce constructive behavior and thought.

The affective approach is phenomenological in that the helping process centers on the uniqueness of each person's perception of reality

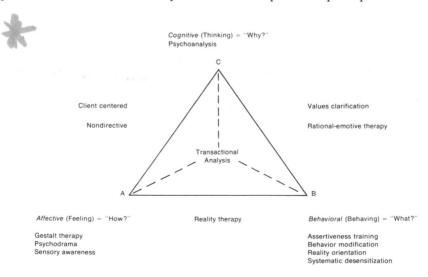

Fig. 11–3
The ABCs of Counseling Theories

and feelings about personal experiences. The counselor encourages focusing on now-centered experiences and feelings rather than "gossiping" about past events. Popular phenomenological counseling approaches are Gestalt therapy, psychodrama, and sensory-awareness processes.

behavioral approaches

Behavioral counseling theorists contend that the way in which a person behaves directly determines how a person feels and thinks. By changing problematic behavior, positive thoughts and feelings about oneself occur. The predominant question asked by behavioral counselors is "What?" "What is the problem behavior?" "What would be a more productive behavior?" "What needs to be done to reinforce positive behavior and extinguish negative behavior?" The behaviorist contends that feeling good about oneself and others and thinking constructive thoughts is a by-product of positive social reinforcement for specific, socially appropriate behavior. Whereas the affective counselor allows the individual's expression of feelings to shape the environment and define the norms, the behaviorist wants the environment and defined norms to shape the individual. Garth Blackham and Adolph Silberman state:

> *Each society, social class, and subculture values, sanctions, and emulates very different behaviors. Acceptable behavior in one society may be socially or legally condemned in another. Adaptive behavior must be socially relevant. Behavior that is not socially relevant evokes all manner of negative consequences and ends up [being] punishing to the offender.*[7]

The behaviorist believes that avoiding punishment by society for maladaptive behavior results in positive feelings and thoughts about self, others, and environment. Learning socially acceptable ways of behaving can result in self-actualization.[8] Among the currently used behavioral approaches are assertiveness training, behavior modification, reality orientation, and systematic desensitization.

cognitive approaches

The psychoanalytic or cognitive approach to counseling has the longest history and the most complex set of assumptions of any of the helping theories. Psychoanalytic theories depend on rational analysis of factors in one's life history, which are understood by pinpointing the involvement of personality structures known as the ego (mastery), id (impulse), and superego (conscience). The basic question asked by psychoanalytic counselors is "Why?" "Why does the present conflict exist?" The answer to any "why" question always begins with "because" and ends with the scapegoat for present behavior called the reason. To the psychoanalyst, conflict (anxiety, neurosis, psychosis, etc.) results when the basic drives of the developing human being acquiesce to social pressures. This process of converting basic drives into socially accepted activities is called sublimation. Sublimation within the individual's power to do so results in creativity. However, when individuals are asked to sublimate beyond their capacity, conflict and unhappiness result. The psychoanalyst believes that this unhappiness comes about because of inadequate or traumatic experiences with sublimation in early childhood, particularly emphasizing conflicts between instinctual drives and social demands. Recounting these early childhood traumas and understanding them is believed to be the path to their solution. To the psychoanalyst, freedom is knowledge; slavery is ignorance.[9] "The more perfect a person's knowledge of himself, the more likely it is that he will operate rationally."[10]

Although most counseling theories have their roots in psychoanalytic theory, most have deviated from the indepth rational analysis required to be an avid follower of Sigmund Freud. Because adherence to strict psychoanalytic theory requires lengthy and demanding training, it is not a practical counseling theory to be pursued by leisure counselors. It is also questionable whether insight into and understanding of historical roots to problems does indeed free the individual from problems in the present. In addition to Freudian theory, Adlerian therapy and Jungian analysis may be considered to be predominantly cognitive.

combined approaches

Many counseling theories are eclectic; they combine concepts, techniques, and assumptions from one or more of the three basic areas of counseling. In the 1940s, Carl Rogers developed *client-centered therapy*, sometimes called Rogerian theory. Its central hypothesis is that

> *the growthful potential of any individual will tend to be released in a relationship in which the helping person is experiencing and communicating realness, caring, and a deeply sensitive non-judgmental understanding.*[11]

In practice, client-centered therapy pulls together techniques and concepts from the affective and cognitive domains. It resembles psychoanalytic theory in that the therapist-client relationship is crucial (although the relationship in psychoanalysis is superficial and designed to allow the client to transfer negative feelings onto the therapist—called transference—while the relationship in Rogerian theory is intended to be genuine). It resembles an affective approach in that expression of genuine feelings is encouraged. The nondirectiveness of client-centered therapy resembles the free association of psychoanalysis. However, it differs from cognitive and affective approaches in that the solution of problems is not believed to depend on either reasoning or feeling. Instead, the client is encouraged to rationalize and/or feel as the need arises, within the safe confines of an accepting relationship. It is this totally accepting relationship that is believed to be healing.

Reality therapy systematically draws on both affective and behavioral areas. As with all affective approaches, expressing feelings within the safe confines of a therapeutic relationship is encouraged. Another affective element is the urgency of living responsibly "in the now." Future events are only discussed as they relate to present behavior. Responsible behavior is the key to reality therapy, and the client is encouraged to make moral judgments concerning right and wrong behavior and then contract responsibly to pursue correct behavior.[12] From this standpoint, reality therapy has a behavioral approach.

Counseling theories that draw from the cognitive and behavioral domains include values clarification and rational-emotive therapy. In both theories, the thinking processes are examined with the belief that altered thinking or clarified thinking results in altered behavior.

Values clarification is based on the premise that "everything we do, every decision we make and course of action we take, is based on our consciously or unconsciously held beliefs, attitudes and values."[13] The theory is not concerned with the specific content of our choices, but rather the process we go through in developing and claiming values. Reexamining what our values are and how we came to have them is believed to be helpful in changing them and in aligning our behaviors with our values. Whenever our behaviors are inconsistent with our stated or unconsciously perceived values, frustration and anxiety result.

The rational-emotive counselor believes that by pointing out faulty logic and assumptions to clients, their belief system will be altered, which in turn alters their behavior.[14] Someone who uses this approach might point out that difficulty in making choices about leisure involvement seems largely to be due to catastrophically high expectations of participation. Understanding this distortion of thinking might remove the obstacle to positive behavior. Rational-emotive therapy holds that

> virtually all serious emotional problems with which humans are beset directly stems [sic] from their magical, superstitious, empirically unvalidatable thinking; and that if disturbance-creating ideas are vigorously and persistently disputed by a rigorous application of the principles of logico-empirical thinking, they can almost invariably be eliminated and will ultimately cease to reoccur [sic].[15]

Logically, ameliorating irrational thinking results in rational behavior.

The dominant counseling theory that seems to draw from all three theoretical areas is *transactional analysis* (fig. 11–3). TA was developed by Eric Berne. The theory is cognitive in that it analyzes the structure of the personality. The basic notion is that we are constantly functioning from one of the three basic ego states: the Parent (P), the Adult (A), and the Child (C). Transactional analysis does exactly what it says: it analyzes transactions that take place within us, among us, and between us and characterizes them as the Parent, Adult, or Child ego states.

The *Parent* stands for all of the controls we have been taught and continue to feel and act on. The Parent has two parts: the Nurturing Parent and the Critical Parent. The Nurturing Parent is the part that maturely loves, nurtures, and takes care of others. The Critical Parent is the prejudicial, biased, judgmental part that assumes authority and control. The Critical Parent uses words such as should, should not, never, always, must, don't, do, right, and wrong. The Critical Parent is heavily obligated to rules, standards, customs, and myths.

The Adult is the ego state that gathers information, analyzes it, and sorts it out into its proper perspectives. It is the part that is objective, organized, adaptable, intelligent, and able to test reality and estimate probabilities.[16]

The *Child* ego state contains all of the impulses that come naturally to a child. It also develops some adaptations due to the influences of the Critical Parent. The three parts of the Child ego state are the Natural Child, the Adapted Child, and the Little Professor. The Natural Child within each person's Child ego is that which would be there naturally if nothing influenced him or her otherwise. It is that expression that is spontaneous, feeling, affectionate, impulsive, sensuous, uncensored, and curious. *The Natural Child is the most important aspect of the personality in relation to play behavior.*

However, due to the tremendous demands placed on the Child ego by significant authority figures (Critical Parents), the Adapted Child emerges as part of the Child ego state. Very early in life, authority figures begin telling the child how to behave and what to do in order to be successful in life. Young children usually learn what they have to do to avoid pain and to get approval. They adapt in many ways to the "oughts," and very often the oughts say, "Be responsible," "Be mature," "Be dependable," "Be strong," "Be perfect," "Do as I say," "Don't be silly," "Don't be loud," "Children should be seen and not heard," and on, and on, and on. The Adapted Child comes to believe that there is something wrong with playing, whereas hard work, duty, and responsible behavior are the keys to happiness. Thus, the individual's ability to play, to be spontaneous, to meet personal needs is diminished by trying to live up to everyone else's idea of what she or he should be. The Adapted Child is likely to be complying, complaining, whining, withdrawing, sulking, blaming, and procrastinating. Adapted Children turn into Critical Parents who are also unable to get their playful needs met later in life.

The Little Professor is the creative, intuitive genius of the Child ego. Combined with the Adult, the Little Professor can build a castle out of sand, create a dragon, write a poem, compose a song, or build a home. Combined with the Natural Child, it makes possible healthy play behavior and attitudes. When people cannot enjoy their Natural Child and their Little Professor, they have certain blocks to meaningful, need-fulfilling leisure and play behavior.[17]

In practice, transactional analysis is affective, in that an attempt is made to facilitate expression of feelings by personifying ego states. New ways of responding to self, others, and environment are taught by having clients change ego states and thus behave differently. Like other behavioral therapists, the TA counselor asks clients for contracts to behave differently and requires homework assignments in which to practice more fulfilling behavioral responses.

Transactional analysis is embodied primarily in *script theory*, which believes that

> *beginning early in life each person fashions a life plan for himself which he thereafter devotes himself to living out in an obsessive and unknowing fashion. Since the action in this script can only advance after proper casting has been accomplished and appropriate motivation supplied via "rackets" and the "games" which support the rackets, most of a person's effort in his lifetime prove to be script-related, if not script determined.*[18]

In TA, every effort is made to help constituents understand their scripts, express their feelings about their life situations, and appropriately change their self-defeating behaviors.

Regardless of the population receiving services defined as rehabilitative or therapeutic, the therapeutic recreator should know the basic premises of the popular counseling theories, and should be skilled in one or more facilitation technique. To maintain credibility with other health-related professionals, therapeutic recreators must be equipped with skills other than basic activity skills. The ability to base interaction on counseling theory is essential, particularly in settings that adhere to specific treatment philosophies.

leisure counseling:
a component of leisure education

The recent notoriety of leisure counseling and the emergence of individuals calling themselves leisure counselors place the responsibility of quality control on professionals in the leisure movement. Chester McDowell's historical review of leisure counseling reveals a multiplicity of philosophies and practices, ranging from simple utilization of participatory checklists to sophisticated practices of individual and group therapy.[19] To some, leisure counseling implies the sharing of information about recreation programs and facilities. To others, it means educating others about specific leisure skills. To still others, leisure counseling includes guided discoveries into personal feelings and values about play behavior. The phrase leisure counseling is used in a number of ways. It is considered a type of program, a process, and a philosophy. Consequently, it also receives mixed reactions. Therapeutic recreators need to agree on a definition of leisure counseling and alleviate the confusion that results from individual interpretations.

Gerald O'Morrow was one of the first professionals to use the phrase *recreational counseling.* O'Morrow's definition was founded on work with psychiatric patients, although it probably can be generalized to other populations. He defines recreational counseling as

> *a technique in the rehabilitation process whereby a professional person uses all information gathered about a person prior to discharge to further explore interests and attitudes, with respect to leisure, recreation, and social relationships, in order to enable the patient to identify, locate, and use resources in the community.* [20]

This definition refers to a technique, yet leaves the process undefined. It does, however, clearly indicate that a socioleisure lifestyle is of central concern.

Because the term leisure counseling has been used so diversely, it is not unusual that a variety of programs and processes have been developed under that term. Chester McDowell has classified the existing leisure counseling orientations into three categories.

1. "Leisure counseling as a leisure resource guidance service." This approach basically attempts to match a client's expressed leisure interests to existing leisure resources. It is an information-sharing process that assumes that the client has interests and skills and is blocked only by a lack of knowledge related to the availability of opportunities or facilities.
2. "Leisure counseling as a therapeutic-remedial-normalizing service." This category encompasses models that relate to client problems with leisure participation that spring from lack of recreational or social skills and knowledge. Programs using this approach are most likely to use structured activities to bring needed leisure and social skills into existence.
3. "Leisure counseling as a lifestyle development-education service." This category contains approaches that deal with problematic leisure involvement based on attitudes, values, and concepts. It does not assume illness in the traditional sense, but rather "felt difficulty" related to leisure as expressed by the client.[21]

Specific models or developed approaches can be identified within each category. They vary from highly formal or structured approaches to rather informal or loosely organized methods. Confusion sets in at this point, since many of the models are descriptions of programs that focus more on content or on organizational procedures than on the interactional or facilitation techniques. Leisure counseling is perhaps best understood when it *consistently indicates a facilitation process.* Program goals or content should be separated, as should administrative procedures. More time and attention need to be directed at specifying the process itself, i.e., defining and refining the facilitation act between counselor and client.

The term leisure counseling needs to be redefined. Bruce Shertzer and Shelley Stone describe counseling as an interaction process between counselor and client that facilitates understanding of self and environment and results in the establishment and/or clarification of values and goals for future behavior.[22] This type of definition is common in the counseling literature. Although it does not specify any particular therapeutic techniques, it does limit counseling to the client-counselor interaction.

The nature of this interaction not only depends on the personality traits of both counselor and client, but also upon the philosophical frame of reference from which the counselor views the client and the resulting facilitation theories and techniques used to promote positive behavioral changes.

McDowell describes a counseling orientation to leisure as having two basic parts: "a philosophical or theoretical construct related to the nature of man and his behavior, and secondly, an established set of techniques for conducting the behavior change."[23] McDowell builds a theoretical base concerning leisure behaviors and the human condition, including leisure and mental health, leisure and self-concept, leisure and attitudes, and leisure and valuing. Based on this material, he designs a counseling method (using techniques of values clarification) with which to develop a leisure counseling program. This systematic approach to leisure counseling contributes to future model constructions within the therapeutic recreation field.

If leisure is a state of being in which the player is allowed optimum freedom of self-expression with a maximum amount of self-regulation, and counseling is a facilitative, problem-solving process that seeks to enhance decision making about self, others, and environment, then leisure counseling must surely focus on self-expression. Concerning leisure counseling, McDowell states:

> The goal of leisure counseling is not necessarily to help the individual in ways to use free time as recreation. We should not be so naive [as] to believe that all people engaging in recreation are necessarily happy, self-fulfilling, problem-free "leisure beings." Is not our mandate one of helping the person to get in touch with his inner resources so that he can experience this state of mind called "lei-

sure"; and having done so see in it a value that can mold a place within a lifelong lifestyle? People may not necessarily value so much what it is they are doing for recreation, but what they are feeling inwardly about doing or having done it. [24]

McDowell defines leisure counseling as "a helping process which facilitates interpretive, affective, and/or behavioral changes in others toward the attainment of their leisure well-being."[25] We consider leisure counseling to be *a helping process that utilizes verbal facilitation techniques to promote self-awareness; awareness of leisure attitudes, values, and feelings; and the development of decision-making and problem-solving skills related to leisure participation with self, others, and the environment.*

counseling theories as applied to leisure counseling

The efficacy of any counseling approach depends on three factors: (1) the personal philosophies of the counselor concerning personality theory and human interaction, (2) the personality, needs, and life situations of clients, and (3) the predominant facilitation style embraced by the agency. Although many counselors vow adherence to an eclectic approach, most claim an allegiance to a particular theory. Counseling is a complex process that depends on many variables, and it is advantageous for the counselor to be comfortable in using a range of techniques to facilitate meaningful growth in clients. Although not exhaustive, the following theories seem to be appropriate to the leisure-counseling process. As previously mentioned, purely cognitive or psychoanalytical theories require extensive training and most often seem riddled with nebulous circumlocution around pertinent issues, resulting in the elusive search for the cause, of the cause, of the cause! For this reason, it is highly advisable to leave purely psychoanalytic approaches to the well-trained professional counselor.

gestalt approach

Because recreation is action-oriented, and because we believe in the inalienable right of self-determination and self-expression, Gestalt awareness techniques seem very appropriate for leisure counseling. Leisure counseling, using Gestalt awareness, tries to help identify and remove the blocks to play behavior, rather than attempt to mold specific outcome behaviors.

Gestalt awareness emphasizes the *here* and *now* of experience. For the individual who resists trying new experiences, appropriate questions would be, "How are you keeping yourself from playing?" "What mistakes are you afraid of making right now?" "How are you feeling about your projection of my response toward your failure?" From the Gestalt viewpoint, in the well-integrated individual the process of need-fulfillment goes on without interruption. Needs are constantly being formed in a dominance hierarchy; as one need is satisfied, it is replaced by another.[26] When any need goes unmet, a block to present awareness develops and inner conflicts result. The Gestalt counselor is concerned with *how* a person prevents himself or herself from getting needs met, or *how* aliveness and life energy are stopped. In order to discover the how, the counselor focuses on the *now* of behavior, attitudes, and awareness. Very often a person's need to respond freely in play is blocked by strong, inhibiting authority messages of right and wrong behavior and overly protective admonitions toward safety. Other blocks to play behavior include imposed structure, fear of making mistakes, lack of experience or knowledge, and environmental barriers. Identifying and removing blocks to play behavior is a fundamental responsibility of the leisure counselor.

The Gestalt therapist assumes that every emotion has a physical counterpart. Therefore, much of how we *feel* can be seen in bodily responses. Various forms of art, music, poetry, and movement have been used successfully by the Gestalt leisure counselor to assist clients in acknowledging, and expressing their feelings.

client-centered approach

Most recreation leaders can claim to be Rogerian in their theoretical approach to counseling, in that establishing warm, genuine relationships is the key to client-centered therapy. Leisure specialists have long professed that establishing caring, accepting relationships with clients brings about positive behavioral change. This approach is useful to the counselor with minimal training because it is nondirective. It is not, however, devoid of techniques, the most important of which are reflective listening and reflective feedback. The counselor is trained to listen carefully and render feedback of both fact and feeling to the client.[27] The client-centered approach provides a sound basis for other counseling skills.

behavioral approach

Of all the counseling theories, the behavioral approach is best known for its marked adherence to the scientific method in evaluating results and designating process variables.[28] There is a keen interest in learning as a form of behavior change. "For the behavioral counselor the function of reward is very important because much evidence exists for the principle that behavior that is rewarded tends to be repeated.[29]

2

The behavioral approach has been used rather extensively to modify or change children's behavior. The leisure counselor, using behavioral counseling, may determine (with the client when possible) the appropriate leisure or leisure-related skills (the "social graces") to be learned, and proceed to reward successful or approximately successful experiences.

Behavior modification is a useful counseling approach with children, particularly with emotionally disturbed and mentally retarded children. Behavior modification has also been attempted with old people, although its success is questionable.

The more appropriate behavioral approaches with adults seem to be systematic desensitization and assertiveness training. In *systematic desensitization*, a socially timid individual would be encouraged to attend a small, nonthreatening group function as a first step toward being able to attend large social gatherings. By allowing the client to risk new behaviors gradually, with the support of the counseling relationship, it is hoped that the goal behavior will ultimately be achieved.

More recently, *assertiveness training* has been viewed as a useful behavioral leisure-counseling technique. As with all behavioral counselors, the person using assertiveness-training techniques believes that frustration and anxiety result when we use self-defeating behaviors. Assertion is defined as the outward expression of feelings *other than* anxiety.[30] Therefore, to reduce frustration and anxiety, attempts are made to help individuals become more assertive so that personal needs can be met and desires can be expressed. Assertiveness training teaches techniques for outwardly expressing our needs in a straightforward, *nonaggressive* manner.[31] Leisure assertiveness-training groups provide an excellent environment in which constituents may learn to assert their leisure needs and say no to those factors that interfere with their play needs being met.

Behavioral techniques definitely have a place in leisure counseling. However, the emphasis on being specific, precise, and objective sometimes tends to place the focus on minute pieces of behavior while ignoring the larger leisure-behavior patterns. Such a narrow approach is antithetical to the concept of leisure. A behavioral approach, however, lends itself well to demands for accountability.

reality therapy approach

The concepts of relatedness and responsibility lend themselves well to leisure counseling efforts with young people. Youths commonly struggle simultaneously to sever the apron strings, to accept adult responsibilities, and yet to maintain safe, meaningful relationships. The leisure counselor has the opportunity, using reality therapy techniques, to bridge the gap between childhood and adulthood by offering an accepting, understanding relationship, while demanding responsible behavior.

Making decisions about leisure pursuits and following through on personal commitments are most appropriate concerns of the leisure counselor who adheres to reality therapy theories.

values clarification approach

Adeptly portrayed by Chester McDowell, values clarification is a significant responsibility of the leisure counselor.

> An important aspect of leisure counseling should be that of allowing the client, either individually or within a group, to personally explore his leisure-work life style, attitudes, and values, among other things. From the beginning of leisure counseling, the client is presented with the opportunity to engage in "concrete" exercises and experiences during a session or throughout the week. Completion of these experiences form [sic] a part of the discussion at each counseling session, and help [sic] in identifying barriers, constraints, as well as alternatives and consequences.[32]

Values clarification lends itself well to leisure counseling in that the activities are fun as well as insightful. Numerous appropriate activities are available in print and can easily be incorporated into leisure-counseling sessions. Additionally, values clarification techniques and concepts are indigenous to the group situation and are oriented toward gaining the greatest possible benefit from group interaction.

rational-emotive therapy approach

Like values clarification and assertiveness training, rational-emotive therapy lends itself well to group interaction, a plus in leisure counseling. As participants discuss their beliefs (fears, pains, etc.) about leisure participation, or lack of it, group members are quick to point out irrational thinking. Group members are also helpful in suggesting appropriate homework assignments geared to risk new behaviors and challenge irrational beliefs.

transactional analysis approach

Transactional analysis is also appropriate to group interaction. There is an abundance of TA literature, rich with activities designed to facilitate awareness of self-defeating behaviors. Although sometimes used excessively, the clear-cut structure of personality and the terminology offer an easy-to-learn counseling framework. It is, therefore, possible to explain behavior to adults and children alike (including higher-functioning retarded children). Many operational techniques in transactional analysis have been borrowed from other sources, including Gestalt, psychodrama, and the behavioral therapies, thus broadening the range of counseling possibilities. Role playing is a must in a TA group and is also an effective technique in leisure counseling. For example, asking an obsequious group member to switch roles with a bully, or to become a dogmatic Critical Parent, may help the client to understand the inhibitions that prevent her or him from playing well.

implications for the leisure-counseling-services delivery system

There is little agreement on what molds the good counselor or what constitutes successful counseling. There is also little agreement concerning the educational processes necessary to prepare one for the counseling role. However, there is a general consensus that counseling involves face-to-face interaction in human relationships, and that, in itself, is complex. It involves knowledge and beliefs concerning values, attitudes, and philosophical ideas about human nature. As counselors work with, relate to, and experience other human beings, what they feel, what they believe, and how they behave influence their counseling efficacy. To be effective, counselors must look beyond their awareness of how a client usually behaves and how best to employ counseling techniques. The counselor must also take a journey into himself or herself. The following broad areas of preparation are some prerequisites to effective leisure counseling and warrant a place in leisure education curricula:

1. comprehensive knowledge about normal patterns of growth and development;
2. knowledge about the implications of abnormal behaviors and developmental patterns—physically, affectively, and cognitively;
3. knowledge about and skills for a variety of facilitation techniques and concepts. Various counseling and educational theories need to be examined and appropriate applications made to problem solving in leisure counseling;
4. opportunities for self-discovery, made available to the student aspiring to be a leisure counselor. Without self-awareness and self-disclosure, little is available to give to others in the helping process.

Leisure personifies self-actualization, which Abraham Maslow defines as

an episode, or a spurt in which the powers of the person come together in a particularly efficient and intensely enjoyable way, and in which he is more integrated and less split, more open for experience, more idiosyncratic, more perfectly expressive or spontaneous, or more fully functioning, more creative, more humorous, more ego-transcending, more independent of his lower needs, etc. He becomes in these episodes more truly himself, more perfectly actualizing his potentialities, closer to the core of his being.[33]

Since leisure counselors are concerned with the self-actualization of their clients, they must take continual journeys into themselves to study their own progress towards self-actualized leisure. They must understand their own personality needs before they can effectively help others to meet theirs.

It has been said that

The self-actualizing counselor tends to stress the concept of identity and experience of identity in human nature. He emphasizes experiential knowledge rather than systems of concepts or abstract categories. He is open to his own experiences, rather than being closed or defensive. . . . The realization is present that he is a growing organism—one that continually assimilates and incorporates experiences into his own being. Such an individual is not easily threatened. To be open means rediscovery, stimulation, reconception, and even rebirth. This individual is better able to understand himself or another being. He tries to perceive the situation as the client sees it, rather than as an individual who is primarily concerned with placing a value judgment on the behavior of another person.[34]

Concepts and techniques of leisure counseling will be discussed. Pontifical theories will be formulated. Numerous leisure counseling models will be drafted, published, and sold as the guiding lights to leisure awareness. But, in the last analysis, the efficacy of leisure counseling will depend upon our personal commitment to examine and reexamine ourselves and our own leisure attitudes, values, and feelings. Doing so puts us in a better position to ameliorate blocks to meaningful play behavior in the lives of others.

a systems approach
to the leisure counseling process

Regardless of the complexities inherent in leisure counseling relationships, training in verbal facilitation techniques and procedural strategies are clearly necessary in order to effect positive behavioral changes. The following systems design specifies: (1) the general requirements (input) for leisure counseling, (2) the process for implementing a leisure counseling program, and (3) the general outcomes (output) of the counseling program. The model does not specify a particular population and can be easily adapted to any setting. Regardless of the population served, the leisure-counseling *process* remains relatively the same and the basic *content areas* of the model are also relatively constant (fig. 11–4).

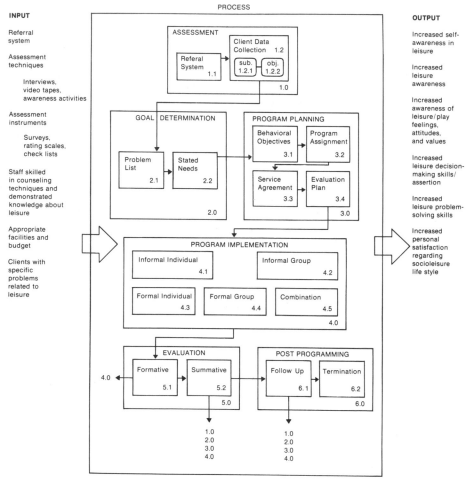

Fig. 11–4
Systems Approach to the Leisure Counseling Process

input

Any counseling program requires that a viable *referral system* be established. In institutional settings, referrals may be made by designated members of the rehabilitation teams, i.e., physicians, social workers, psychologists, etc. In community-based programs, referrals may be made by teachers, parents, or directly by the constituents.

Assessment is a prerequisite to any effective programming. Program design, in fact, depends on the assessment of needs. Therefore, one requirement for leisure counseling is to determine specific assessment techniques (interviewing, videotaping, and awareness activities) and assessment instruments (surveys, rating scales, and check lists).

Perhaps the most essential ingredient in effective leisure counseling is a staff skilled in counseling techniques (specific verbal facilitation skills) and knowledgeable about leisure. Guidance requires experiential knowledge; in leisure counseling, we simply cannot take people any farther than we have come ourselves.

process

Assessment. When a referral is made to a leisure counseling program, it is imperative that the counselor gather the necessary information for effective program planning. Subjective information is perhaps the most important. This constitutes the direct input of the client regarding problems and needs. Objective information is also helpful. This is the input from sources other than the client (parents, friends, past records, other members of the rehabilitation team, and test results). Examination of this information allows the counselor, and when possible, the client, to determine the program goals.

Goal Determination. Based on the assessment information, a list of specific problems can be formulated. This problem list should show the priority of problems. For example, if a client is both "withdrawn in social situations" and "afraid of failure in unfamiliar leisure activities," it would be preferable first to focus on improving social skills. After priorities are determined, specific needs of the client should be detailed. It is at this point that actual program planning may begin.

Program Planning and Implementation. If the client needs to increase social skills, the leisure counselor may begin program planning by stating the behavioral objectives for each problem or need. Stating these objectives makes it possible to evaluate the client's progress throughout the program and to give feedback on implementation strategies. A behavioral objective includes: (1) a concise statement of the behavior to be attained, (2) the condition under which the behavior is expected to occur, and (3) the criteria used to judge acquisition of the behavior. A behavioral objective for a client needing to increase social skills might read:

> During four informal gatherings (condition), the client will demonstrate the ability to relate effectively with others (behavior) by voluntarily introducing himself or herself to three people and, during the course of a casual conversation, sharing and receiving the following introductory information:
> 1. name,
> 2. occupation,

3. favorite leisure activities, and
4. the happiest happening in their life over the past three weeks (criteria).

In order to achieve this objective, the client may benefit from participating in a formal counseling group where fears are discussed and means of overcoming them are practiced, i.e., a leisure assertive-training group. If this seems like a viable means of achieving the leisure objective, a program assignment is made.

Leisure counseling programs will vary in their composition and use different facilitation styles. The composition of leisure counseling relationships may be: (1) informal meetings on an individual basis, (2) informal meetings of groups, (3) formal meetings on an individual basis, and (4) formal meetings of a group.[35] Some clients may be assigned to a combination of counseling situations. Facilitation strategies may be as diverse as the range of possible counseling styles.

Having agreed on the type of counseling program appropriate to achieving the counseling objective, client and counselor may want to sign a contract. This service agreement ensures that both parties clearly understand the intentions and requirements of program participation as well as the fee structure and length of involvement. Before implementing a program, the staff should complete the details of evaluation planning to ensure program accountability. This may include: (1) acquiring the necessary forms for evaluation; (2) reserving audio-visual equipment, if needed for videotaping or tape recording clients; (3) soliciting volunteer observers; and (4) finalizing observation schedules. Program implementation may begin after all phases of program planning are completed.

Evaluation. Evaluation makes it possible to improve programs and to make various decisions to improve a program's effectiveness. Evaluation follows program implementation and assessment. Assessment is necessary to determine either total program goals or individual program goals. It is also necessary to determine specific, measurable objectives, implementation strategies, and evaluation strategies. Evaluation takes place while a program is being implemented and at its completion. Formative evaluation takes place during program implementation and should result in immediate program improvement, such as a leisure counseling session being extended to one hour as opposed to thirty minutes, when it is realized that there is not enough time for program content to be covered.

Summative evaluation can only be conducted by summarizing formative evaluation data. Summative evaluation data may result in overall changes in any or all phases of the leisure-counseling process. Summative evaluation leads to recommendations about whether clients should continue in or leave a program. In addition, summative evaluation makes it possible to compare programs for their effectiveness.

Postprogramming. After a client has achieved individual program goals, recommendations may be made for continued independent participation outside the counseling program. However, it is always advisable to follow up on a client's continuing progress. Assuming that, over time, the client continues to be satisfied with her or his newly acquired socioleisure life style, final termination from the program is in order.

output

An effective leisure counseling process will result in specific individual behaviors for each client. However, the generally expected results of an effective leisure-counseling process are

1. increased self-awareness in leisure;
2. increased leisure awareness;
3. increased awareness of personal feelings, attitudes, and values regarding leisure and play behavior;
4. increased decision-making skills regarding leisure participation;
5. increased problem-solving skills relative to leisure; and
6. increased personal satisfaction regarding socioleisure life styles.

It is to these ends that leisure counseling addresses itself. The efficacy of leisure counseling depends on: (1) systematic processes of service delivery and (2) the sophisticated knowledge, skills, and experiences necessary to be facilitative helpers.

instructional techniques

Assisting clients in acquiring activity skills, social-interaction skills, and more awareness of the potential of leisure and leisure resources, requires that the therapeutic recreator employ certain teaching methods. Granted, some people are natural teachers and their methods are naturally good. On the other hand, most of us can benefit from studying different teaching styles and by increasing the range of techniques available for our use. Also, clients respond to different teaching strategies. The therapeutic recreator's job is to facilitate their learning, which may mean trying a variety of techniques before finding the most appropriate ones.

Most of us are familiar with at least three instructional techniques. Common to most activity instruction programs is the standard "describe, demonstrate, practice, and correct" method of group instruction. Equally common is the straight verbal description of some action or procedure. Other times, a basic imitative or modeling technique easily shows students the behavior or action we wish them to acquire. These standard techniques have been used successfully for decades and, indeed, have their merits. It may be useful also to become aware of a few more instructional methods.

Muska Mosston has identified six instructional strategies designed for group physical education programs. These techniques appear to be appropriate for other types of activity programs as well. Although designed for nonhandicapped people, most of the techniques need little or no modification to be easily used with special populations. The strategies are teaching: (1) by command, (2) by task, (3) with a partner, (4) in a group, (5) by guided discovery, and (6) by problem solving.[36]

teaching by command

In this technique, the instructor is in control of the material or action to be learned as well as the process of the instruction. The teacher determines in advance what is to be taught, how it will be taught, what amount of time will be designated for the different activities, and what organizational patterns will be used for the group. Once into the actual teaching phase, all students perform the *same activity at the same time* with the instructor designating beginning and ending points. The basic instruction is usually implemented by verbal or visual demonstration, followed by the group's controlled participation. Corrections can be made by stopping the whole group and giving comments and further demonstrations or by assisting students individually while the rest of the group routinely practices an activity skill.

The technique is a common one and is often used without considering that other strategies may be more appropriate for individuals with differing levels of functional ability. Special populations are among those groups that may need alternative strategies that take into account the various functional or developmental stages.

teaching by task

Teaching by task is similar in many ways to the command method. The instructor determines the activities, the organizational patterns, and the basic structure of the session. And the instructor describes and demonstrates the activity or action. The major difference occurs when the students are asked to perform. At this point, the instructor does not attempt to regulate the action. Students are free to initiate performance of the task at their own rates. They are free to repeat the task or terminate the task at will. Individuals thus take control of their behaviors during the performance of the designated task. No one is expected to engage simultaneously in the same action. Handicapped individuals obviously have a high degree of success with this method, since it allows them to focus on the task without the stress of trying to conform to a predetermined pace. The instructor is also able to assist individuals as needed.

reciprocal teaching—use of a partner

Reciprocal teaching relies on the observational and feedback skills of a partner. It is often used when an exact motion or action is required in an activity, but when the group is too large for a single instructor to observe everyone easily. The instructor still describes and demonstrates an activity or motion, and students are asked to observe the instruction carefully. Next, students are paired off. A student then practices the task while the other partner observes and gives positive or corrective feedback. Later the roles are switched. The instructor is free to circulate and give advice or assistance. However, when helping, the instructor *gives the information to the observer* who then relays it to the participating partner.

This strategy allows students to gain additional information about the task and how it is done. The ability to observe, analyze, and correct a partner usually improves the performance of the observer when the roles are reversed. The major problem occurs when an observing student does not understand the action or observes poorly and thus gives inappropriate or inaccurate information to his or her partner. With special populations great care should be given to the assignment of partners, since peer authority as well as differences in functional ability could be a problem.

teaching by small group

The small group style is a take-off on the reciprocal teaching method. Instead of partners, three or more students are assigned to a group. One is assigned the role of doer, one or more to the role of observer, and one or more to the role of recorder. This latter role is a clerical one of note taking and reporting.

Although this instructional style has several social and communicative values, it leaves much to be desired in terms of actual participation, since only one person is engaged in the action at any given time. It does provide for some checks and balances if the observer is unable to correct the doer adequately. Generally speaking, however, it doesn't allow for enough on-task time for participants.

teaching by guided discovery

Guided discovery requires the use of cognitive skills to a greater extent than other methods. It also requires a great deal more preparation by the instructor. The teacher asks a series of questions that clue the students to certain responses or actions. The teacher never gives the answers but guides students to the appropriate responses. Thus, a set of well-thought-through questions must be logical and sequential in order to assure appropriate responses. Here is an example of this process:

Leisure Education Class with mildly mentally retarded individuals
Topic: Leisure Resources

Instructor: "I'm thinking of a place where we can go to get some books to read. Who knows where we might go?"
Students: "The book store?"
Instructor: "It's a building that we pass on the way to the swimming pool."
Students: "The drug store?"
Instructor: "The books there are free for us to borrow."
Students: "The library?"
Instructor: "Right on! Who would like to go tomorrow?"

This technique can also be used to teach action-oriented activity skills. Although cluing for the discovery of some action is a little more difficult, it is a viable approach to learning. In teaching the flutter kick in swimming, for example, the student could be guided to the awareness that keeping the legs relatively straight is much more effective than kicking with the knees bent. Students are much more likely to remember what they learn through this process. The major drawback is the amount of teaching time this process takes. Another potential disadvantage is that the students must exercise cognitive skills to deal with alternatives and arrive at solutions.

teaching by problem solving

The problem-solving technique is one that can be used with subjects or activities that have *no single procedure that must be followed in order to participate successfully*. The process requires that students come up with their own methods of creating something or performing a task. It is an ideal method for teaching some skills, but very inappropriate for others. For example, it would be a delightful method for teaching about different media in a crafts program, but a poor choice for teaching a specific motor skill such as a standard overhand throw.

Problem solving as a teaching method relies heavily on the students' cognitive abilities. It is therefore an excellent technique when program goals are broader than just teaching specific motor skills. When used in small groups, problem solving encourages social interaction and the ability to cooperate. One point must be made clear about the problem-solving method: the instructor must be willing to accept the product, action, or behavior that results from the process. The end product is an entirely creative effort and should not be judged right or wrong.

Before selecting this method, the instructor should determine whether the intended activity is conducive to total freedom of choice. Problem solving also requires that the instructor be prepared to answer practical questions related to the task. This method encourages students to be independent—to make their own decisions and find their own solutions.

other instructional methods

In the past few years, a great deal of attention has been paid to the development of instructional techniques and strategies within the field of education. Methods have been designed that relate to social skills and affective skills as well as to cognitive and academic areas. Teaching strategies have been developed for people with specific disabilities. Perhaps most noteworthy are the techniques designed for the mentally retarded. The studies of learning theory and individual developmental differences have resulted in such instructional techniques as backward chaining, modeling, environmental manipulation, and physical manipulation. Principles of behavior modification have also been employed. Techniques have also been developed for use with other special populations. More teaching materials and methods now exist for the elderly and the emotionally disturbed. When designing therapeutic recreation instructional programs, investigation of these techniques could be most useful once a specific population and age are determined.

leadership techniques

When a therapeutic recreation program falls into the category of recreational participation as opposed to leisure education or therapy, the facilitation approach would most appropriately be called leadership. Of all the facilitation techniques, leadership is probably the least defined or described in the professional literature. Many therapeutic recreators assume that leadership is a phenomenon that evolves because of the character and personality of the staff member. Relying on charisma and experience, an individual acquires a style of working with people. The traditional and over-used leadership classifications—democratic, authoritarian, and laissez-faire—are seldom described behaviorally so that they can be taught to students and staff, let alone regulated.

Selecting an appropriate leadership technique for a program

should be based on the type of clients and the nature of the goals and objectives. Once a choice is made, the designer can then specify the characteristics or attributes of the interaction as part of the program plan. The absence of well-defined leadership techniques in the literature leaves the program designer with a difficult task in describing the attributes of the leadership style chosen. However, several aspects of leadership have been identified and can be helpful in specifying the desired interaction. The basic issue of concern is the amount of *control* the leader asserts over the group.

Robert Schmidt and Robert Tannenbaum have established a five-category description of leadership styles that moves from leader-centered to group-centered control.[37] Thomas Stein and Douglas Sessoms describe those five patterns as follows:

> *Telling.* Telling is the most autocratic leadership form; the leader makes the decision and announces the course of action to be followed. Although the interests of the members may be considered, they do not participate directly in the decision-making process. The power is vested in the leader and coercion may or may not be used or implied.
>
> *Selling.* The leader who employs the selling style of leadership makes a decision and attempts to persuade the group to accept it. He describes the benefits of the alternative he has chosen and how it relates to their needs and the needs of the organization. It is a sugar-coated form of telling.
>
> *Testing.* When the leader begins to involve the group in the decision-making process by asking for their ideas and questions, he is using the testing technique. Although he may ultimately disregard the opinions of the group (he makes the final decision), he is honest in his attempts to seek their reactions to his plan and to modify his approach if their reactions and comments indicate his thinking is faulty.
>
> *Consulting.* The consulting pattern is a group-centered form of leadership in which the group members have a chance to influence the decision from the outset. The leader presents the problem and the pertinent information to the group, but allows the group to develop the plan, to consider the various alternatives, and to recommend a course of action. Inasmuch as the group members are involved in the planning process, the leadership generally involves them in the implementation phase.
>
> *Joining.* The ultimate in group-centered leadership is the joining style, in which the leader participates as a member of the group and agrees, in advance, to carry out the decisions the group makes. The power is vested in the group; it contains the authority and it must accept the responsibility for its actions. The leader is simply the executor of the group's decision.[38]

This information gives the planner some major categories from which to choose. These patterns, however, are still described too briefly to be adequate for the level of specification needed in systems design.

Elliott Avedon has identified eight leadership roles that further refine the different ways leaders can interact with a group. His leadership roles are described behaviorally and include information about the populations for which each would be appropriate.

Controller. *The Controller makes all decisions regarding action. He decides what activity will be engaged in, who will engage in it, for what period of time, and in which place. He checks and regulates participant involvement in the activity. He sets the rules, sees that they are followed, and defines the limits in which the participant may operate. He exercises restraining power over participants, and dominates the situation.*

It is obvious from this description that the role lends itself to situations in which patients or clients have little internal control and a considerable degree of external control must be exercised. This role is often played with small children and with adolescents and adults who are hyperactive or who are not responsible for their behavior. It is also played with persons who have difficulty in making decisions as a consequence of illness, and at times is used in operant conditioning programs with the mentally retarded child. Sometimes an activity may pose a hazard to certain patients or clients and this role is utilized to permit continued participation.

Director. *The Director actively leads, but does not make all the decisions. He allows the participant some personal latitude. The Director decides where, when, how, and who concerning action. He causes participants to follow a specific course of action. He points out the right way to act. He regulates the action and the course of his action. He gives orders or instructions in an authoritative manner. He commands, manages, and guides the selection of behavioral effects to be produced, and the means to be used. He indicates the appropriate tempo, moods, and intensity of the action.*

Although in this role some degree of internal participant control is assumed, the participant has need to know all of the limits of action in order to behave effectively. He relies on the leader to set these limits. This role is often played with children and adults who are mentally ill, and at times with others who as a result of disability are relearning to live within the scope of an altered life situation. The role is sometimes played in correctional institutions with persons who manifest asocial behavior.

Instigator. *The Instigator starts action, gets participants involved, and then moves out of a direct leadership role. He sets minimal limits and expects some degree of participant control. He respects individuality and encourages expressions of self-determination. He goads and urges participants to act. He provokes and incites them, getting them to move forward.*

This role is used with persons who are lethargic, depressed, bored, spiritless, indifferent, preoccupied, and apathetic. The intent is to get them involved. As an Instigator, the leader may wish to have a participant become actively involved to express real feelings—feelings that may be negative. For example, in a communal living situation for the elderly, a client may be quite angry that he is there, but may be unable to say so. As a consequence, the client bottles up angry feelings and thus begins to suffer a number of uncomfortable physical symptoms. It may be the specialist's function (using this role) to provoke the client into expressing his anger. In a psychiatric setting, a patient may consistently reject certain negative ideas about his behavior during psychotherapeutic interviews by indicating that he never behaves in a specific manner. A psychiatrist may request that the specialist play the role of instigator, inciting certain behavior in the patient so the patient may be presented with tangible evidence that heroes indeed behave in the ways he has denied. This latter task is especially difficult and requires considerable supervision and experience.

Stimulator. The Stimulator generates positive interest in activity and stands by to encourage and assist participation when necessary. He excites, stirs, impels, and rouses participants.

This role is often used in work with mentally retarded young persons, also those with a physical disability who are relearning patterns of behavior, and at times with elderly persons in nursing homes and related facilities.

Educator. The Educator teaches skills which the participant wishes to learn so that he may become more active and more socially involved. The leader not only teaches activity skills per se, but is concerned with the conduct of self and effective social behavior.

This role is played in a number of settings. It assumes that a participant is self-determining and requests direct help from the leader. The role is sometimes played by a special volunteer who has a degree of expertise with specific activity media.

Adviser. The Adviser makes suggestions to participants concerning involvement and behavior. He also makes recommendations regarding decisions or courses of action. He may counsel or give guidance and information.

This role may be played with persons in a correctional setting or with mentally ill persons during the predischarge period. It may also be played with patients or clients in congregate living situations who have difficulty in social situations, or with persons who have a degree of physical disability and are endeavoring to take their place in society once again.

Observer. The Observer watches the participant as he engages in activity. He takes notice of behavior and recognizes the underlying meaning of various actions. He considers the meaning of what the participant does, and marks attentively what is happening. He perceives, evaluates, and makes appropriate responses to expressions of attitudes and feelings.

In this role, the leader is primarily offering sanction and realistic response by his physical presence at an activity and by what he says to the participant. It is a time when the participant is testing his wings and seeks a referent to determine his effectiveness. The role may be played in any number of settings as a consequence of treatment termination. In effect, in this role the leader is the good parent, or the "fan." However, the leader playing this role goes beyond observation in a physical sense by responding appropriately to the participant's request for response—be it approbation, critique, or chastisement.

Enabler. The Enabler assists the participant when asked. He provides the kind of assistance the participant wishes when the participant wishes it. He gives strength or authority to the participant's purpose, and makes practicable or easy his action. He provides means and opportunities for the participant to engage in *the activity of the participant's choice. The leader enhances the self-esteem and self-determination of the participant.*[39]

Drawing on information about leadership behavior, the program designer can specify the leadership intervention style desired for a program. Again, it is important to write with enough detail to enable the program implementors to be consistent in their method of conducting the program so that it can be both replicated and evaluated.

One additional style of leadership should be considered and indeed is used in many recreation participation programs. It is the *supervision* of groups. Basically, a supervision technique is used when groups or individuals are capable of self-initiated and directed leisure behavior, but when conditions of safety or well being need to be monitored. In this case, the role of the supervisor is to protect the individual in potentially hazardous situations. The interaction between client and specialist is limited to those verbal or nonverbal exchanges that ensure everyone's safety.

summary

Selecting an appropriate facilitation technique is of central importance in systems-designed therapeutic recreation programs. The nature of the technique varies according to the purpose of the program. Within each of the three basic domains of therapeutic recreation service, countless facilitation techniques prevail. The program planner selects techniques based on the nature and needs of the population served, the setting and its philosophy, and the staff employed to conduct the program.

As the therapeutic recreation profession expands and becomes more sophisticated in its delivery of services, there is a growing need for the therapeutic recreation professional to develop new and different methods of interaction. Defining and refining facilitation techniques not only remains a requirement of systems-designed programs, but also brings credibility and respect to the profession and improvement of services to clients.

 notes

[1] James E. Christensen and Rick Crandall, "Leisure Education for a State of Mind," *Leisure Today, Journal of Health, Physical Education and Recreation,* March 1976, p. 34.
[2] Edwin J. Staley, "The Struggle for Significance," *Leisure Today, Journal of Health, Physical Education and Recreation,* March 1976, p. 27.

[3] John Neulinger, "An Issue of Attitude Change," *Leisure Today, Journal of Health, Physical Education and Recreation,* March 1976, p. 28.

[4] Buford Stefflre, "Counseling in the Today Society: A Primer," in *Counseling and Guidance in the Twentieth Century,* ed. William H. Van Hoose and John J. Pietrofesa (New York: Houghton Mifflin Co., 1970), pp. 252–53.

[5] C. G. Wrenn, *The Counselor in a Changing World* (Washington, D.C.: American Personnel and Guidance Association, 1962), p. 33.

[6] John J. Pietrofesa and William H. Van Hoose, *The Authentic Counselor,* ed. George E. Leonard (Chicago, Ill.: Rand McNally, 1973), p. 6.

[7] Garth J. Blackman and Adolph Silberman, *Modification of Child and Adolescent Behavior,* 2d ed. (Belmont, Calif.: Wadsworth Publishing Company, 1975), p. 3.

[8] Ibid., p. 5.

[9] Reuben Fine, "Psychoanalysis," in *Current Psychotherapies,* ed. Raymond Corsini (Itasca, Ill.: F. E. Peacock Publishers, Inc., 1973), p. 7.

[10] Ibid., p. 8.

[11] Betty D. Meador and Carl R. Rogers, "Client-Centered Therapy," in *Current Psychotherapies,* ed. Raymond Corsini (Itasca, Ill.: F. E. Peacock Publishers, Inc., 1973), p. 119.

[12] William Glasser, *Reality Therapy: A New Approach to Psychiatry* (New York: Harper and Row Publishers, 1965).

[13] Sidney B. Simon, Leland W. Howe, and Howard Kirschenbaum, *Values Clarification: A Handbook of Practical Strategies for Teachers and Students* (New York: Hart Publishing Company, 1972), p. 13.

[14] Albert Ellis, *Reason and Emotion in Psychotherapy* (Secaucus, N.J.: Citadel Press, 1977).

[15] Albert Ellis, "Rational-Emotive Therapy," in *Current Psychotherapies,* ed. Raymond Corsini (Itasca, Ill.: F. E. Peacock Publishers, Inc., 1973), p. 172.

[16] Muriel James and Dorothy Jongeward, *Born to Win: Transactional Analysis with Gestalt Experiments* (Reading, Mass.: Addison-Wesley Publishing Company, 1971), p. 18.

[17] Scout L. Gunn, "Leisure Counseling: An Analysis of Play Behavior and Attitudes Using Transactional Analysis and Gestalt Awareness," in *Expanding Horizons in Therapeutic Recreation III,* ed. Gerald Hitzhusen and Gary Robb (Columbia, Mo.: Department of Recreation and Park Administration, Technical Education Services, 1975), pp. 38–39.

[18] Glen A. Holland, "Transactional Analysis," in *Current Psychotherapies,* ed. Raymond Corsini (Itasca, Ill.: F. E. Peacock Publishers, Inc., 1973), p. 353.

[19] Chester F. McDowell, *Leisure Counseling: Selected Lifestyle Processes* (Eugene, Oreg.: University of Oregon, Center of Leisure Studies, 1976).

[20] Gerald S. O'Morrow, "A Study of Recreation Service to Psychiatric Patients in Relation to Pre-discharge Planning and Aftercare" (Ed.D. dissertation, Columbia University, Teachers College, 1968), pp. 18–19.

[21] McDowell, *Leisure Counseling,* p. 21.

[22] Bruce Shertzer and Shelley C. Stone, *Fundamentals of Counseling,* 2d ed. (Boston, Mass.: Houghton Mifflin Co., 1974).

[23] McDowell, *Leisure Counseling,* p. 29.

[24] Ibid., p. 1.

[25] Ibid., p. 26.

[26] Richard Wallen, "Gestalt Therapy and Gestalt Psychology," in *Gestalt Therapy Now: Theory, Technique and Application,* ed. Joan Fagan and Irma Shepherd (New York: Harper and Row, 1970), p. 9.

[27] Charles B. Truax and Robert R. Carkhuff, *Toward Effective Counseling and Psychotherapy: Training and Practice* (Chicago, Ill.: Aldine, 1967).

[28] Alan Goldstein, "Behavior Therapy," in *Current Psychotherapies,* ed. Raymond Corsini (Itasca, Ill.: F. E. Peacock Publishers, Inc., 1973), p. 207.

[29] Lawrence Brammer, *The Helping Relationship: Process and Skills* (Englewood Cliffs, N.J.: Prentice-Hall, Inc., 1973), p. 43.

[30] Joseph Wolpe, *Psychotherapy by Reciprocal Inhibition* (Stanford, Calif.: Stanford University Press, 1958).

[31] Manuel J. Smith, *When I Say No, I Feel Guilty* (New York: Bantam Books, 1975).

[32] McDowell, *Leisure Counseling*, p. 71.

[33] Abraham H. Maslow, *Toward a Psychology of Being*, 2d ed. (Princeton, N.J.: D. Van Nostrand, 1968), p. 91.

[34] Pietrofesa and Van Hoose, *Authentic Counselor*, p.149.

[35] Shirley Bushell, "Recreation Group Counseling with Short-term Psychiatric Patients," *Therapeutic Recreation Journal*, 7, no. 3 (1973), 26–30.

[36] Muska Mosston, *Teaching Physical Education* (Columbus, Ohio: Charles E. Merrill Publishing Company, 1966).

[37] Robert Schmidt and Robert Tannenbaum, "How to Choose a Leadership Pattern," *Harvard Business Review*, 36, no. 2 (March-April 1958), 95–101.

[38] Thomas A. Stein and H. Douglas Sessoms, *Recreation and Special Populations* (Boston, Mass.: Holbrook Press, Inc., 1973). p. 37.

[39] Elliott M. Avedon, *Therapeutic Recreation Service: An Applied Behavioral Service Approach,* © 1974, pp. 157–59. Adapted by permission of Prentice-Hall, Inc.

———————— *suggested references* ————————

ACUFF, S. H., "Recreation Counseling as an Aspect of Programming for the Short-term Psychiatric Patient," *Recreation in Treatment Centers*, 5 (1966), 5–7.

AVEDON, E. M., *Therapeutic Recreation Service: An Applied Behavioral Science Approach*. Englewood Cliffs, N.J.: Prentice-Hall, Inc., 1974.

BLACKHAM, G. J., AND A. SILBERMAN, *Modification of Child and Adolescent Behavior* (2d ed.). Belmont, Calif.: Wadsworth Publishing Company, 1971.

BRAMMER, L., *The Helping Relationship: Process and Skills*. Englewood Cliffs, N.J.: Prentice-Hall, Inc., 1973.

BUSHELL, S., "Recreation Group Counseling with Short-term Psychiatric Patients," *Therapeutic Recreation Journal*, 7, no. 3 (1973), 26–30.

CORSINI, R., ed., *Current Psychotherapies*. Itasca, Ill.: F. E. Peacock Publishers, Inc., 1973.

DICKASON, J. G., "Approaches and Techniques of Recreation Counseling," *Therapeutic Recreation Journal*, 6, no. 2 (1972), 74–78, 95.

DOWNING, J., *Gestalt Awareness: A Collection of Essays on the Many Faces of Gestalt Therapy*. New York: Perennial Library, 1976.

ELLIS, A., *Reason and Emotion in Psychotherapy*. Secaucus, N.J.: Citadel Press, 1977.

FAGAN, J., AND I. L. SHEPHERD, eds., *What Is Gestalt Therapy?* New York: Harper and Row Publishers, 1970.

———, *Gestalt Therapy Now: Theory, Techniques, Applications*. New York: Harper and Row Publishers, 1970.

FAIN, G. S., "Leisure Counseling: Translating Needs into Action," *Therapeutic Recreation Journal*, 7, no. 2 (1973), 4–9.

GLASSER, W., *Reality Therapy: A New Approach to Psychiatry*. New York: Harper and Row Publishers, 1965.

GUNN, S. L., "Leisure Counseling: An Analysis of Play Behavior and Attitudes Using Transactional Analysis and Gestalt Awareness," in *Expanding Horizons in Therapeutic Recreaction III*, ed. Gary Robb and Gerald Hitzhusen. Columbia, Mo.: University of Missouri, Department of Recreation and Park Administration, Technical Education Services, 1975, pp. 35–42.

———, "Leisure Counseling Using Techniques of Assertive Training and Values Clarification," in *Expanding Horizons in Therapeutic Recreation IV*, ed. Gerald Hitzhusen et al. Columbia, Mo.: University of Missouri, Department of Recreation and Park Administration, Technical Education Services, 1976, pp. 35–41.

GUNN, S. L., AND C. A. PETERSON, "Therapy and Leisure Education: A Component of Therapeutic Recreation Services," *Parks and Recreation*, November 1977, pp. 22–25, 51–52.

HITZHUSEN, G., "Recreation Counseling for Adult Psychiatric and Alcoholic Patients," *Therapeutic Recreation Journal*, 7, no. 1 (1973), 16–22.

HOFFMAN, C. A., AND B. ELY, "Providing Recreation Counseling in a Psychiatric Hospital: A Vital Community Link," *Therapeutic Recreation Journal*, 7, no. 3 (1973), 3–7.

HOLLAND, G. A., "Transactional Analysis," in *Current Psychotherapies*, ed. Raymond Corsini. Itasca, Ill.: F. E. Peacock Publishers, Inc. 1973.

JAMES, M., AND D. JONGEWARD, *Born to Win: Transactional Analysis with Gestalt Experiments*. Reading, Mass.: Addison-Wesley Publishing Co., 1971.

JOSWIAK, K. F., "The Design, Implementation and Evaluation of Leisure Counseling Program Materials for Use with Mentally Impaired Adults in a Group Home Setting." Unpublished master's thesis, Michigan State University, 1975.

LEDERMAN, J., *Anger and the Rocking Chair: Gestalt Awareness with Children*. New York: McGraw-Hill, 1969.

MASLOW, A. H., *Toward a Psychology of Being* (2d ed.). Princeton, N.J.: D. Van Nostrand, 1968.

McDOWELL, F., Jr., *Leisure Counseling: Selected Lifestyle Processes*. Eugene, Oreg.: University of Oregon, Center for Leisure Studies, 1976.

———, "Toward a Healthy Leisure Mode: Leisure Counseling," *Therapeutic Recreation Journal*, 8, no. 3 (1974), 96–104.

McKECHNIE, G. E., "Psychological Foundations of Leisure Counseling: An Empirical Strategy," *Therapeutic Recreation Journal*, 8, no. 1 (1974), 4–16.

MOSSTON, M., *Teaching Physical Education*. Columbus, Ohio: Charles E. Merrill Publishing Co., 1966.

NEULINGER, J., "An Issue of Attitude Change," *Leisure Today, Journal of Health, Physical Education and Recreation* (March 1976), pp. 28–29.

O'Morrow, G. S., "A Study of Recreation Service to Psychiatric Patients in Relation to Pre-discharge Planning and Aftercare." Unpublished doctoral study, Columbia University, Teachers College, 1968.

———, "Social Recreation Counseling for the Ill and Disabled," *Therapeutic Recreation Journal*, 6, no. 2 (1972), 69–73.

Overs, R. P., "A Model for Avocational Counseling," *Journal of Health, Physical Education and Recreation*, 41, no. 2 (1970), 36–38.

Perls, F. S., *Gestalt Therapy Verbatim*. Lafayette, Calif.: Real People Press, 1969.

Pietrofesa, J. J., and W. H. Van Hoose, *The Authentic Counselor*, ed. G. E. Leonard. Chicago, Ill.: Rand McNally, 1973.

Stein, T. A., and H. D. Sessoms, *Recreation and Special Populations*. Boston, Mass.: Holbrook Press, Inc., 1973.

Shepard, M., *Fritz: An Intimate Portrait of Fritz Perls and Gestalt Therapy*. New York: Bantam Books, 1976.

Shertzer, B., and S. C. Stone, *Fundamentals of Counseling* (2d ed.). Boston, Mass.: Houghton Mifflin Co., 1974.

Shostrom, E. L., *Man, the Manipulator*. New York: Bantam Books, 1968.

Simon, S. S., L. W. Howe, and H. Kirschenbaum, *Values Clarification: A Handbook of Practical Strategies for Teachers and Students*. New York: Hart Publishing Company, 1972.

Smith, M. J., *When I Say No, I Feel Guilty*. New York: Bantam Books, 1975.

Stefflre, B., "Counseling in the Total Society: A Primer," in *Counseling and Guidance in the Twentieth Century*, ed. W. H. Van Hoose and J. J. Pietrofesa. New York: Houghton Mifflin Co., 1970.

Stevens, J. O., *Awareness: Exploring, Experimenting, Experiencing*. New York: Bantam Books, 1973.

Tannenbaum, R., I. R. Weschler, and F. Massarik, *Leadership and Organization: A Behavior Service Approach*. New York: McGraw-Hill Book Company, 1961.

Thompson, G., "Outline for Development of a Recreational Counseling Program," *Therapeutic Recreation Journal*, 6, no. 2 (1972), 83–85, 96.

Truax, C. B., and R. R. Carkhuff, *Toward Effective Counseling and Psychotherapy: Training and Practice*. Chicago, Ill.: Aldine, 1967.

Weertz, D. J., J. R. Healy, and R. P. Overs, "Avocational Activities Inventory," *Milwaukee Median for Rehabilitation Research*, Report 5, 1968.

Wolpe, J., *Psychotherapy by Reciprocal Inhibition*. Stanford, Calif.: Stanford University Press, 1958.

Wrenn, C. G., *The Counselor in a Changing World*. Washington, D. C.: American Personnel and Guidance Association, 1962.

CHAPTER TWELVE

specifying the implementation plan

PURPOSE: To present information pertinent to the implementation plan for systems-designed programs. Included is material related to the length and number of sessions; sequencing; input requirements, such as staff, facilities and equipment; and other program requirements for desired and optional program operation.

A systems-designed program specifies terminal performance objectives, which are then broken down into enabling objectives (EOs) with corresponding performance measures(PMs). Each EO and PM is then task analyzed to produce content and process for bringing the desired behaviors into existence. Although the program planners design a program with general implementation considerations in mind, up to this point the implementation strategy has not yet been delineated. This step, however, is vitally necessary and must be in accordance with the program's objectives and content.

In a system's approach, the designer is saying that a particular program, implemented in a particular manner, should produce the desired results. If desired results are not achieved, then a variety of factors can be analyzed and changed, if necessary, to improve the likelihood of success. The program, its implementation plan, and the evaluation plan are closely interrelated. Many times programs do not work, not because of their content, process, or objectives, but because the implementation strategy was deficient. Obviously, it is easier to revise the implementation plan than it is to rewrite the program.

number, length, and content of sessions

When a designer decides to run a program for ten weeks for an hour and a half each week, the designer is indicating that the objectives and performance measures should be possible to achieve within that time. In evaluating such a program, the amount of time spent on each EO is compared to the results achieved. Discrepancies or program failures can then be realistically analyzed relative to the amount of time needed to accomplish the program content. Revisions based on data can then be made. For example, a program may require more sessions or a longer time in each session to produce the desired outcomes.

In other cases, the content of the program may need to be cut to allow for the achievement of the objectives within the time available. A *sequence sheet* is often employed to delineate the number of sessions and their content and is very useful. Breaking down each session by the number and nature of the EOs to be achieved gives the designer a reasonable idea of the program's feasibility in terms of time. The sequence sheet also describes how the program was designed to be implemented. Later, when the program is being operated and evaluated, the sequence sheet serves as the master plan for scheduling and conducting the sessions. Important evaluation data can be gathered and decisions made for possible revisions and improvements relative to the adequacy of time distribution for each EO.

The breakdown on the sequence sheet requires the designer's best judgment in the planning process. The amount of time assigned to each EO and the order in which the EOs are presented are important planning decisions. The sequence sheet helps in choosing good estimates because the whole program is laid out before it is implemented. Two typical, completed sequence sheets appear in tables 12–1* and 12–2.** They designate the number, length, and content of the program sessions for two different programs.

Some programs do not lend themselves to having a set number of sessions. The program is designed to be ongoing, with the EOs presented when appropriate. Other programs are designed in such a way that many EOs are being worked on simultaneously. These variations are common in many treatment settings in which clients are admitted and discharged at various times and with no set length of treatment designated. Many recreational participation programs are also of this type, since the clients voluntarily choose when they wish to initiate or terminate program involvement. Even in these types of programs, session implementation

*Material used with permission of the designer, Joan Henn.

**Material used with permission of the designer, Charles Bullock.

STATE TECHNICAL INSTITUTE AND REHABILITATION CENTER

Sequence Sheet

TENNIS

TPO	EO	DESCRIPTION	SESSION NUMBER	ESTIMATED TIME (minutes)
2	2	A. Give overview of course	1	10
		1. General description of what course will cover		
		2. Discuss important criteria for purchase of racket		
		3. Give handout—A Guide for Tennis Players		
1	2	B. Introduce forehand drive		5
		1. Grip		
		2. Body position and ready position		
		3. Racket swing and point of contact		
1	3	C. Introduce courtesy serve and practice stroke		10
		D. Introduce backhand drive		5
		1. Grip		
		2. Body position		
		3. Racket swing and point of contact		
		E. Introduce and practice backhand courtesy serve		5
		F. Practice forehand and backhand: Rally between two using courtesy serve to start ball in play		
1	2	G. Introduce footwork		10
1	2, 3	H. Practice forehand and backhand: Rally		10
				15
1	2, 3	A. Review and practice footwork	2	10
1	2, 3	B. Review forehand, backhand, and courtesy serves		15
		C. Practice		20
1	5	D. Cover rules listed under general play		10
		E. Rally between two		20
1	5	A. Cover rules governing serve	3	5
		B. Practice serving on courts		20
1	5	C. Cover rules governing serve receive		5
		D. Practice serve and serve receive		15

		Week	Activity	Time
1	1	4	A. Review full swing serve and ball toss	10
1			B. Practice serve and serve receive	15
1	2, 3		C. Review and practice forehand and backhand	15
1	2, 3		D. Introduce and practice cross-court shots	10
1			E. Cover scoring	10
1	5		F. Play singles game, keeping score	15
1	2, 3	5	A. Review and practice cross-court shots	10
1	2, 3		B. Introduce and practice down-the-line shots	10
1	1		C. Review and practice serve and serve receive	10
1	5, 6		D. Review rules; cover court etiquette	10
1	7		E. Play one set of singles thinking about strategy	25
1	7		F. Discuss game strategy	5
2	1		G. Discuss where one may find tennis courts within the community	5
1	2, 3	6	A. Review and practice cross-court and down-line shots	10
1	1		B. Review and practice serve and serve receive	10
1	4		C. Introduce volley 1. Court position and rules governing net play 2. Technique	10
1	5		D. Practice volley	15
1	4		E. Discuss game strategy in relation to net play	5
1	7		F. Play singles game, coming to net when appropriate	20
1	7		G. Discuss game strategy	5
1	4	7	A. Review and practice volley	15
1	1		B. Practice serve and serve receive	10
1	2, 3		C. Practice forehand and backhand drives	10
1	7		D. Play singles games and discuss strategy	40
		8 and 9	A. Open practice and warm up	15
			B. Play singles round-robin tournament	60
			C. Complete check sheets for skills	

TPO	EO	DESCRIPTION	SESSION NUMBER	ESTIMATED TIME (minutes)
1	1, 2, 3, 4	A. Practice strokes	10	15
1	7	B. Introduce doubles play		20
1	7	1. Court position of players		
1	5	2. Strategy		
1	7	3. Rules specific to doubles play		
		C. Play doubles games		40
1	1, 2, 3	A. Open practice and warm up	11	15
		B. Play doubles round-robin tournament		60
		C. Complete check list for skills		
1	5	A. Written test	12	30
		Free play		45

Table 12-1

Sequence Sheet for a Program with a Set Number of Sessions—
Instructional Tennis Program for Vocational Rehabilitation Students

PROGRAM SEQUENCE SHEET

TPO	EO	DESCRIPTION	SESSION[a]	ESTIMATED TIME
1	1	Basic terminology	1	90 minutes
1	2	Social ecological involvement	2	30 minutes
1	3	Specific terminology	2	30 minutes
2	1	Self-examination	3	45 minutes
2	2	Soliciting feedback	Any session as needed—at least by session 3	15 minutes
2	3	Log presentation	All sessions after 3	15 minutes
2	4	Consequences	4	60 minutes
2	5	Verbal assertiveness exercises	5-8b	75 minutes
2	6	Physical assertiveness exercises	6-9b	75 minutes
3	1	Preparation of self-directed program	After last physically assertive exercise	120 minutes
3	1	Presentation of self-directed program	Final session	120 minutes

[a] Program designed to run a minimum of 8 sessions and a maximum of 12 sessions

[b] Depending on the size of the group

Table 12-2

Sequence Sheet for a Program with a Set Number of Sessions—
Assertiveness Training Program for Psychiatric Patients

should be described. Such a description will designate the length of the sessions and present the general format for each session.

The implementor picks the content for a given session from the program materials (EOs and TLAs), based on the client needs.This method still allows for evaluation of the appropriateness of the enabling objectives and the corresponding use of content-and-process sheets. The session formats can also be evaluated as long as the program was implemented as designed. Although such programs cannot be tightly implemented and evaluated, they still meet the requirements of systems design. The more detail provided by the designer on the implementation plan, the greater likelihood that the implementor will be able to follow the intended program concept. An example of such a description follows.

> Aspects of an Implementation Plan for a Program that Is Ongoing—Peer-Interaction Program for Developmentally Disabled and Emotionally Disturbed Children*
>
> *Agency and Population Description.* The facility is a short-term residential treatment center for fifty emotionally disturbed and developmentally disabled children ages five to fifteen. The stay for each child may be from three months to a year or more.
>
> *Statement of Purpose.* To help emotionally disturbed and developmentally disabled children to interact socially in play.
>
> *System.* The peer-interaction program is an *on-going program* that meets in the gym *four times each week for one hour each time.* The program helps the participants learn cooperative play. At any one time there are *six to fifteen children;* however, children move in and out of the group as they are admitted and discharged from the facility.
>
> *Implementation Strategy.* When children are admitted to the facility, their social skills are assessed and they are assigned to the peer-interaction group, if needed. Games are introduced to the children through a several-month period. As the children grasp the rules of one or two games, another game is taught. When one-half of the children can play one-half of the games when given external cues, new games are introduced. The session begins with a familiar game and then a new game is taught. Sessions continue to include familiar games to help the continuity of the activity and to give the children continued success.
>
> *Sample Session Format*
>   1. Fifty minutes of teaching and playing games:
>   Duck, Duck, Goose
>   Stone
>   Fox and Squirrel
>   Flying Dutchman
>   2. Five minutes of quiet rest.

*Materials presented with permission of the designer, Mary Patricia McCreary.

3. Five minutes of clapping time:

Children who did a "super job" (super job means that children played the games with external cues and attended to the activity throughout to the extent that they did not disrupt the ongoing activity) that day will get clapped for. Children's names are called individually and if they did a good job they are clapped for. This gives the children reinforcement for a job well done!

Program materials. The leader selects appropriate enabling objectives (EOs) and corresponding teaching-learning activity (TLA) sheets from the program materials, based on the assessed level of the individual children and the level of the group. A full description of techniques for working on that EO is found in the process column of the TLA. Twenty-six games are provided in the appendix of the system. They are rated by level of difficulty in terms of interaction requirements. (Note: Sample enabling objectives and TLAs for this system are found in figures 9–1 and 9–2.)

Whether the program under consideration is an "ongoing" program or a "set-number-of-sessions" program, part of the implementation plan is to discuss the length and nature of the sessions, either through a sequence sheet or a general format description. Other information related to sessions, such as their number and frequency, should also be covered. A systems-designed program always revolves around its objectives and performance measures. Making appropriate implementation decisions is vital if the program is to achieve its intended outcomes. Some other factors in the implementation plan also relate to whether a program is successful.

description of population

Systems programs are generally designed for specific populations. It is therefore usual to describe the target population in the implementation plan. If the program is designed for educable mentally retarded, the materials and interactions designed take into account certain characteristics that might make the program inappropriate for another population. The more specifically designed a program is for a given population, the more information is needed for the implementation plan. An instructional swimming program for individuals with cerebral palsy should describe the levels of severity and types of CP for which the program is intended. If the program is designed for general populations (mild disabilities or mixed disabilities), the population description can note that information, thus telling the implementor that modifications may need to be made in the materials when working with certain other individuals.

The description of the specific population may also include such factors as the age range and group size for which the program is designed. The importance of these factors vary, but could be critical when evaluating results or making judgments about the appropriateness of a program for a population other than the one for which the program was intended.

description of staff

Most programs are designed with certain constraints and re-sources in mind. The implementation plan needs to identify these factors. Staffing requirements are central to the effective implementation and out-comes of the designed program. The implementation plan identifies the number of staff needed as well as the qualifications required. Here is an example of such a description for a bowling program for the physically handicapped:

> Staff: therapeutic recreation specialist with knowledge of bowling, physically handicapping conditions, and methods of adapting or modifying bowling equipment and procedures. One adult volunteer or staff assistant for each alley used.

The failure of a program is often attributed to something as seemingly minor as the absence of the appropriately trained staff or number of staff, as described in the implementation plan.

description of required facilities and supplies

Program plans are also designed around some assumptions about needed or available facilities or supplies. Since these resources may not always appear in the actual program plan (terminal performance sheets and teaching-learning activity sheets), they should simply be identified in a section of the implementation plan. Occasionally a program requires an unusual or unique piece of equipment not related to the program's con-tent but to the teaching of or interacting with clients. The use of a video-tape machine, for example, might be central to a program's design and thus be important to identify in the implementation description.

summary

An implementation plan is vital to a systems-designed program. The program itself designates objectives and performance measures, and details the activities and interactions needed to bring about the desired

244

outcomes. However, the program plan does not identify many factors and conditions necessary for the program operation. They should be delineated in the implementation plan. An implementation plan states pertinent information about the target population, needs for staffing, facilities, and supplies. It also describes the nature and format and the length and number of sessions.

---

suggested references

BENJAMIN, A., *The Helping Interview*. Boston, Mass.: Houghton Mifflin Co., 1969.

BERGEVIN, P., D. MORRIS, AND R. SMITH, *Adult Education Procedures*. Greenwich, Conn.: Leabury Press, 1963.

BRAMMER, L. M., *The Helping Relationship: Process and Skills*. Englewood Cliffs, N. J.: Prentice-Hall, Inc., 1973.

KRAUS, P. G., AND B. J. BATES, *Recreation Leadership and Supervision: Guidelines for Professional Development*. Philadelphia, Pa.: W. B. Saunders Company, 1975.

REIK, T., *Listening with the Third Ear*. New York: Grove Press, 1948.

SCHULMAN, E. D., *Intervention in Human Services*. St. Louis, Mo.: C. V. Mosby Co., 1974.

program evaluation

PURPOSE: To provide a rationale for and information about an evaluation process to be used with systems-designed programs. The methodology presented makes possible data-based decisions for program and revision improvement, and provides a foundation for making statements about program effectiveness. Sample data-collection instruments are presented.

Evaluation! The term panics the average practitioner and student. Some envision vast amounts of statistics complicated by computer language. Others see outsiders surveying their programs briefly and with insensitivity, and then pronouncing harsh judgments about inadequate staffing or the absence of clients. Still others resent the concept (whatever it is) because they believe it interferes with vital client time and produces massive amounts of paper work. Although most agree that there is a desperate need to determine the effects of programming in order to justify service, there still remains a dread and fear of the evaluation process.

It would be impossible to respond to all of the evaluation phobias. We simply would like to impart some information about the evaluation process and provide some useful tools to assist the professional in conducting basic evaluations, with the intention of improving program operation and effectiveness.

The evaluation information presented interrelates with program design and implementation. It is evaluation meant to be conducted by those individuals who plan and conduct programs. It assumes a desire to improve services rather than to make irrelevant judgments about staff, facilities, funding, or the nature of a client's status.

description of evaluation

The word evaluation is used in many different ways, within many diverse contexts, and often on a variety of levels. As a result, it is hardly strange that confusion and misinterpretation surround its existence. However, common to all usage is the concept of judging the merit of some phenomena. Program evaluation, aided by new techniques in evaluation research, is attempting to make the judging process more accurate and objective. This is accomplished by determining in advance the criteria by which to judge outcomes.[1] Systems-designed programs fall neatly into the category of entities that can be evaluated by certain predermined criteria, since specific behavioral objectives and performance measures, which serve as standards for judgment, are inherent in program design. Evaluating a program that has been designed with a systems methodology is, thus, a relatively easy process compared to evaluating other programs that have no predetermined and specifically stated outcome behaviors or standards.

The process is still not all that simple or automatic. Information (data) needs to be systematically and consistently collected, which enables the evaluator to compare performance with standards. To make good evaluations, the evaluator must first ask the right questions and develop the appropriate information-gathering tools (instruments and records), in order to make accurate and useful judgments.

Thus, evaluations judge the value of programs. The process, however, takes advantage of the established concepts, procedures, and methods provided by evaluation research. Specifically, the discrepancy evaluation model (DEM)[2] and Stake's evaluation model[3] provide the background for the information presented. Both models rely on the assumption that evaluation is an integral part of program planning and operation and that meaningful evaluation requires the specification of standards in the program-design stage.

the purposes and functions of evaluation

What does worth or merit mean in terms of a program? *First, evaluation, systematically conducted, leads to information related to program improvement.* Most of us want to know where and how to improve what we do. Observing our programs for the purpose of improving services are reasonable and justifiable expenditures of time and effort. A systems-designed program, coupled with discrepancy evaluation, produces explicit information about what revisions need to be made for program improvement.

The second major purpose of evaluation is related to judging the effectiveness of programs. Programs designed with a systems methodology have clearly stated objectives, along with specific procedures for achieving them. These procedures, accompanied by systematic evaluation, allow professionals to state accurately the effects or outcomes of their programs. Evaluation of this type does not rely merely on intuitive feelings or on random success stories, but on rather accurate, data-based statements of achievement. For example, stating that "80 percent of the clients reached the designated objectives" is a definitive and supportable report of the program's operation. Although a program may not prove to be totally effective, at least criteria can be established and decisions made based on actual performance compared with predetermined standards. Objective judgment and accurate reporting related to program outcomes are necessary responsibilities of professionals in the human-services fields. Systems evaluation allows for this level of accountability.

Whether evaluation is conducted for program revision and improvement or for judging program effectiveness, the systems approach to evaluation serves the vital function of facilitating decision making. Information is systematically gathered on major aspects of design and operation, which enable objective decisions to be made. Programs can be expanded, maintained, revised, or terminated. Such decisions, which in the past have often been made without adequate evidence, can now be based on actual program performance.

rationale for evaluating programs

Evaluation takes time. It requires paper work. It adds additional responsibilities to program implementors and administrators. "So why bother?" some professionals might ask. The answer comes back loud and clear—accountability! All kinds of human services are having to justify their existence. Accountability and justification go hand in hand. People want to know the reason for programs and their effects. Three groups of people are usually interested in accountability. Although their interests differ, they each have a concern and a right to hold therapeutic recreation services accountable.

clients

The individuals who receive therapeutic recreation services are the primary group to which we need to be accountable. All too often they are the last ones to understand why they are scheduled for certain programs or what outcomes should result from their participation. Systems-designed and evaluated programs can resolve these issues. Clearly stated objectives and performance measures enable clients to know what is expected of them and how well they are doing. Program evaluation ensures that they are receiving the most effective services possible.

the funding source

Funding of therapeutic recreation services comes from a variety of sources: taxpayers, insurance companies, direct fees, granting agencies, and voluntary contributions. The funds are controlled, managed, and distributed by the sponsoring agency. Administrators at different levels are accountable for the allocation of the funds. Tighter controls, seemingly fewer resources, and more demands for services describe the contemporary agency. Justification for services and accountability are demanded in such a situation. Administrators want to know why programs are needed, what exact objectives and procedures will be employed, and how program effectiveness will be determined. Again, systems-designed and evaluated programs meet the requirements for this level of justification and accountability. Program results are easily determined and can be objectively recorded and reported.

the therapeutic recreation profession

One of the marks of a profession is that there are established procedures related to its area of services. Therapeutic recreators have had a difficult time delineating such procedures. Systems-designed and evaluated programs contribute greatly to this goal. Over time, information can be gathered and distributed that can standardize procedures. Therapeutic recreation specialists can say, "This program, with these objectives, implemented in this way, produces these results." Program evaluation is obviously needed to substantiate and support such statements. The profession stands to gain credibility and respect through such efforts. We are accountable to ourselves for the development and utilization of professional procedures. Program-planning and evaluation methods are among the procedures that need standardization.

types of evaluation

Two types of evaluation are related to program planning and decision making. Although they serve different functions, each contributes to the total process.

formative evaluation

Formative evaluation refers to evaluation efforts and processes that are conducted while a program is being planned or during its implementation. *The purpose of formative evaluation is to improve the program's effectiveness.*[4] Data are collected to help decision makers revise and improve the program. The revisions can be made at any time: before the program is actually put into operation, during the implementation, or after a program is concluded. Sophisticated formative evaluation plans might call for the collection of data and revisions at all three stages. Regardless of the depth of the evaluation, the concern is the same: gathering information to further develop and improve the program's effectiveness. Much of the evaluation discussed in this chapter is formative in nature.

summative evaluation

Summative evaluation is conducted on a program in operation to determine its value. Its purpose is to judge the program's effectiveness.[5] Normally, summative evaluation requires comparative studies between programs with similar goals but with different procedures in order to make judgments about the best or most efficient way of conducting a program. In therapeutic recreation, we rarely have the time or resources for such in-depth comparative studies. It is important to note, however, that statements about a program's effectiveness can be made from data collected during formative evaluation. The same evaluation questions, asked for the purpose of improving and revising systems-designed programs, can also yield basic information necessary for making basic judgments about a program's effectiveness.

practical concerns about evaluation

Programs must be evaluated practically. Three concerns emerge as useful in this regard. First, the evaluation needs to be *efficient*. In other words, the evaluation should take as little time as possible. Evaluation, after all, is not the primary focus of therapeutic recreators; service to clients is. Consequently, any evaluation effort should be possible within the time available and keep program delivery central.

Second, program evaluation should be *feasible*. The staff members who conduct the evaluation must have the necessary skills. To be meaningful, evaluation efforts require the support of the staff and administrators. Actions that are subverted or resisted destroy the intent and value of program evaluation. Part of feasibility includes the willingness of administrators to allow the time for evaluation efforts as well as to provide other necessary resources, such as secretarial help and financial assistance.

Third, meaningful program evaluation must be *appropriate within the context of the setting.* Agency attitudes and philosophies must be considered, as well as operational priorities. No one is going to get excited about program evaluation if it disrupts the entire agency schedule and operation on a day-to-day basis. This does not mean evaluation is not important; it does mean that it needs to be tempered with good judgment and some public-relations efforts.

characteristics of program evaluation

Basic program evaluation, as presented in this chapter, has a variety of characteristics that are important to identify and that refine our understanding of the term.

Program evaluation is part of *comprehensive program planning.* Sequentially, the steps are to

1. conceptualize the program;
2. design the program, including terminal objectives, enabling objectives, performance measures, and the content and process (TLAs) for each EO;
3. develop the implementation plan; and
4. design the evaluation plan.

Determining at the outset what information, procedures, and levels of evaluation are needed or desired simplifies the total process and makes it more relevant. Discrepancy program evaluation cannot be conducted after a program is terminated. Data need to be collected throughout the program and that means that the plans for its collection must be determined and developed prior to implementation.

Program evaluation is also an ongoing process during *program operation.* The basic evaluation questions normally asked in program evaluation are ones that require continuous attention. The most useful data are collected after each session. No staff member should be expected to remember details about some activity or session that occurred ten weeks before. Useful and accurate information is best obtained as the program is implemented on a regular basis.

Program evaluation is part of the *implementation strategy.* Time needs to be built into the implementation schedule for the required evaluation tasks. For some programs, allocated evaluation time is a regular aspect of each session. For other programs, it is every fourth session. And for yet others, it is at the end of the program. This does not mean that the evaluation is necessarily separate from the program's operation. Many performance measures can be assessed while regular program activities are going on. Nevertheless, program evaluation takes time and thus should be considered in scheduling and planning.

In addition to the observations that take place when clients are present, time is also needed to assemble and record the data. This time should be counted as part of the implementation and operation of the program.

Program evaluation is conducted primarily by *the person who conducts the program*. Program evaluation, at the level we are presenting it, is within the expertise and assumed responsibilities of the therapeutic recreator who conducts the program. Few agencies have the resources to hire outside evaluators or to have their own staff evaluation expert. Although there is some controversy over who can conduct evaluations objectively, we feel that practicality and feasibility must be taken into account. It is worth sacrificing some objectivity in order to have program evaluation operate on a wide-scale basis.

Program evaluation has many levels of sophistication. The characteristics we have identified place our version of evaluation somewhere between massive evaluation efforts conducted by teams of experts and evaluation efforts that may ask good questions but do not systematically collect and analyze data. The references suggested at the end of this chapter supply the reader with countless resources if higher levels of evaluation design and research are of interest.

discrepancy evaluation

The method of program evaluation we favor is called discrepancy evaluation.[6] In simplest terms, discrepancy evaluation compares actual outcomes with desired or planned outcomes. The area of difference, or discrepancy, between the real and intended outcomes isolates the area for investigation. It leads to the identification of factors that can be changed to improve the program. Answers to questions relevant to the components of the program's design and operation help to explain the discrepancies. Evaluation is concerned with three basic areas: inputs, process, and outcomes (fig. 13–1).

input

Input refers to necessary people and objects involved in the program. Normally, the input of a therapeutic recreation program is comprised of (1) staff, (2) clients, (3) supplies, (4) facilities, and (5) funding.

The program and implementation plans, as presented in chapters nine and twelve, describe the need to specify the characteristics of input

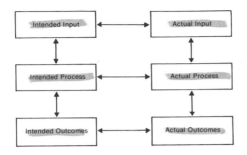

Fig. 13–1
Discrepancy Evaluation Model*

in the design stage. Later, during evaluation, the question will be asked, "Was the program implemented as designed?" The actual input will be compared to the intended input. If there is a discrepancy between the two, it may well explain why desired outcomes were not achieved. For example, suppose that the implementors did not have the required training and that certain staff skills were necessary to enable clients to achieve the program objectives. This discrepancy could explain deficient program results and point to an area of program improvement, e.g., provide the necessary staff training or select staff who have the training. If this was the true cause of the problem, and if staff changes were made or training provided, one would expect the program to come closer to its desired performance the next time it was implemented.

The clients are considered to be input. Programs are usually designed for specific individuals. When there is a discrepancy between the actual clients involved in a program and the description of clients for whom the program was intended, program revisions or a different screening procedure may be in order.

Designated supplies, facilities, and funding are also considered input. Discrepancy between actual and intended outcomes can often be explained by investigating differences in these areas.

process

Process refers to the actions (TLAs) described in the program plan. A systems-designed program specifies the content and process that are to be used to achieve the program's objectives. In the evaluation, a careful investigation of the process is undertaken. There are two major areas of concern. First, were the designated content and process followed? Sec-

*Adapted from Robert E. Stake, "The Countenance of Educational Evaluation," *Teachers College Record*, 68, no. 7 (April 1967), 523–40.

ond, were the activities and processes that were implemented appropriate and useful in achieving the objectives? Here again is the concept of intended versus actual. If a program was not implemented as designed, one can understand its failure to achieve objectives. Sometimes implementation problems have nothing to do with the program, per se. Other priorities at a treatment facility, for example, could prevent sessions from taking place or disrupt the operation of a given session. In this case, the evaluator can explain the failure of the program, but may not need to make program revisions. In other cases, the program may not have been feasible to implement as designed because of problems in the program's design, e.g., too much or too little content for a given session. Here the evaluator has specific information to work with in actual program revision.

Part of the process of evaluation is to investigate the activities and interactions designed for the program. The designer wants to know how well they worked and what improvements can be made. The implementor is, therefore, asked to keep an account of the session's process in order to provide information for revision. The best ideas of the designer can prove inadequate in the actual operation of a program. Much of the task of evaluation, consequently, is checking out and attempting to improve the content and process of the program, thus increasing the probability of achieving desired objectives.

outcomes

Intended outcomes are the terminal performance objectives (TPOs) and enabling objectives (EOs) of a program. The designer selects them with great consideration and formulates the performance measures to assess the achievement of the desired outcomes. In the evaluation process, the implementor checks and records the progress toward the attainment of the objectives. Usually the first evaluation question asked is, "Did the clients achieve the objectives?" Normally some standard is predetermined for a program, e.g., "We will consider this program effective if 80 percent of the clients reach 90 percent of the objectives." Checking intended outputs against program results provides the necessary information for judging program effectiveness.

The gap between actual and intended outcomes is equally important for revision decisions. The question, Did we reach our desired level of attainment of objectives? must be followed with the question, What aspects of the program contributed to or hindered the achievement of the objectives? The evaluator wants to know precisely what parts of the program were good or bad. Only this type of information will lead to solid revisions. It is always possible for clients to reach objectives by chance or even despite the program. The program designer is, consequently, interested in knowing if the designated activities and process of the program contributed to the achievement of the objectives. Questions about why the program did or did not work focus on inputs and process of the program.

The discrepancy evaluation model depends on well-constructed programs that show logical relationships between input, process, and outcomes. Thus, program results can be compared to the intended plan, and changes can be made about its design and operation.

evaluation questions

The four evaluation questions that follow are central to a basic evaluation plan. They provide the mechanism to collect the data about program effectiveness. Although the questions are simple, the answers provide meaningful evidence for later decision making and program improvement.

what are the effects (or outcomes) of the program?

Central to all evaluation is information related to the program's effectiveness. In a systems-designed program, this question is answered by looking at how many clients achieved how many objectives. A performance score sheet (table 13–1) provides the instrumentation needed to record program results. This form provides a format for the implementor to record when clients have achieved the designated objectives of the program. Basic mathematical calculations can be used to determine the percentage of clients who achieve the objectives.

In addition to reporting results, the performance score sheet allows the implementor to discover quickly the *enabling objectives that are problematic* for clients in general. The vertical columns can easily be scanned and problem EOs identified. This information should immediately alert the designer and implementor. Problems surrounding an EO can be involved with implementation or with the designed process and content. In either case, investigation and possible revisions are called for.

Scanning the horizontal rows indicated *individuals* who are having difficulty. This information can then be related to input descriptions. Are these individuals who do not fit the characteristics of the population for which the program was designed? If this is true, it may mean that the program is still effective and appropriate, but that the individuals in question should not have been involved in the program. If the individuals having difficulty are of the target population, investigation and revisions to the program are definitely called for.

Regardless of whether the program is judged effective or not, information from the performance score sheet should be used to help un-

PERFORMANCE SCORE SHEET

Term _Fall_

Course _Drama_

Instructor _Brothers, Warner_

X = Able to perform before instruction
O = Not able to perform before instruction
⊖ = Unable to perform after instruction
⊗ = Able to perform after instruction

	TPO 1:EO 1 - Voice Projection	EO 2 - Voice Inflection	EO 3 - Facial Expression	EO 4 - Eye Contact	EO 5 - Gestures	EO 6 - Gracefulness	TPO 2:EO 1 - Charm	EO 2 - Beauty	EO 3 - Versatility
1. Charming, Prince	⊗	⊗	⊗	⊗	⊗	⊗	⊗	⊖	
2. Ella, Cinder	⊖	⊗	⊗	⊗	⊗	⊗	⊗	⊗	
3. Fudd, Elmer	⊗	⊗	⊗	⊗	⊗	⊖	⊗	⊗	
4. Hood, Robin	⊗	⊗	⊗	⊗	⊗	⊗	⊗	⊗	
5. Mouse, Minnie	⊗	⊖	⊗	⊗	⊗	⊗	⊗	⊗	
6. Ridinghood, Red	⊖	⊗	⊗	⊗	⊗	⊗	⊗	⊗	
7. Robin, Christopher	⊗	⊗	⊗	⊗	⊗	⊗	⊗	⊖	
8. Oil, Olive	⊗	⊗	⊖	⊖	⊗	⊗	⊖	⊗	
9. Vanwinkle, Rip	⊖	⊗	⊗	⊖	⊖	⊖	⊖	⊖	
10. White, Snow	⊗	⊗	⊗	⊗	⊗	⊗	⊗	⊗	
11. Zel, Rapun	⊗	⊗	⊗	⊗	⊗	⊗	⊗	⊗	

Table 13-1

derstand the program's design and operation. If the program was effective, the designer will want to know if effectiveness was the result of the program's process and content or of chance factors. If the program had problems, the evaluator will want to know where the problems are and how they may be corrected. Both concerns require that the evaluator ask additional questions.

was the program implemented as designed?

If a program does not achieve its desired objectives, the first area of investigation is implementation. Programs are planned with specific numbers of sessions, lengths of sessions, and content for sessions. If there is a disruption in the implementation of these sessions, program effects can be described and explained. There may be no need for a program to be revised. Examples are sessions constantly missed due to conflicting scheduling or outdoor programs canceled due to bad weather. In these cases, improvement could result simply by rescheduling or extending the programs.

A *post session report* form is used for gathering information about implementation. This form can be a simple checklist or ask for short, narrative answers. Questions are of this nature:

1. Was the content on the sequence sheet followed in this session? If not, why not?
2. Was the time designated on the sequence sheet followed? If not, why not?

An example of a monitoring form appears in figure 13–2.

Information of this nature gives vital input to judging program effectiveness and indicates areas for possible change. Such a form is completed at the end of each session when information is fresh and easily recalled by the implementor.

If a program has specific requirements for equipment, supplies, and facilities, the evaluator needs to know if they were available and used. Again, the postsession report form can be of value here. Questions about whether necessary supplies and facilities were available can be added to the form for easy, continuous recording.

Staffing is another input area that is related to implementation. In most cases, the evaluator can simply observe the staff members involved and determine whether they meet the specifications on the implementation plan. No instrumentation is needed. However, the evaluator must still determine whether staff implemented the program as designed.

The last area of vital concern regarding implementation relates to clients. Program results need to be cross-checked with the designated

LEISURE LEARNING EXPERIENCE MONITOR FORM

TPO _____
EO _____

1. The amount of time spent on this LLE was that amount recommended by the materials. If not, why not?

   _____   _____
   YES   NO

2. The presentation medium used on this LLE was that which
   was specified by the materials. If not, why not?

   _____   _____
   YES   NO

3. The content of this LLE was stated similarly to that specified
   in the materials. If not, why not?

   _____   _____
   YES   NO

4. The sequence of the session content was similar to that specified in the materials. If not, why not?

   _____   _____
   YES   NO

5. The content of this LLE was implemented as specified in the
   materials. If not, why not?

   _____   _____
   YES   NO

6. List the subjects not present for this LLE.

7. Other comments:

Fig. 13–2*

clientele described on the implementation sheet. "Were the right clients
involved in the program?" The basic instrument for collecting this information is a client information sheet (fig. 13–3). This form covers all the
necessary information about a client. The content of the form varies with
different populations or settings. In essence, however, it should identify
all factors that might relate to client achievement. Such a form allows the
evaluator to determine whether individuals fit the designated population
description as well as to identify other characteristics related to the
achievement of program objectives.

The client information sheet can be completed by several different
methods. Sometimes the information needed is readily available from
existing records within the agency. In other situations, it is filled out by
the client or during an interview with the client. In some community-
based recreation or instructional programs, the information can be obtained as part of the registration process. Regardless of the method of

*Used with permission of the designer, Ken Joswiak

CLIENT INFORMATION SHEET

SEX _____

AGE _____

MARITAL STATUS _____

RESIDENCE

    STREET _____

    CITY _____

    PHONE _____

LIVING SITUATION _____
_____

EMPLOYMENT _____
_____

EDUCATION _____
_____

PRIMARY MODE OF TRANSPORTATION _____
_____

SOCIOECONOMIC BACKGROUND _____
_____

LEVEL AND TYPE OF DISABILITY _____
_____
_____

Fig. 13–3

collection, the instrument should contain all items that the program designer feels are necessary in determining possible reasons (or explanations) for success or failure within the program.

was the process of the program appropriate?

Assuming that the program was implemented as designed, the
evaluator turns to questions regarding the actual activities and interactions specified in the program plan. The major interest here is determin-

ing whether the program's content and process were appropriate to the achievement of the objectives. This information is of concern basically for the revision and improvement of the program. The designer wants to know, as specifically as possible, whether the designated content and process facilitated the achievement of the performance measures. The implementors, again, are the best persons to make suggestions for improvement. They can evaluate the specific activities and designated interactions, and give opinions about sequencing and time allotments. The instrument most useful for collecting this data is the *postsession report* form. Along with the implementation factors on the form, questions can be asked about the activities used and their appropriateness, the designated processes of the session, sequencing, timing, and any other considerations of interest. Again, the format can be of several different types: checklists, open-ended questions, narratives, or scales. Examples of such instrumentation appear in figures 13–4 and 13–5. The amount of detail for this instrument is left to the designer and depends on the time available and level of evaluation necessary. The more detail asked for on the form, the more accurate and specific the revision.

It is common to ask clients and/or staff to give their impressions of the program. Figures 13–6 and 13–7 illustrate sample questionnaires for this purpose. Normally, such questionnaires are administered at the conclusion of a program and thus detailed information about specific enabling objectives or sessions is not as easily identified.

what were the unanticipated outcomes of the program?

Many unexpected things happen in therapeutic recreation programs: some good, some bad, and some in between. An evaluation plan should consider these factors along with the predetermined questions that are asked. Although no specific instrument is used to collect this information, the implementor should keep an ear and an eye out for any information about the program. Both effectiveness statements and revision decisions can be made on such information. Jotting down anecdotes, observations, and comments from others is a good way to preserve this important information. Often, information gathered in this way comes from clients and staff. A statement such as, "I never realized how important play is to my recovery and health," is perhaps as significant a result of a program as is the achievement of a set of objectives. Unsolicited information still needs to be documented and reported as part of the final evaluation.

Many unanticipated things affect the outcomes of programs. Staff attitudes change, money becomes available, families get involved, clients

Date _____

LEISURE COUNSELING SESSION EVALUATION FORM

TPO _____

EO _____

Please fill out the following form using the key provided. One (1) indicates strongly agree and five (5) indicates strongly disagree on the scale. Please make any comments in the space provided.

1. The time allowed for this leisure-counseling session was sufficient to allow the subjects to learn the material presented.
   Comments:

1	2	3	4	5
SA				SD

2. The presentation media used were helpful in the instruction of the subjects.
   Comments:

1	2	3	4	5
SA				SD

3. The content of this leisure-counseling session was appropriate for the leisure education of the subjects.
   Comments:

1	2	3	4	5
SA				SD

4. The content of this leisure-counseling session was presented clearly and in an orderly sequence.
   Comments:

1	2	3	4	5
SA				SD

5. General comments:

Fig. 13–4*

*Used with permission of the designer, Ken Joswiak.

Session Number _____

POSTSESSION REPORT

APPROACH

	Strongly Agree				Strongly Disagree
1. The sequence of activities is appropriate. Observations and comments.	1	2	3	4	5
2. The activities are appropriate to the population. Observations and comments.	1	2	3	4	5
3. The time allotment for the activities is appropriate. Observations and comments.	1	2	3	4	5
4. The interaction techniques are appropriate to the population. Observations and comments.	1	2	3	4	5

Fig. 13–5*

Name _____

Date _____

POSTPROGRAM SUBJECT INTERVIEW

1. What did you like about the leisure counseling program? Why?

2. What didn't you like about the leisure counseling program? Why?

3. What were the benefits for you of the leisure counseling program? Explain.

Fig. 13–6**

*Used with permission of the designer, Bob Frost.

**Used with permission of the designer, Ken Joswiak.

POSTPROGRAM STAFF INTERVIEW

1. Have you witnessed any beneficial effects of the leisure counseling program?

2. Have you witnessed any negative effects of the leisure counseling program?

3. What were the program's best qualities?

4. What leisure issues did the program fail to address?

5. Was there enough time adequately to cover the subject of leisure counseling?

6. Could you make any suggestions or comments concerning the leisure counseling program?

Fig. 13–7*

grow. It is significant to record and report such information. Noting these unanticipated changes allows the implementor and evaluator to become sensitive to and aware of both advantages and problems.

the evaluation plan

The designer develops the evaluation plan as part of the total program plan. This plan, accompanied by the developed program materials and implementation plan, completes the comprehensive program design. The evaluation plan indicates what information is needed to evaluate the program's effectiveness, as well as to identify areas for revision. The plan, which is developed prior to program implementation, specifies what major evaluation questions will be addressed and when and how data will be collected. This information then allows for the development of instrumentation and for the determination of a schedule for collecting data, which will be followed throughout the program. *A basic evaluation plan describes six stages of development for each evaluation question asked.* An evaluation plan worksheet helps to clarify the stages and tasks involved. A sample evaluation worksheet appears in figure 13–8. A description of each of the six steps follows.

*Used with permission of the designer, Ken Joswiak.

EVALUATION PLAN WORKSHEET

Evaluation Question	Variables	Source of Data	Method of Collecting Data	When Data Is To Be Collected	Treatment of Data

Fig. 13–8

steps

*Step 1. **State the Evaluation Question.*** Four basic evaluation questions have previously been discussed. The evaluation plan starts by asking one of them. In addition to the four questions already presented, other questions could be asked, such as:

1. Are the program objectives appropriate for the designated population?
2. Are the program objectives theoretically valid?

*Step 2. **Determine the Variables.*** Each evaluation question is broken down into subquestions called variables. These are the specific questions asked in order to obtain the information needed to answer to broader concern. For example, the evaluation question dealing with implementation might have the following variables:

1. number of staff involved,
2. qualifications of staff involved,
3. number of clients involved,
4. disabilities of clients involved,
5. presence of necessary supplies,
6. availability of required facility,
7. number of sessions completed,
8. length of sessions, and
9. content of session as specified.

Each of these variables would be stated in question form. For example, the first variable would be phrased, "Were the designated number of staff present to conduct the program?"

*Step 3. **Sources of Data.*** Each variable is analyzed to determine the appropriate source of data to answer the question. The source of data for variable one would be the program implementor. This individual could readily determine if required staff were present throughout the program.

*Step 4. **Method of Collecting Data.*** This step identifies the instrument or method for collecting the needed information. In the case of variable one, an item could easily be added to the postsession report form to record the presence or absence of required staff.

*Step 5. **When Data Are Collected.*** Some information is collected continuously. An illustration is the absence or presence of required staff. This information would need to be recorded after each session. Evaluation variables have different times for collection. "The characteristics of clients involved in the program," for example, would only need to be collected once. The appropriate time for collecting this data would be at the beginning of the program. Thus, column 5 in figure 13–8 might read, "Before or within the first week of implementation."

Step 6. Treatment of the Data. This step indicates how the information related to each variable will be treated. In discrepancy evaluation, the basic form of treatment is simply to describe the data. This implies writing down the answers to subquestions. Objectively reporting the information allows the decision maker to survey the material and decide on what needs to be done. At the level of evaluation presented in this chapter, no complicated statistics need to be used. In more sophisticated evaluation plans, data might involve statistical analysis.

analysis

The evaluation plan worksheet provides a column for each variable. At the end of the process, the designer has a complete picture of what data are needed, how and when they should be collected, and what instruments need to be developed for collecting the information. Necessary instrumentation is then designed, followed by the scheduling for data collection.

At this point in the planning process, preparation for program implementation can begin. The program materials are ready, the implementation schedule determined, and the evaluation plan and instruments developed. Necessary preparation may include staff training, ordering of supplies, scheduling of rooms, or whatever is required to launch the program. Once under way, continuous monitoring and data recording are completed as scheduled. Designated evaluation periods are used for analysis of data, revision decisions, and judgments of program effectiveness.

summary

Program evaluation planning is the third and final aspect of total systems-program design. It serves the vital function of specifying what information is needed to substantiate the program's performance, as well as indicating areas for possible revisions for improvement. Evaluation conceptualized in this manner is part of the comprehensive program-planning and implementation effort and is cyclical in its contribution to program effectiveness. Its levels of sophistication vary, but its purpose remains the same: improvement of the delivery system to enhance the development of the leisure life styles of clients engaged in therapeutic recreation services.

notes

[1] Carol H. Weiss, *Evaluation Research: Methods of Assessing Program Effectiveness* (Englewood Cliffs, N.J.: Prentice-Hall, Inc., 1972), p. 1.

[2] Diane Kyker Yavorsky, *Discrepancy Evaluation: A Practitioner's Guide* (Charlottesville, Va.: University of Virginia, Evaluation Research Center, 1976).

[3] Robert E. Stake, "The Countenance of Educational Evaluation," *Teachers College Record*, 68, no. 7 (April 1967), 523–40.

[4] Michael Scriven, "The Methodology of Evaluation," in *Perspectives of Curriculum Evaluation*, ed. Ralph Tyler, Robert M. Gagne, and Michael Scriven (Chicago, Ill.: Rand McNally and Company, AERA Monograph Series on Curriculum Evaluation, no. 1, 1967), pp. 39–83.

[5] Ibid.

[6] Information presented on discrepancy evaluation is adapted from two evaluation models and approaches, primarily taken from Stake, "Countenance of Evaluation," pp. 523–40, and Yavorsky, *Discrepancy Evaluation*, pp. 47–84.

suggested references

AMERICAN INSTITUTES FOR RESEARCH, *Evaluative Research Strategies and Methods.* Pittsburgh, Pa.: American Institutes for Research, 1970.

ARONSON, S. H., AND C. C. SHERWOOD, "Researcher Versus Practitioner: Problems in Social Action Research," *Social Work*, 12, no. 4 (1967), 89–96.

BATEMAN, W., "Assessing Program Effectiveness: A Rating System for Identifying Relative Program Success," *Welfare in Review*, 6, no. 1 (1968), 1–10.

BEATTY, W. H., ed., *Improving Educational Assessment and an Inventory of Measures of Affective Behavior.* Washington, D.C.: Association for Supervision and Curriculum Development, NEA, 1969.

BLOOM, B. S., ed., *Taxonomy of Educational Objectives, Handbook I: Cognitive Domain.* New York: Longmans, Green, 1956.

BLUM, H. L., AND A. R. LEONARD, "Evaluation Research and Demonstration," in *Public Administration: A Public Health Viewpoint*, pp. 286–322. New York: Macmillan Publishing Company, 1963.

BONJEAN, C. M., R. J. HILL, AND S. D. McLEMORE, *Sociological Measurement: An Inventory of Scales and Indices.* San Francisco, Calif.: Chandler Publishing Co., 1967.

BORGATTA, E., "Research Problems in Evaluation of Health Service Demonstrations," Part 2, *Milbank Memorial Fund Quarterly*, 44, no. 4 (1966), 182–99.

BRIM, O. G., JR., "Evaluating the Effects of Parent Education," *Journal of Marriage and Family Living*, 19 (February 1957), 54–60.

BROOKS, M. P., "The Community Action Program as a Setting for Applied Research," *Journal of Social Issues*, 21, no. 1 (1965), 29–40.

BRUNNER, E. DE S., "Evaluation Research in Adult Education," *International Review of Community Development*, nos. 17–18 (1967), 97–102.

BUROS, O., ed., *Sixth Mental Measurements Yearbook*. Highland Park, N.J.: Gryphon Press, 1965.

CAMPBELL, D. T., "Administrative Experimentation, Institutional Records, and Nonreactive Measures," in *Improving Experimental Design and Statistical Analysis*, ed. J. C. Stanley, pp. 257–91. Chicago, Ill.: Rand McNally & Company, 1967.

CARO, F. G., "Approaches to Evaluative Research: A Review," *Human Organization*, 28, no. 2 (1969), 87–99.

———, "Issues in the Evaluation of Special Programs," *Review of Educational Research*, 41, no. 2 (1971), 87–114.

———, ed., *Readings in Evaluation Research*. New York: Russell Sage Foundation, 1971.

CHERNEY, P. R., ed., *Making Evaluation Research Useful*. Columbia, Md.: American City Corporation, 1971.

DAILY, E. F., AND M. A. MOREHEAD, "A Method of Evaluating and Improving the Quality of Medical Care," *American Journal of Public Health*, 46, no. 7 (1956), 848–54.

DENISTON, O. L., I. M. ROSENSTOCK, AND V. A. GETTING, "Evaluation of Program Effectiveness," *Public Health Reports*, 83, no. 4 (1968), 323–35.

DOWD, D. J., AND S. C. WEST, "An Inventory of Measures of Affective Behavior," in *Improving Educational Assessment and an Inventory of Measures of Affective Behavior*, ed. W. H. Beatty, pp. 90–158. Washington, D.C.: Association for Supervision and Curriculum Development, NEA (1969).

ERIC, Clearinghouse on Tests, Measurement and Evaluation. Princeton, N.J.: Educational Testing Service.

EVANS, J. W., "Evaluating Social Action Programs," *Social Science Quarterly*, 50, no. 3 (1969), 568–81.

FERMAN, L. A., "Some Perspectives on Evaluating Social Welfare Programs," *Annals of the American Academy of Political and Social Science*, 385 (September 1969), 143–56.

FOX, D. J., "Issues in Evaluating Programs for Disadvantaged Children," *Urban Review*, 2 (December 1967), 7, 9, 11.

GRONLUND, N., ed., *Readings in Measurement and Evaluation*. New York: Macmillan Publishing Company, 1968.

GUBA, E. G., AND D. L. STUFFLEBEAM, *Evaluation: The Process of Stimulating, Aiding and Abetting Insightful Action*. Columbus, Ohio: Ohio State University, Evaluation Center, 1968.

HAYES, S. P., *Evaluating Development Projects: A Manual for the Use of Field Workers*. Paris: UNESCO, 1966.

HERZOG, E., *Some Guide Lines for Evaluative Research*. Washington, D.C.: U.S. Department of Health, Education and Welfare, 1959.

HESSELING, P., "Principles of Evaluation," *Social Compass*, 11, no. 1 (1964), 5–22.

HILL, M. J., AND H. T. BLANE, "Evaluation of Psychotherapy with Alcoholics," *Quarterly Journal of Studies on Alcohol,* 28, no. 1 (1967), 76–104.

HUTCHISON, G. B., "Evaluation of Preventive Services," *Journal of Chronic Diseases,* 11, no. 5 (1960), 497–508.

HYMAN, H., AND C. R. WRIGHT, "Evaluating Social Action Programs," in *The Uses of Sociology,* ed. P. F. Lazarsfeld, W. H. Sewell, and H. L. Wilensky, pp. 741–82. New York: Basic Books, Inc. Publishers, 1967

JAMES, G., "Planning and Evaluation of Health Programs," in *Administration of Community Health Services,* pp. 114–34. Chicago, Ill.: International City Managers Association, 1961.

KELMAN, H. R., "An Experiment in the Rehabilitation of Nursing Home Patients," *Public Health Reports,* no. 77 (April 1962), 356–66.

LEMKAU, P. V., AND B. PASAMANICK, "Problems in Evaluation of Mental Health Programs," *American Journal of Orthopsychiatry,* 27, no. 1 (1957), 55–58.

LERMAN, P., "Evaluative Studies of Institutions for Delinquents: Implications for Research and Social Policy," *Social Work,* 12, no. 4 (1968), 55–64.

LEVINSON, P., "Evaluation of Social Welfare Programs: Two Research Models," *Welfare in Review,* 4, no. 10 (1966), 5–12.

LORTIE, D. C., "Rational Decision-Making: Is it Possible Today?" *The EPIE Forum,* 1 (1967), 6–9.

MCINTYRE, R. B., AND C. C. NELSON, "Empirical Evaluation of Instructional Materials," *Educational Technology,* 9, no. 2 (1969), 24–27.

MEDLEY, D. M., AND H. E. MITZEL, "Measuring Classroom Behavior by Systematic Observation," in *Handbook of Research on Teaching,* ed. N. L. Gage. Chicago, Ill.: Rand McNally, 1963.

MEYER, H. J., AND E. F. BORGATTA, *An Experiment in Mental Patient Rehabilitation.* New York: Russell Sage Foundation, 1959.

MILLER, D. C., *Handbook of Research Design and Social Measurement.* New York: David McKay Co., Inc., 1964.

OTT, J. M., "Classification System for Decision Situations: An Aid to Educational Planning and Evaluation," *Educational Technology,* 9, no. 2 (1969), 20–23.

PATTISON, E. M., R. COE, AND R. J. RHODES, "Evaluation of Alcoholism Treatment: A Comparison of Three Facilities," *Archives of General Psychiatry,* 20, no. 4 (1969), 478–88.

RIECKEN, H. W., "Memorandum on Program Evaluation," in *Evaluating Action Programs: Readings in Social Action and Education,* ed. Carol H. Weiss, pp. 85–104. Boston, Mass.: Allyn & Bacon, Inc., 1972.

ROSENBLATT, A., "The Practitioner's Use and Evaluation of Research," *Social Work,* 13, no. 1 (1968), 53–59.

SCHULBERG, H. C., AND F. BAKER, "Program Evaluation Models and the Implementation of Research Findings," *American Journal of Public Health,* 58, no. 7 (1968), 1248–55.

SCHULBERG, H. C., A. SHELDON, AND F. BAKER, eds., *Program Evaluation in the Health Fields*. New York: Behavioral Publications, Inc., 1970.

SCRIVEN, M., "The Methodology of Evaluation," in *Perspectives of Curriculum Evaluation*, ed. R. W. Tyler, R. M. Gagné, and M. Scriven, pp. 39–83. AERA Monograph Series on Curriculum Evaluation, no. 1. Chicago, Ill.: Rand McNally & Co., 1967.

SJOGREN, D. D., "Measurement Techniques in Evaluation," *Review of Educational Research*, 40, no. 2 (1970), 301–20.

STAKE, R. E., "The Countenance of Educational Evaluation," *Teachers College Record*, 68, no. 7 (1967), 523–40.

———, "Objectives, Priorities, and Other Judgment Data," *Review of Educational Research*, 40 (1970), 181–212.

STEWARD, M. A., "The Role and Function of Educational Research, I," *Educational Research*, 9, no. 1 (1966), 3–6.

STUFFLEBEAM, D. L., "Evaluation as Enlightenment for Decision Making." Address delivered at the Working Conference on Assessment Theory, sponsored by the Commission on Assessment of Education Outcomes and the Association for Supervision and Curriculum Development, Sarasota, Florida, January 19, 1968. Columbus, Ohio: Ohio State University, College of Education, The Evaluation Center.

———, "Evaluation as Enlightenment for Decision Making," in *Improving Educational Assessment and an Inventory of Measures of Affective Behavior*, ed. W. H. Beatty, pp. 41–73. Washington, D.C.: Association for Supervision and Curriculum Development, NEA (1969).

STUFFLEBEAM, D. L., et al., *Educational Evaluation and Decision Making*. Itasca, Ill.: F. E. Peacock Publishers, Inc., 1971.

SUCHMAN, EDWARD A., "A Model for Research and Evaluation on Rehabilitation," in *Sociology and Rehabilitation*, ed. Marvin B. Sussman, pp. 52–70. Washington, D.C.: American Sociological Association, 1966.

———, *Evaluative Research: Principles and Practices in Public Service and Social Action Programs*. New York: Russell Sage Foundation, 1967.

TRIPODI, T., I. EPSTEIN, AND C. MACMURRAY, "Dilemmas in Evaluation: Implications for Administrators of Social Action Programs," *American Journal of Orthopsychiatry*, 40, no. 5 (1970), 850–57.

TYLER, R. W., R. M. GAGNÉ, AND M. SCRIVEN, *Perspectives of Curriculum Evaluation*. AERA Monograph Series on Curriculum Evaluation, no. 1. Chicago, Ill.: Rand McNally & Co., 1967.

WALBERG, H. J., "Curriculum Evaluation: Problems and Guidelines," *Teachers College Record*, 71, (1970), 557–70.

WEBB, E. J., D. T. CAMPBELL, R. D. SCHWARTZ, AND L. B. SECHREST, *Unobtrusive Measures: Nonreactive Research in the Social Sciences*. Chicago, Ill.: Rand McNally & Co., 1966.

WEISS, CAROL H., ed., *Evaluating Action Programs: Readings in Social Action and Education*. Boston: Allyn & Bacon, Inc. 1972.

WILLIAMS, WALTER, "Developing an Evaluation Strategy for a Social Action Agency," *Journal of Human Resources*, 4, no. 4 (1969), 451–65.

WORTHEN, B. R., "Toward a Taxonomy of Evaluation Designs," *Educational Technology*, 8, no. 15 (1968), 3–9.

YAVORSKY, D. K., *Discrepancy Evaluation: A Practitioner's Guide*. Charlottesville, Va.: University of Virginia, Evaluation Research Center, 1976.

3

management
concerns
in therapeutic
recreation

management philosophies and principles

PURPOSE: To discuss approaches to program management and staff utilization that attempt to capitalize on all available resources and allow for both individual and collective accountability and responsibility in the process of service delivery. Important variables in the management of client-centered programs are discussed, along with some basic principles of effective communication and staff motivation.

The preceding chapters have dealt with the process of program conceptualization, design, implementation, and evaluation. However, even the best-designed programs suffer without sound managerial philosophies and operational principles to back them up. Effective organizational management is being researched for all facets of service delivery; management research easily encompasses volumes. It would, indeed, be presumptuous for us to attempt to cover effectively, in this brief section, all of the managerial philosophies that relate to therapeutic recreation services. We have, however, found that certain basic, underlying managerial principles are particularly effective in our work, and offer them as food for thought. We refer those who want to know more to the selection of readings that appears at the end of the chapter.

The measurable variables that contribute to effective management include a balanced blending of all the elements presented in the preceding chapters. However, the personal characteristics and charisma of management staff, although unable to be measured, appears to contribute significantly to effective programming. We often comment on the "power of pizazz" and wish we knew how to build it into our educational and

275

professional development programs! Gerald O'Morrow states that management "is a tool for achieving objectives."[1] It provides the framework for maximizing human energy while maintaining orderliness and consistency. Unlike management designed to produce tangible, uniform products, the manager of a human-services delivery system must appreciate the uniqueness of each consumer. Organizational styles may sound good on paper but often conflict with client development. Therefore, we want to point out the *philosophical* differences between the traditional organizational flow charts and to introduce one that is specifically designed to facilitate appreciation for, and development of, individual client needs.

philosophies of organizational style

The traditional organizational flow chart appears intrinsically to perpetuate responsibility upward to superiors (fig. 14–1).

This style of autocractic governance most often assigns responsibility according to education and experience. Rarely discussed, it is assumed that lower-level staff members are responsible to and often seek to meet the expectations of the immediately superior supervisor. The hierarchy is maintained to the highest level of management. In industry, often the "top dog" presumably knows best, and the style has proven to be

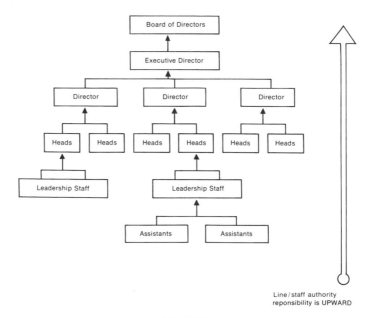

Fig. 14–1
Traditional Organizational Flow Chart

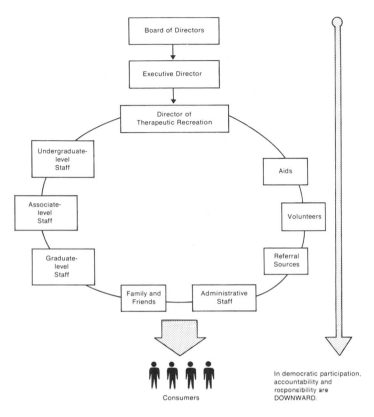

Fig. 14–2
Client-centered Organizational Flow Chart

effective. However, in human services, the top dog is very often too far removed from the needs of the consumers to know best, and should ideally use his or her power to facilitate the staff in their efforts to meet client needs. The philosophical difference is illustrated in figure 14–2. This diagram illustrates the necessary commitment by all staff members to meet the needs of the clients. Each employee and volunteer is responsible for effectively meeting these needs. Accountability for doing so is both individual and collective.

The traditional organizational flow chart shows the management assumption that the more educated and experienced individuals can provide the most effective and knowledgeable services, e.g., a therapeutic recreator with a master's degree is usually presumed to be a better counselor than the volunteer with no special education. In reality, this is often not true. We once observed a graduate-level musician who insisted that he was the most competent to facilitate group musical experiences, when, in fact, an untrained volunteer guitarist proved to be far superior. The point is simple: effective managers realize that effective leadership does not consistently correlate with educational status.

In therapeutic recreation, effective leadership often appears to correlate most highly with the quality of interpersonal relationships established between staff members and clients. For this reason, we strongly advocate the client-centered team approach to program implementation. The team member who is most effective with specific individuals or groups in specific activities should, whenever possible, be granted the leadership role, irrespective of status. Other team members, regardless of status, should then assist in all possible ways to facilitate their team member in meeting client needs.

When this management approach is used, we have noted the following positive effects on programming and staff morale:

1. There appears to be an increased sense of individual and group responsibility and accountability. Rather than competing for individual status, staff members learn from, share with, and assist each other in tasks.
2. Each staff member's repertoire of skills is expanded by working with other team members, e.g., the individual skilled in sports may work with the musically inclined staff member, thereby acquiring additional skills in facilitating musically oriented activities.
3. The possibility for creative programming is greatly increased by various staff members working together, e.g., a music specialist may provide a mood for an art specialist to encourage visual expressions of self.
4. Evaluation of various programs is more objective in that staff members are able to observe each other and clients in a variety of settings.
5. Continuity of programming is more likely to be achieved because all of the staff is working toward the same end, that of meeting client needs.

This management philosophy is not intended to preempt existing organizational structures, nor should it be presumed that all therapeutic recreators can work together as a team. Certain decentralized programs operate with individual units, such as day camping programs or institutional programs having several residential units. In these cases, this managerial philosophy extends beyond therapeutic recreators to all disciplines involved in programming, including volunteers.

interaction philosophies

In terms of a personal, philosophical commitment to have meaningful encounters with clients in various therapeutic recreation settings, we encourage staff to adhere to the following beliefs:

We believe in the client's inalienable right to self-determination (to the greatest possible extent) throughout the treatment, education, or recreation process. As therapeutic recreation leaders, we believe in confrontation with support, and in the total staff and/or therapeutic community working together within a reality-based environment. Specifically, this means that we believe in the concepts of:

1. staying in touch with the "here and now," with the clients and with ourselves;
2. personal involvement with clients and involvement of clients in their own therapeutic process;
3. achievable objectives in terms of success;
4. contract and commitment between staff and clients, and ongoing assessment and evaluation of status, because we believe that both staff and client can and should learn to take responsibility for their actions and feelings.

effective communication in management

When staff is asked to identify problems with management, invariably effective communication wins. We are certainly convinced of the necessity of effective communication in the management process; we are also convinced that the responsibility for facilitating it is *not* the *sole* responsibility of top management. Several managerial decisions help to open up communications, but the process succeeds or fails at the level of *individual* interaction.

individual responsibility

Three major factors contribute to the breakdown of communication between individuals: (1) lack of self-awareness about basic feelings of pain, anger, fear, and joy; (2) if and when feelings are recognized, an unwillingness or inability to express those feelings effectively; and (3) the ease with which blaming others allows individuals to discount personal responsibility for communicating effectively.

Most of us learn very early to deny, discount, or ignore our basic feelings. Most typically, little boys are asked to fake it when feeling pain or fear, and little girls are often denied the right to their anger. It is usual also to subdue our expressions of joy when we reach maturity lest we appear childish. As adults yearning for open communication, we often overlook the necessity of acknowledging our feelings about situations that occur in both our personal and professional lives. A common incident on the job, which invariably breaks down communication, is when a staff member feels that her or his opinion has been overlooked or discounted, and, in defense of self, responds angrily to cover over the deeper feeling of hurt. Compare "If you don't care about my opinion, then I won't help with that assignment" (anger), to "I felt overlooked in the decision-making process and am, therefore, having difficulty enjoying my work." Honestly *identifying* personal feelings is the first step to effective communication.

Effectively *expressing* feelings is the second step to meaningful communication and requires claiming rather than blaming. The blame game always begins with an actual or implied *you*—"You ignored me" or "You made me angry." When you is implied or stated, a misunderstanding follows. Claiming rather than blaming involves four components of expression:

1. a restatement of the stimulus situation ("A decision was made without my input.");
2. an acknowledgement of the behavioral response ("I lost interest in helping.");
3. claiming the *feeling* (" . . . because I felt left out and ignored.");
4. asking for what is wanted or needed (" . . . and, in the future, I would appreciate it if you would ask my opinion before decisions are made that affect my work.").

Claiming rather than blaming requires a few simple but critical changes in communication styles:

1. "You's" are replaced with "I's."
2. "It's" are replaced with "I's." E.g., "It makes me angry" is replaced with "I feel angry."
3. Desires for future action are expressed.
4. The appropriate person is confronted. E.g., rather than talking about someone, talk *to* that person.

managerial responsibilities

Managers can and should enhance the individual communication process by adhering to these principles:

1. Consistently seek input from all staff and implement as many changes as possible relative to the acquired input.
2. Inform staff immediately about decisions made by managers and explain the rationale behind the decisions. Decisions made on the basis of "because-I-say-so" logic is not effective with children and certainly not with adults. Staff should also receive relevant information directly and promptly from managers, rather than via the grapevine.
3. When inhouse problems occur, bring in all persons involved and confront them *together* about the situation. Individual interviews with staff members involved in conflict very often only intensify the problem, whereas open confrontation forces the issue and pressures individuals to resolve conflicts fairly.

blocks to staff motivation

The topic of motivation has been researched extensively. "How do I motivate my staff?" is a common question that managers ask and one that is most often dealt with philosophically rather than realistically. It is our firm belief that managers cannot motivate anyone to do anything! However, managers can recognize the factors that keep individuals from being motivated and remove those blocks to motivation.

Blocks to motivation depend on the situation. However, we have consistently identified the following factors as major elements that impair staff motivation:

Blocks to Staff Motivation	Managerial Action
1. Failure to recognize the value of staff members' input into decision making and problem solving.	1. Consistently seek input from staff.
2. Failure to acknowledge staff for good work.	2. Appropriately praise staff.
3. Failure to pinpoint the shortcomings of staff.	3. Confront staff with shortcomings and offer constructive assistance and support.
4. Failure to provide direction when needed.	4. Some staff need more direction than others. Recognize this need and be available to give needed direction.
5. Lack of ongoing growth opportunities.	5. Structure ongoing, consistent opportunities for inservice education and staff development.
6. Lack of open communication.	6. Model and encourage others to follow approaches to open communication.

summary

Managerial philosophies within human-services delivery systems are distinctly different from the organizational management philosophies of industry. Management must believe in their clients' inalienable rights of independence and self-determination. This requires that staff and clients work together in supportive, reality-based environments that are conducive to growth. It requires a firm belief in the rights and abilities of all staff and clients to behave responsibly about their feelings, thoughts, and actions. Managers in all therapeutic recreation settings must hold the clients' well-being in the highest regard and strive to facilitate the greatest degrees of growth and enjoyment in the learning process. Managers must be firmly commited to the value of play behavior in the fully functioning person.

note

[1] Gerald S. O'Morrow, *Administration of Activity Therapy Service* (Springfield, Ill.: Charles C. Thomas, 1966), p. 247.

suggested references

BANNON, J. J., *Leisure Resources: Its Comprehensive Planning*. Englewood Cliffs, N.J.: Prentice-Hall, Inc., 1976.

BLAU, P. M., AND M. W. MEYER, *Bureaucracy in Modern Society* (2nd ed.). New York: Random House, 1956.

BRAMMER, L. M., *The Helping Relationship: Process and Skills*. Englewood Cliffs, N.J.: Prentice-Hall, Inc., 1973.

CAPLOW, T., *Principles of Organization*. New York: Harcourt Brace Jovanovich, 1964.

CARKHUFF, R. R., *Helping and Human Relations*. New York: Holt, Rinehart and Winston, Inc., 1969.

CARKHUFF, R. R., AND B. G. BERENSON, *Beyond Counseling and Therapy*. New York: Holt, Rinehart and Winston, Inc.,1967.

HALPIN, A. W., *Theory and Research in Administration*. New York: Macmillan Publishing Company, 1972.

MARCH, J. G., AND H. A. SIMON, *Organizations*. New York: John Wiley and Sons, Inc., 1958.

MICHAEL, J., *Personnel Management*. Homewood, Ill.: Richard D. Irwin, Inc., 1967.

MILLER, S., E. W. NUNNALLY, and D. B. WACKMAN, *Alive and Aware: Improving Communications in Relationships*. Minneapolis, Minn.: Interpersonal Communication Programs, Inc., 1975.

NEGGISON, L. C., *Personnel: A Behavioral Approach to Administration*. Homewood, Ill.: Richard D. Irwin, Inc., 1967.

O'MORROW, G. S., *Administration of Activity Therapy Service*. Springfield, Ill.: Charles C. Thomas, 1966.

SIMON, H. A., *Administrative Behavior* (2nd ed.). New York: Macmillan Publishing Co., 1957.

THOMPSON, J. D., *Organizations in Action*. New York: McGraw-Hill Book Co., 1967.

staffing and staff development

PURPOSE: To outline procedures for acquiring and keeping qualified staff members through systematic recruitment and selection processes and through ongoing staff development and training programs.

Acquiring and keeping qualified, effective staff members is one of the major functions of the program manager and is an integral part of a systems-designed program. Program conceptualization, design, implementation, and evaluation depend largely on the quality of staff involved in the process. For this reason, we want briefly to present procedures for acquiring qualified staff, and provide a procedural outline for conducting ongoing staff development that is relevant to the needs of individual agencies.

staffing

Hiring staff generally involves three aspects: (1) prerecruitment planning, (2) recruitment, and (3) selection.

prerecruitment planning

Efficient planning for staff hiring is very often the most tedious part of staffing. Perhaps because of this, its significance is often discounted. The following steps are critical and must precede actual recruitment:

1. Develop a specific and, when possible, comprehensive job description appropriate to the job. This is important to do for all jobs, regardless of level. If a job description already exists, it should be updated, using input from the staff most directly related to the tasks outlined. The job description should include the following information (see fig. 15–1):
   a. correct job title and position;
   b. general description of the job;
   c. specific job duties, including expected hours of work; and
   d. necessary qualifications—education and experience.
2. Establish the recruitment procedures to be followed. They include:
   a. establishing the time schedule for announcing the position, terminating applications, interviewing applicants, and making the final selection;
   b. determining the specific tasks to be performed, including preparing the announcement, determining the audience to receive the announcement, mailing the announcements, receiving and reviewing applications, interviewing applicants, selecting the staff member, and informing all applicants of the selection;
   c. assigning the responsibility for completing the tasks to appropriate persons.

JOB DESCRIPTION

DEPARTMENT OF THERAPEUTIC RECREATION

POSITION: Coordinator of therapeutic recreation services

DUTIES AND RESPONSIBILITIES:

GENERAL:

1. Supervise development of comprehensive therapeutic recreation programs for the CMHC catchment area and the General Hospital. Therapeutic recreation will focus on developing various kinds of activity programs designed to promote the mental, social, and physical well-being of the clients served.
2. Coordinate with other departments and/or agencies the rendering and receiving of TR services.
3. Coordinate the continuing educational training (CET) activities for the Department of Therapeutic Recreation in cooperation with the director of CET.

SPECIFIC:

1. Serve as a consultant and supervisor for the various program directors, relating treatment programs to unique client needs.
2. Assist in the ongoing development and revision of departmental program philosophies, policies, procedures, forms, etc.
3. Serve as chief consultant for the Therapeutic Recreation Department.
4. Assume responsibility for personnel selection.

Fig. 15–1

5. Advise CMHC administration of facility, equipment, and personnel needs, as well as current departmental status. This information will be related to the administrator of the General Hospital and the director of the CMHC, depending on the nature of the presenting situation.

6. Assume responsibility for staff meetings to maintain communication and coordination between all therapeutic recreation staff and programs.

7. Serve as the chief liaison between the TR department and appropriate medical and administrative staff of the CMHC and the General Hospital, in order to ensure medically approved plans and policies that will meet the needs, capacities, and interests of clients, assisting in their general rehabilitation.

8. Serve as the chief liaison between the TR Department, the community service agencies, and the total administrative and treatment staff.

9. Represent the Department of TR at all department head meetings, and serve as a member of the CMHC Executive Board.

10. Supervise the preparation of the various budgets for all TR programs, personnel, equipment supplies, and facilities.

11. Assume the primary responsibility for the maintenance and compilation of records and reports concerning the ongoing status of the Department of TR.

12. Assume the responsibility for the development and provision of training and orientation programs for TR staff, students, and volunteers.

13. Assist other members of the psychotherapy and medical teams, as well as community members, in evaluating and providing for individual needs.

14. Assume primary responsibility for the coordination of ongoing staff development programs.

15. Assume primary responsibility for staff and program evaluations, encouraging optimum utilization of all resources.

16. Assume primary responsibility for keeping the TR staff cognizant of current research, programs, articles, etc. relating to the TR field.

17. Coordinate the utilization of the TR staff with program directors and the Department of CET.

18. On a monthly basis report departmental progress and status to director of the CMHC, administrator of the General Hospital, the editor of the CMHC news, and the coordinator of CET.

19. Direct community and CMHC surveys, evaluating needs and services rendered by the department.

20. Conduct research for developing new techniques and adaptive procedures and methods in accordance with treatment goals.

21. Be available to work one weekend per month.

QUALIFICATIONS:

Must have a master's degree in therapeutic recreation; be registered accordingly with the National Therapeutic Recreation Society; and, have two years of full-time experience in the field of therapeutic recreation.

Fig. 15–1 *(cont.)*

recruitment

Announce the position using the procedures determined, and receive applications until the termination date.

selection

The selection process depends on the agency. However, the following procedures are fairly standard:

1. After receiving all application materials, have a selection committee of three or more persons individually rate the applicants and select the top three to five candidates.
2. Meet together to compare ratings and determine the final applicants.
3. Notify the applicants and schedule interviews.
4. Interview the applicants. The interview may break down into these parts:
   a. Begin with small talk to put the applicant at ease.
   b. Describe the position, organization, general expectations, and basic employee benefits.
   c. Question the applicant, using a list of prepared questions. Ask both general and specific questions. Listen carefully and observe the applicant's reactions. It may also be useful for the applicant to role play a specific situation with you.
   d. Close the initial interview. Have the applicant wait while you summarize responses immediately, before touring the facility and meeting other staff members.
   e. Tour the facility and meet with other staff members and when possible with clients. Continue to observe interactions. It may sometimes be expedient to observe the applicant interacting independently with the clients. It is also often useful to observe the applicant during casual, informal meetings with staff members, such as lunch and coffee breaks.
   f. When specific knowledge is necessary for a job, such as medical or legal terminology, a written exam may be given.
5. Evaluate the applicants. Often a weighting system allows for more objectivity and would rate: application, education, experience, references, exam (when given), interview, and interactions with staff and clients. Again, the selection committee should make their judgments individually and then meet together to compare ratings and to make a final determination of who will fill the position.

Interviewing and selecting the right person to fill a position is an art that is best developed through experience. Additional readings concerning this skill appear at the end of this chapter.

staff development

Having hired the appropriate staff, the manager is now responsible for retaining good staff members and providing them with opportunities in which to grow and to maintain an optimum level of job performance and satisfaction. An effective staff development program is often the key to continuous quality work, in that it directly relates to both problem solving and creative programming. A comprehensive program of staff development may build staff cohesion, confidence, creativity, and cooperation. Continuing opportunities for professional development and growth enable staff members to be innovative, enthusiastic, and dynamic.

goals

The purpose of staff development is to heighten employee understanding of job tasks and responsibilities, to improve specific skills, and to enhance professional growth and development.[1] Ongoing learning is a lifetime process and appears to be an integral part of job satisfaction. Typical staff development goals are:

1. to increase knowledge about agency policies and procedures;
2. to increase ability to perform job-related skills;
3. to increase staff cohesion, confidence, creativity, and cooperation;
4. to improve the quality of services rendered to clients;
5. to decrease staff turnover rates;
6. to enhance both personal and professional growth; and
7. to acquire new skills to meet changing program needs.

Specific, measurable objectives for staff development programs are formulated according to the procedures presented in previous chapters.

types of staff development

There are numerous ways in which ongoing staff development may be offered. A diversity of educational opportunities is most often advisable in order to meet the multiplicity of individual staff needs. The following types of staff development programs are most common in therapeutic recreation:

1. Conferences and counseling sessions with individual staff members. Traditionally, one-to-one encounters between supervisor and staff member engender fear or anxiety in the supervised staff member. However, it is important to realize that these sessions need not always center around solv-

STAFFING AND STAFF DEVELOPMENT

ing problems. The effective manager takes the time simply to rap with staff members about job perspectives. Often when this occurs, it is the manager who learns. Individual sessions of this nature contribute considerably to the personal and professional growth of staff.

2. Regular staff meetings provide an anticipated and ongoing vehicle for problem solving and professional sharing. The frequency of these staff meetings varies, but should generally be held at least twice a month. Often problems and issues that would otherwise absorb much time by conferring with staff individually can be easily placed on a meeting agenda. Staff meetings can also reduce the cost of paperwork significantly. Staff members need to have a regularly scheduled time in which concerns can be aired. If these meetings are not available, communication lines tend to deteriorate.

3. Special, inservice training sessions are excellent ways to provide information about concerns that arise during ongoing programming. For example, a session might be given on the interaction techniques to use with a client who is particularly difficult to work with, such as a brain-damaged child with destructive tendencies.

4. Inservice training courses provide another means of developing staff. Courses that teach new record-keeping procedures, explain recent implementation strategies for legislation, discuss sexual problems of handicapped clients, teach new counseling techniques, or explore improved assessment procedures are only a few of the courses that may be relevant to therapeutic recreation services.

5. Workshops in specific program areas may also be provided, either by the agency or other professional organizations. It is important to encourage as many staff members as possible to attend and report back to the rest of the staff.

6. Professional conferences and symposia provide another educational opportunity. In addition to learning current techniques and skills in the profession, staff members also have the opportunity to exchange ideas with professionals from other areas.

7. College courses also promote the goals of staff development and should be encouraged.

8. Orientation programs are important for initial staff development and can set the standard for ongoing development. Orientation programs should be available to all persons concerned with programming, including volunteers.

planning procedures for staff development

Certain types of staff development programs are most appropriately scheduled as ongoing programs. Such is the case with regularly scheduled individual staff conferences, regular staff meetings, and orientation programs. Other staff development programs are offered by external agencies and need not be specifically designed by the manager. These include workshops, conferences, symposia, and college courses. Special, inservice training sessions and staff development courses must be specifically designed to meet the unique staff needs. The following ten steps are helpful in developing these sessions:

1. Identify a need for, or a particular interest in, a training area. It is often helpful for the manager to keep a list of the problems incurred in programming or by staff. Repeated problems or an expressed need for greater learning generally identify the staff training needed. It is essential that all staff be allowed to offer input into final decisions about training.
2. Define the topics to be covered. Brainstorming sessions with staff can be useful in specifying the particular problems, questions, issues, or concerns to be covered.
3. Determine the goals and specific objectives for the staff development sessions. Goals will clarify what is hoped to be accomplished. Objectives will specify the criteria for measuring program success.
4. Identify the appropriate resources with which to conduct the program. Resources are personnel or training media that are available and that are related to the topic.
5. Select the appropriate educational and learning activities. These activities may include lectures, panels, discussions, site visits, demonstrations, audience participation, written materials, audio-visuals, experiential exercises, role playing, and staff rotation.
6. Outline the sessions, including the assignment of responsibilities to appropriate persons.
7. Publicize the sessions.
8. Implement preparation for the sessions.
9. Conduct the sessions.
10. Evaluate the effectiveness of the session (see the strategies described in chapter thirteen). The importance of evaluation in staff development should not be overlooked. Unfortunately, most staff development programs are seldom evaluated. In order to transmit information that is relevant to the staff, training sessions might be judged for their effectiveness and the resulting information used continually to improve programming.

summary

Lack of personal and professional growth and development, lack of self-confidence in job-related tasks, and lack of effective communication contribute to job dissatisfaction and high rates of staff turnover, all of which are disruptive to effective programming. Well-designed, implemented, and evaluated staff development programs appear significantly to influence both staff retention and quality job performance. For this reason, staff development must be viewed as an integral part of all therapeutic recreation program operations.

notes

[1] Richard G. Kraus and Barbara J. Bates, *Recreation Leadership and Supervision: Guidelines for Professional Development* (Philadelphia, Pa.: W. B. Saunders Co., 1975), p. 148.

[2] Portions of these procedures were adapted from Paul Bergevin, Dwight Morris, and Robert Smith, *Adult Education Procedures* (Greenwich, Conn.: Leabury Press, 1963).

suggested references

BEATON-MAMAK, M., "Education That 'Turns On' Staff," *Dimensions in Health Services*, 53, no. 7 (July 1976), 40–41.

BEAUDRY, M. L., "Inservice Education: An Investment in People," *Hospital Programs*, 56, no. 1 (January 1975), 8, 10.

BENGSON, E. M., "Training Programs for Activity Directors," *American Journal of Occupational Therapy*, 28 (February 1974), 102–3.

BERNARD, H. S., "Inservice Training of Non-professionals in a Correctional Institution Setting," *Bulletin of American Academy of Psychiatry Law*, 3, no. 3 (1975), 175–84.

BUTLER, R. J., "Behavior and Rehabilitation: Development of an Inservice Training Course," *Nursing Times*, 72, no. 5 (February 1976), 191–93.

CABOT, E. E., "Videocassettes: Using Show and Tell to Teach Employees," *Modern Hospital*, 121 (November 1973), 108.

CANTER, L., "A College Credit Model of In-school Consultation: A Functional Behavioral Training Program," *Community Mental Health Journal*, 10, no. 3 (Fall 1974), 258–75.

CONVENUTO, S., "Giving Zest to Inservice," *American Journal of Nursing*, 74, no. 10 (October 1974), 1835.

DISTEFANO, M. K., "Effect of Brief Training on Mental Health Knowledge and Attitudes of Nurses and Nurses' Aides in a General Hospital," *Nursing Research*, 24, no. 1 (January-February 1975), 40–42.

"Employee Training: From Paperwork to Patient Care," *Nursing Outlook*, 22 (June 1974), 390–93.

ERIKSEN, M. K., "Changing Staff Behavior," *Canadian Nurse*, 71, no. 4 (April 1975), 30–40.

FELTON, G. S., "Training Mental Health Workers to Better Meet Patients' Needs," *Hospital Community Psychiatry*, 25 (May 1974), 299–302.

GLASSMAN, S. M., "Organizing a Staff Development Department: The Fort Logan Model," *Hospital Community Psychiatry*, 26, no. 12 (November 1975), 14–15.

HICKEY, T., "Attitudes Toward Aging as a Function of Inservice Training and

Practitioner Age," *Journal of Gerontology*, 31, no. 6 (November 1976), 681–86.

————, "Inservice Training in Gerontology: Toward the Design of an Effective Education Process," *Gerontologist*, 14, no. 1 (February 1974), 57–64.

HITCHINGS, C. R., "The Royal Free Hospital: Modular Training," *Nursing Times*, 70, no. 42 (October 17, 1974), 1621–22.

LEWIS, C. J., "The Royal Free Hospital: Commissioning Training," *Nursing Times*, 70, no. 40 (October 3, 1974), 1530–31.

LEYASMEYER, E., AND L. A. WHITMARSH, *Continuing Education in the Health Professions: An Annotated Bibliography*. St. Paul, Minn.: Northlands Regional Medical Program Inc., 1969.

LLOYD, BROWN, AND WILSON, *A Selected and Annotated Bibliography on Continuing Medical Education and Other Subjects*. Los Angeles, Calif.: Division of Research in Medical Education, University of Southern California School of Medicine, 1969.

MAALOUF, "Zaire: Establishing an Inservice Education Program," *International Nursing Review*, 21, no. 5 (September-October 1974), 143–44.

MACEACHERA, B., "P.E.I. Leads East Coast Hospitals: Inservice Education on Team Concepts," *Dimensions in Health Services*, 51 (July 1974), 44–45.

NATIONAL ADVISORY HEALTH COUNCIL, ALLIED HEALTH PROFESSIONS EDUCATION SUBCOMMITTEE, *Education for Allied Health Professions and Services*. Washington, D.C.: U.S. Government Printing Office, 1967.

NIMH CONTINUING EDUCATION PROGRAM, *Mental Health Digest*. Washington D.C.: National Clearinghouse for Mental Health Information, 1967.

PENNINGROTH, R. E., "Control of Violence in Mental Health Settings," *American Journal of Nursing*, 75, no. 4 (April 1975), 606–9.

POLLEY, G. W., "Mental Health Training for County Welfare Social Work Personnel: An Exercise in Education and Community Organization," *Community Mental Health Journal*, 7 (March 1971), 29–38.

PURVIS, J. R., "Orientation to Deafness for General Counselors," *American Rehabilitation*, 1, no. 1 (September-October 1975), 30–31.

SCHECHTER, D. S., "Hospital Trainers Tell Problems and Needs," *Hospitals*, 48 (May 16, 1974), 67–78.

SHORE, H., "Designing a Training Program for Understanding Sensory Losses in Aging," *Gerontologist*, 16, no. 2 (April 1976), 157–65.

SIGNELL, K. A., "An Interaction Method of Teaching Consultation: Role Playing," *Community Mental Health Journal*, 10, no. 2 (Summer 1974), 205–15.

SMITH, S. L., "The Training and Role of the Nurse Therapist in a General Hospital Psychiatric Unit," *Hospital Community Psychiatry*, 26, no. 1 (January 1975), 21–24.

STOPERA, V., "A Staff Development Model," *Nursing Outlook*, 22 (June 1974), 390–93.

UNITED STATES DEPARTMENT OF HEALTH, EDUCATION, AND WELFARE, *Annotated*

Bibliography on Inservice Training for Allied Professionals. Washington, D.C.: U.S. Government Printing Office, 1969.

WAX, D. E., "A Collaborative-Interactive Model for Mental Health Consultation: Teacher Inservice Education by Psychiatric Clinicians," *Child Psychiatry and Human Development,* 5, no. 2 (Winter 1974), 78–88.

WRIGHT, R., "Accountability: The Key to Training Effectiveness," *Hospital Programs,* 55 (March 1974), 604.

techniques
of charting—
writing records
and reports

PURPOSE: To present a rationale for and specific techniques of problem-oriented, goal-directed charting, record keeping and reporting in therapeutic recreation services.

Chapter six and seven outlined systematic procedures for assessing individuals and groups and for program planning. Chapter thirteen discussed the basic techniques of evaluation. Making programming decisions depends on reliable assessment and evaluation procedures, which in turn rely on efficient methods of charting, e.g., recording and reporting information.

recording and reporting
in therapeutic recreation

The very thought of keeping records and writing reports often conjures up fantasies of someone hidden behind a desk piled high with papers that are filled with fancy rhetoric aimed at satisfying administrators and funding agencies. This does not need to be the situation. Written evidence of program accountability should be concise, precise, and invaluable to overall program operation. Good writing habits ease program problem solving and decision making. Here are some reasons why:

293

1. Records and reports allow for more effective administrative control. Program priorities can easily be monitored. For example, records make it simple to detect that a substantial portion of the budget is spent on equipment and supplies that are rarely used or used by only a few participants. In this event, the program director may decide to reallocate money to promote interests in other areas. When facilitation techniques (as discussed in chapter eleven), are recorded and their effects on participants are discussed, decisions may be made about their continued use, devoid of guess work.

2. Written records and reports enhance program effectiveness because programs are given immediate feedback and successes and failures are readily apparent.

3. It is impossible to assess clients and evaluate program effectiveness without records and reports.

4. Self-evaluation is possible by comparing and analyzing the effects of various activities, implementation strategies, and facilitation styles.

5. Records and reports facilitate the team approach to programming by providing a consistent means of communication.

6. The program is more easily interpreted to family, clients, and other professionals when it is recorded and reported properly.

7. Educational and staff development needs may be easily detected by consistently recording and reporting the elements of programming.

8. Consistent record keeping in ongoing programs, particularly treatment programs, makes it possible for someone else to take over when the program leader is ill or on vacation.

9. Meaningful research is more likely to be identified when consistent records are kept. When properly done, records and reports often provide meaningful data for research studies.

10. Very often in both treatment settings and externally funded programs, consistent record keeping and reporting are required to receive payment for services. Richard Patterson reports that in order to receive payment for services through Medicare, Medicaid, and third-party carriers in a hospital setting, services must be *documented*. He states that "the treatment furnished should be documented in the medical records in a manner and with such frequency as to provide a full picture of the therapy administered, as well as an assessment of the patient's reaction to it."[1]

definitions of records and reports

Very often the terms record and report are used synonymously. However, administratively, they are different. A record is defined as "a statement set down in writing or otherwise recorded for the purpose of preserving memory, or presenting authentic evidence of facts and events."[2] Recording is done on a frequent and regular basis as significant events occur. The frequency of recording a client's progress in certain activities, or recording the use of specific techniques, depends on a program's purpose. For example, if the client is in a treatment program designed to overcome specific problems, recording the progress occurs more frequently, very often daily. If the client is in a leisure-skills development program, progress may only need to be recorded when aspects of skills are obtained or at the end of each week. Recording the progress of groups also depends on the need for ongoing monitoring. Most often, clients in therapeutic or rehabilitation programs require more frequent monitoring. The overall program philosophy also affects the frequency of recording. The following progress notes depict the records, kept regularly and frequently, of a client's progress in a structured therapy program, in which the goal is to develop basic functional skills:

Day one. The client reported to the therapeutic recreation program and sat quietly removed from the group. No acknowledgment of the therapist or other clients was observed.

Day two. During the music session, the client moved from his chair set apart from the group and voluntarily sat with a group of five other clients. His head remained bowed when the client next to him or the therapist spoke to him. He occasionally stared at members of the group, but did not respond to any verbal interaction.

Day three. The client came immediately into the room and voluntarily joined the group. He observed the client next to him playing the autoharp. On the third attempt by the therapist to involve the client, he quickly took the autoharp and clutched it on his lap, staring straight ahead. The client appeared to be aware of what was going on and he seemed to recognize his group, in that he joined them immediately.

A review of these daily records indicates to the therapist that in three days the client has increased his tolerance for social interaction and is displaying some reality-based behavior. Left just to recall, this sort of progress might go unnoticed.

A report is defined as "a formal statement of the result of an investigation or an account of occurrences for the purpose of circulating related facts."[3] A report summarizes a sequence of events; it is a summary of records. It does not take the place of records. Without consistent records, it is impossible to construct a meaningful report. A report may reflect the results of a program. It may also reflect the progress of a client at the end of a specific time period, e.g., forwarding a psychiatrist a weekly report on a client who participates in a daily activity program. For the purposes of funding some recreation programs, it is important to keep ongoing records of attendance in order to formulate monthly, semiannual, and annual reports. The following is an example of a weekly progress report that summarizes the content of the previously mentioned daily records:

> During the first week of the program the client progressed from sitting apart from the group to joining his group voluntarily and holding an autoharp in his lap. He appears to be aware of where he is and what he is doing, although he still does not verbally interact with the group.

content of records and reports

The nature of the records and reports varies according to a program's purpose and goals. Within the three domains of therapeutic recreation services—rehabilitation, education, and recreation—the following differences may exist.

records in rehabilitation services

As discussed in chapters six and seven, gathering client information in treatment programs may be a more critical and arduous task than in other types of programs. When the overall purpose of programming is to increase a client's basic functional skills, all accessible client information should be contained in the record. This would include, although not be limited to, the following kinds of information:

1. Identification information—name, age, family status, vocational status, educational status, and leisure status.
2. Condition on admission to program—reasons for admission; physical, mental, and social status at time of admission.
3. Assessment information important to therapeutic recreation programming—impressions from client interviews and from observing the client; test results when appropriate.
4. Specific presenting problems—weaknesses and strengths.
5. Needs in relation to client's problems.
6. Individual goals for programming.
7. Individual program objectives.
8. Individual program plan.
9. Progress notes—regular, frequent observations and impressions of the client's participation.
10. Supplemental information—incidences that may affect programming, such as family problems and medication.

The specifics regarding this type of information are discussed in chapter six. When treatment focuses on a group rather than on individuals, the same type of information is recorded on the group. Group assessment is discussed in chapter seven.

reports in rehabilitation services

The following types of reports are common in treatment programs:

1. Summary of the initial assessment of the client at the time of admission—the condition of the client at the time of entry and his or her potential adjustment and progress in the program.
2. Treatment plan—summary of the treatment program as initiated; interim program summaries, e.g., weekly or monthly, and a summary of any program changes instituted.
3. Progress during treatment program—periodic summary of daily progress notes or records.
4. Final evaluation of program participation—summary of the results of participation and recommendations.

records in leisure education programs

Information recorded in programs directed toward "awareness of leisure attitudes and values and the development of leisure skills," may include the following types of information:

1. Leisure profile—past participation in leisure, interest in leisure, awareness of the concepts of leisure and play, knowledge of leisure resources, and attitudes toward self relative to leisure.
2. Reasons for participation—identification of areas of learning to be addressed, e.g., attitude development, social-skills development, activity skill development, or knowledge-of-leisure-resources development.
3. Program assignment—may include leisure counseling programs or specific classes in social or activity-skills development.
4. Level of functioning at entry—in order to evaluate the end results of programming, the programmer must define the level of functioning before program implementation. In leisure activity skills classes, this may only require recording the skill level, such as beginner, novice, intermediate, or advanced. When a program's goal is to increase knowledge of new leisure skills, the therapeutic recreator may only need to record the number and types of activity skills possessed by the client at the onset of the program. When the goal is to increase positive feelings toward self in leisure, a subjective statement of the participant recorded before, during, and after a leisure counseling class may serve as a measure of the program's success.
5. Progress notes—a simple checklist noting the date and level of skill acquired may be sufficient. This information may be recorded daily, weekly, or at the time the skill is acquired. For leisure counseling programs, periodic, subjective or objective statements and observations may be recorded.

reports in leisure education programs

The following types of reports are common in programs with educational goals:

1. Initial program information—this may include a summary of the number of participants enrolled; number of staff and the budget available; and the general level and status of the participants—individually or collectively, including program goals.
2. Program plan—a summary of the program's goals, objectives, implementation strategies, and measurement criteria as initiated.
3. Participant progress reports—periodic summary statements about the participants' progress in the program, usually weekly or monthly.
4. Final participant evaluation—this usually includes a summary statement about the number of participants originally enrolled and the number completing the program. It also indicates the beginning status of the participants compared with their skills levels leaving the program. The evaluation may also give reasons for successes and failures and any unexpected outcomes.
5. Final program evaluation—this summary statement answers the following questions:
   a. Were the program objectives appropriate to the population served?
   b. Were the learning activities appropriate for achieving the learning objectives?
   c. Was the program implemented as designed?

Reports addressing these concerns are essential for making decisions about and improving programs. Information of this type allows the programmer to compare the effectiveness of one program to another.

records and reports in recreation programs

Supervised recreation programs designed to offer opportunities for self-regulated play require a minimum amount of record keeping and report making. Records only need to include client information and relay necessary precautions related to specific disabilities. It is also highly desirable to record user satisfaction with available programs and facilities. Periodic reports that summarize total services to handicapped populations in general recreation programs do not need to be any different from reports required for all recreation services.

when to write

Recording and reporting should be viewed as a meaningful part of programming, essential to ongoing program improvement. Ideally, recording client status should be done whenever the information has direct implications for decision making. Recording for the sake of recording is both frustrating and unproductive.

Schedules for recording client progress vary among agencies. In treatment programs it is common to find regularly scheduled times for writing in the clients' records, i.e., a daily "staffing" on each client's progress. In this instance, the staff members who work directly with the clients meet together on a daily or weekly basis to discuss and record significant events. Other agencies want significant events to be recorded as they occur by the staff member witnessing the event. This is the best way to ensure that meaningful information is not forgotten by the end of the day. For the therapeutic recreator, it is often helpful also to record pertinent information immediately following regularly scheduled activities.

Reporting also varies among programs. Essentially, reports about client status should be written when change is obvious and it is important for other staff members to know about it. Reports should always be written when programs end, when programs are extended, and at regularly scheduled intervals throughout program implementation. Reports are also helpful when diverse regressions, failures, successes, and plateaus occur.

how to write

One of the most common complaints among the supervisors of therapeutic recreation programs is that staff members don't know how to chart. For this reason, we feel it is important to include a discussion concerning the skills needed to chart (record or report) effectively. The two skills essential for effective charting are: (1) observation and (2) writing.

observation

Before we can record and report effectively, we must see and hear accurately. All of us see, hear, think, and feel selectively, based on our own personal experiences. The tendency to project our own life experiences onto what we observe others doing or saying is perhaps one of the most difficult personal behaviors to overcome. The ability to be *objective* observers is a skill that requires much practice in listening and looking. The following listening skills are important to objective observation:

1. Voice inflection—emphasis on selected words very often reveals particular biases. For example:
   a. Jenny was BUSTED for selling dope!
   b. JENNY was busted for selling dope!
   c. Jenny was busted for selling DOPE!

In the first instance, being arrested appears to be surprising, which may indicate Jenny's perceived social position. In the second response, the judgment is directed against Jenny—of all people! The third remark clearly reflects a value system that prohibits the use of dope.

2. Word usage—
   a. "Like, uh . . . ya know . . . I mean like" indicates uncertainty.
   b. "I agree with you, but . . . " indicates disagreement. The word but generally erases everything that precedes its use. "I agree with you, but . . . " generally means "I *don't* agree with you and it's tough for me to tell you that."
   c. "I can't because . . ." most often means "I won't, and I'm uncomfortable asserting myself, so I'll blame it on someone or something else."
   d. "If only . . . " indicates that personal responsibility has been shifted to someone or something else.
   e. "Do ya see? . . . Do ya understand?" very often subtly asks the question "Do you approve of *me*?"
   f. "Should," "shall," "must," "never," "right," and "wrong" are words that clearly imply control and judgment.
   g. "Nasty," "dirty," "perverted," "sick," and "crippled" clearly imply moral judgments.
   h. "I'll try . . . " usually means "I won't, and I'm uncomfortable revealing that."
3. Pronunciation—listen for pronunciations that reveal clarity, slurring, put-ons, bookishness, and particular dialects.
4. Speed of speech—slow, rapid, jerky, smooth.
5. Voice control—breaks, trembles, chokes, clearing of throat.
6. Pitch of voice—whining, highness, nasality, hoarseness.
7. Breathing—deep, rapid, shallow, even, restrained, constrained.

Looking and seeing are also essential skills of objective observation. The following *physical* cues may reveal a client's present status:

1. Fatigue.
2. Posture—closed, open, erect, slumping.
3. Movement—fast, aggressive, cautious, clumsy.
4. Social distancing—moving away from, turning away from, ignoring, moving close to, touching.
5. Foot movement—tapping, shuffling, sliding.
6. Leg movement—swinging, crossed, open, relaxed.
7. Arm movement—crossed, hidden behind, freely moving.
8. Hand movement—rubbing eyes, wringing, patting, holding head.
9. Handshake—firm, clammy, flimsy.
10. Head position—cocked, down, erect.
11. Hair—well kept, casual, unkempt.
12. Lips—pursed, dry, quivering.
13. Jaws—clenched.

14. Eyes—moist, red, looking away, maintaining direct contact.
15. Neck—red, protruding veins.
16. Dress—sloppy, casual, immaculate.
17. Odor—heavily perfumed, sweaty, offensive.

Observing ecological cues surrounding the client can also be important: (1) weather conditions; (2) temperature; (3) interaction patterns; (4) cultural cues—speech, dress, choice of music, choice of foods; (5) objects in immediate environment; and (6) people in immediate environment.

writing

Recording and reporting a client's progress require simplicity, specificity, honesty, and accuracy. The astute observer will, most likely, record fairly. The following elements, when included in records and reports, will improve writing skills and preserve fairness in recording client data:

1. Accuracy—recorded information must be correct, including exactly what has been seen and heard, nothing more, nothing less; i.e., "The client sat in a chair apart from the group."
2. Honesty—all feelings, assumptions, and perceptions about the client's behavior must be clearly *your* perceptions, *documented with facts*. Base such phrases as "the client seems to be" or "the client appeared to" on the facts—what the client stated and did.
3. Thoroughness—pay careful attention to all facts. Omit nebulous terms such as:
   a. "The client's behavior was inappropriate." State specifically the behavior in question.
   b. "The client was hostile" (or depressed, senile, withdrawn, aggressive, uncooperative, etc.). Describe the specific behavior and the related incident. No client is always hostile, aggressive, or uncooperative. People behave in these ways in certain situations. Cite these specific situations.
   c. "The client has a poor relationship with family and state." What is indicative of a poor relationship?
4. Eliminate empty phrases—be concise, short, and to the point. Avoid over using phrases such as *so as to, so that, in case of,* and *such as.*
5. Avoid flowery, descriptive passages and the overuse of scientific words. As unbelievable as it may seem, the following passage actually appeared in a client's report:

   In lieu of the garrulous manner in which the client exchanged verbal intercourse with other members of their peer group, it would seem, indeed, preposterous to postulate prolonged difficulty in regard to social interactions. It would appear that her paranoid, withdrawn condition has been ameliorated.

This information could have been recorded simply as:

The client was observed freely talking with other clients, and appears no longer to have difficulty relating to peers.

protocol in charting

Although most agencies are not too concerned with strict adherence to formal absolute standards in charting, it is generally advantageous for the therapeutic recreator to conform to some standard protocol. In so doing, all records and reports must be signed with full signatures and appropriate titles, e.g., "Warren Withit, MTRS." The time and date of charting should also be noted. Finally, references to individuals should be in the third person, e.g., "the client" rather than "Mr. Jones"; and in the passive voice, e.g., "It was observed" rather than "I observed." Although this style of charting may be seen as rigid and lacking in warmth, it protects the writer from unnecessary accusations about having undue familiarity with the client and lacking personal objectivity.

abbreviations used in charting

Therapeutic recreators are often required to read the charts and progress notes on their clients in order to program meaningful therapeutic activities. The therapeutic recreator must be familiar with the language used in charting, or else be at a loss to interpret the information in client records.

While different facilities may prefer using certain abbreviations, the ones that follow are generally accepted in treatment settings.[4]

Abbreviation	Meaning
$\bar{a}$	before
$\overline{aa}$	of each
ac	before meals
bid	twice a day
$\bar{c}$	with
d	day
hs	hour of sleep
noc	night
$\bar{o}$	other
$\bar{p}$	after
pc	after meals
$\bar{q}$	every
qid	four times a day
qod	every other day

Abbreviation	Meaning
s̄	without
tid	three times a day
x̄c	except
ad lib	as patient can tolerate
AMA	against medical advice
B & B	bowel and bladder
BJM	bones, joints, muscles
BM	bowel movement
BMR	basal metabolic rate
BP	blood pressure
BRP	bathroom privileges
C-5	cervical lesion at the fifth vertebra
Ca	cancer
cap	capsule
cath	catheterize
CN	cranial nerves
CNS	central nervous system
CP	cerebral palsy
CVA	cerebral vascular accident—stroke
CVR	cardiovascular respiration
D & C	dilatation and curettage
D & V	diarrhea and vomiting
DD	developmental disability
DOA	dead on arrival
DTR	deep tendon reflexes
DTs	delirium tremens
ECG/EKG	electrocardiogram
ECT	electroconvulsive therapy
EEG	electroencephalogram
EST	electroshock therapy
FUO	fever of unknown origin
FWB	fully weight-bearing
fx	fracture
GI	gastrointestinal
GU	genitourinary
Hb	hemoglobin
HT	hypertension
IM	intramuscular (into the muscle)
IQ	intelligence quotient
IUD	intrauterine device
IV	intravenous (into the vein)
L-5	lumbar lesion at the fifth vertebra
LD	learning disability
LKS	liver, kidney, spleen
MA	mental age
MD	muscular dystrophy
ML	midline
MS	multiple sclerosis

Abbreviations	Meaning
n	normal
NP	neuropsychiatric
NPO	nothing by mouth
NSR	normal sinus rhythm
NWB	no weight-bearing (as in crutch walking)
OBS	organic brain syndrome
OD	overdose
OR	operating room
PND	postnasal drip
post op	after surgery
pre op	before surgery; also means pre op medication
prep	prepare for surgery
PRN/prn	given as needed
PWB	partially weight-bearing
ROM	range of motion
Rx	prescription/treatment
sig	instructions (when to take drugs)
SOB	shortness of breath
stat	immediately
T–5	thoracic lesion at the fifth vertebra
tab	tablet
tach	tachycardia
T & A	tonsils and adenoids
TB	tuberculin/tuberculosis
up ad lib	allow patient to move around as much as patient feels is possible
VD	venereal disease
VDG	gonorrhea
w/c	wheelchair
♀	female
♂	male
EMR/EMH	educable mentally retarded or handicapped
LPN	licensed practical nurse
MTRS	master therapeutic recreation specialist
OT	occupational therapy
OTR	registered occupational therapist
pt	patient
PT	physical therapy
RN	registered nurse
RT	recreation therapist
TMR/TMH	trainable mentally retarded or handicapped
TRS	therapeutic recreation specialist
TR	therapeutic recreation

summary

Accountability in therapeutic recreation requires that meaningful, evaluative data be systematically recorded and reported. Recording client progress is a systematic, frequent account of behaviors. Reporting involves summarizing recorded information. The content of records and reports varies among settings and according to client needs and program philosophies. Writing is appropriate when it benefits the client, and should be done objectively and honestly. Continued program improvement depends on more than systematically designed programs and implementation. Records and reports, when properly done, contain valuable program evaluation data, and are therefore important tools for therapeutic recreators.

notes

1 Richard Patterson, "The Development of a Self-Sufficient Therapeutic Recreation Service," *Expanding Horizons in Therapeutic Recreation III*, ed. Gary Robb and Gerald Hitzhusen (Columbia, Mo.: University of Missouri, Technical Education Services, 1976), p. 50.

2 Helen S. Willard and Clare S. Spackman, eds., *Occupational Therapy* (Phildelphia, Pa.: J. B. Lippincott Company, 1963), p. 32.

3 Ibid.

4 Scout Lee Gunn, *Basic Terminology in Therapeutic Recreation and Other Action Therapies* (Champaign, Ill.: Stipes Publishing Co., 1975), pp. 73–77.

consultation

PURPOSE: To discuss the consultative process, the dominant roles of consultants in therapeutic recreation, and the basic principles for effectively employing consultants in systematic programming. Effective consultative techniques are touched on.

The term *consultation* is used in many different ways in relation to therapeutic recreation services. Some use the term to denote almost any professional activity carried out by a specialist. For example, when involved in individual conferences or staff meetings, a manager may state, "I am in consultation." Others use the term to refer to a professional dialogue with a person who is external to the therapeutic recreation setting. For example, a therapeutic recreator may consult with a social worker or physician. Still others restrict the term to the activities of a highly specialized, full-time consultant. To discuss consultation within such a broad frame of reference would only result in confusion. We have, therefore, chosen to use this definition of a consultation: "[a] process of interaction between two professional persons—the consultant, who is a specialist, and the consultee, who invokes the consultant's help in regard to a current work problem which he [or she] has decided is within the other's area of specialized competence."[1] The consultee is responsible for initiating appropriate action about the information obtained from the consultant. The consultant may offer helpful advice, but it is the consultee who accepts or rejects it. The consultant assumes no administrative responsibility for implementing suggestions and no professional responsibility for the outcome of actions based on his or her advice. The consultant is engaged to render advice, not to provide direct service.

The need for consultative services is rapidly increasing in the field of therapeutic recreation, along with expanding requirements for services and more sophisticated techniques. No therapeutic recreator can be expected to know everything about everything and, therefore, must turn to professional advisors in order to extend knowledge, increase insights, and acquire new skills. Sometimes therapeutic recreators simply need firm assurance that what they are doing is worthwhile. Consultants, therefore, assume the roles of educators, trainers, advisors, and counselors. They are not activity leaders, operators, policy setters, administrators, or directors. A consultant's best contribution is to assist the consultee to better understand problems, consider viable alternatives, locate and use appropriate resources, and capitalize on potential abilities.

types of consultation in therapeutic recreation

Four types of consultation are commonly used in therapeutic recreation.[2]

client-centered case consultation

With the decentralization of large, institutional programs, the trend toward mainstreaming handicapped populations, and the increased use of individual program plans, the therapeutic recreator is often confronted with clients who require special attention. Mentally retarded or physically handicapped children who engage in regular community recreation programs may present certain problems in programming. Mentally ill clients who are admitted to nursing homes can create dilemmas when the therapeutic recreator is not trained to deal with abnormal behaviors. The primary goal of consultation in these cases is to assist the therapeutic recreator to design or adapt programs that will assist the clients in question. Hopefully, the insights gained can be transferred to clients with similar problems in the future. The consultant in therapeutic recreation will apply special knowledge and skills to assess the nature of a client's problem and the potential impact of effective programming. The consultant will recommend how the situation can best be dealt with, considering available resources. To arrive at her or his conclusions, the consultant reviews the client's records and observes the client; has a consultation session with the consultee, centering on a discussion of the specific problem; and finally, makes suggestions for assessment, program planning, implementation, evaluation, and precautions to take.

client-centered, staff-development consultation

Often clients have similar problems and present ongoing dilemmas for the staff. For example, staff members are often unsure about how to handle overt sexual expressions of mentally retarded children, such as

307

masturbation in public, overtures to staff or other clients, or unexpected questions posed to staff members. This situation may warrant consultation about the clients' sexual expressions and methods for handling uncomfortable situations. In this case, a consultant may be asked to advise the total staff. The problems of the clients are discussed with the consultees for the purpose of staff development and training.

agency-centered, staff-development consultation

This type of consultation focuses on structural and interpersonal problems that exist within a particular program or agency. Legislative mandates that affect the delivery of services or reallocations of staff often cause confusion and unrest. Therefore, it is usually expedient to employ a consultant to explain the implications of these types of changes. Sometimes, a therapeutic recreation staff has problems dealing with the administrative structure of an agency, such as when social workers or nurses are unwilling to reveal relevant information about clients that would increase effective programming in therapeutic recreation. A consultant may best be able to identify and effectively deal with the communication problems between allied professionals. Agency-centered, staff-development consultation may be useful when staff members experience confusion about record keeping. A consultant may be asked to provide administrators and staff with specific techniques aimed at skill development and personal growth.

agency-centered, program-development consultation

This type of consultation helps the administrators of a program or agency to conceptualize, design, and evaluate specific or agencywide programs. For example, consultation may be helpful before initiating a new program in therapeutic recreation within a larger community recreation program or within an existing institutional program. This type of consultation may also be used to revise an existing therapeutic recreation program.

In accepting an assignment as a consultant or in using a consultant, it is imperative that the specific type of consultation be identified. Confusion and poor quality of services result when the purpose of a consultation is not clearly understood by both consultant and consultee.

problems in consultation

The consultant's role is to advise and persuade rather than to direct and implement. Therefore, it is imperative that the consultant be sensitive to the consultee's anxieties. Jesse Nirenburg lists six human tendencies that appear to work against a meeting of minds:

1. *Resistance to change.* People have difficulty in exchanging old beliefs, ideas, and practices for new ones, particularly if the old modes are based on long-held attitudes.
2. *Distraction by personal concerns.* Consultants are competing with the inner thoughts and feelings of the consultees, which tend to distort the listening process.
3. *Talking before thinking.* Conversation may change direction numerous times because people sometimes speak before their ideas are clearly formed.
4. *Wishful hearing.* All too often, people hear what they want to hear rather than what is actually being said.
5. *Jumping to conclusions.* Both speaker and listener often make assumptions about each other's knowledge, skills, or understanding without checking out the assumptions.
6. *Habitual secretiveness.* Ingrained in the minds of many people is the belief that the less another person knows about them, the better it is.[3]

Rather than merely exchanging words and marking time with each other, consultee and consultant must find ways to deal effectively with these tendencies in order to facilitate a cooperative spirit of thinking together.

H. Curtis Mial identifies the following problems that are intrinsic to the role of consultant:

1. *The consultant is an outsider.* The consultee may assume that a stranger couldn't possibly understand the problem at issue. When this occurs, the consultant is defeated before beginning.
2. *Resistance on the part of the consultee.* This natural resistance may best be handled by the consultant taking the time to understand the problems and limitations of the agency and by initially offering viable alternatives that are not drastic in nature. In this way, a nonthreatening spirit of experimentation can be fostered.
3. *Undefined status and conflict of roles.* Role conflict occurs when the consultant and consultee have different expectations about the nature of the consultation. It is the responsibility of the consultant to understand clearly the consultee's expectations and to establish a statement of purpose and goals that are agreed on by both parties.
4. *Compulsion to see quick results.* The consultant may be tempted to plunge in and prove professional worth immediately, and the consultee may expect to have a problem solved immediately. Some problems can be handled in a short period of time, but most often long-range goals are jeopardized when the problem-solving process is rushed.
5. *Inadequate preparation.* It is often assumed that a consultant can walk into an agency cold and immediately begin working on a problem. Perhaps the most common mistake made by both consultant and consultee is in failing to prepare for the consultative services. The consultee is responsible for providing the consultant with as much information as possible *before* the actual consultation. The consultee must also have available any information requested by the consultant at the time of arrival. The con-

sultant is responsible for his or her preparation, and can, in fact, help to alleviate skepticism and fear by appearing knowledgeable about the problem at the outset.

6. *Insecurity on the part of both consultant and consultee.* The consultee may feel judged by the consultant and may therefore be overly defensive. The adept consultant is sensitive to this and gently alleviates fears. On the other hand, consultants may encounter situations that they cannot handle effectively, and they must be willing to admit to their lack of insight, knowledge, or skill. Good consultants admit their limitations and seek assistance when needed.

7. *Closure.* Most people enjoy being needed and may hesitate to relinquish a position when problems have been solved. Conversely, consultees may enjoy having someone to lean on, and, therefore, prolong services longer than necessary. Good consultants generally work themselves out of a job. They are able gradually to accept from the consultee the power to assist in problem solving, and then gradually to release that power back to the consultee. It is this severing of professional symbiosis that many find most difficult. However, it is vital for the growth and development of both consultant and consultee.[4]

skills related to consultation

Consultative services in therapeutic recreation range from full-time, specialized positions as consultants to periodic requests for expertise in specific areas. No one consultant, regardless of experience or education, can be expected to know everything about therapeutic recreation services. However, if the standards and quality of therapeutic recreation services are to continue to be upgraded, consultants on all levels must demonstrate skills in at least these areas:

1. *Demonstrated experience and skills* in working with the population served by the consultee agency, unless the consultation does not concern specific populations, such as advising about legislation, record-keeping skills, or communication skills between staff members. The consultant should always possess expertise in the area of service for which the consultation is requested. Consultants with experience only in mental retardation should not accept an offer to consult in a geriatric program.

2. *Empathy.* The ability to empathize with the problems and situations in any agency is directly related to the consultant's experience. Being sensitive and responsive to the needs of staff who work with specific populations are tendencies that can only be acquired by personal experience.

3. *Active listening.* The ability to hear both words and feelings and to reflect them back to the sender is a must in consultative work (as it is in all areas of therapeutic recreation services).

4. *Pacing.* This is a skill related to timing that, again, is acquired with experience. Knowing the most receptive moment for suggesting change very often determines whether ideas are accepted. The consultant must be sensitive to the mood of staff members and know when to slow down, stop, go, or move cautiously.

5. *Flexibility.* There is rarely only one way to solve a particular problem. It is essential for the consultant to be able to adjust to unexpected circumstances while constantly moving toward improved services.

6. *Organizational skills,* such as those inherent in systems approaches, can be invaluable in both designing new programs and describing existing ones.

7. *Counseling skills* that center on reality, responsibility, and supportive confrontation enhance the consultant's ability to sort out problems, offer realistic alternatives, and relinquish power when appropriate to the consultee. The consultant must constantly be careful not to attempt to rescue the consultee in areas in which assistance has not been solicited.

8. *Creative use of resources.* The consultant must always be aware of the available strengths within any program or staff, and be able to capitalize on those talents and energies.

9. *Assertiveness.* The ability to use assertiveness successfully rather than adapting, placating, and behaving aggressively usually results in both the needs of the consultant and the consultee being met.

10. *Appropriate level of communication.* The consultant may often need to reduce complex concepts to simple language and communicate the essential meaning without forfeiting quality and correctness.

summary

The consultant-consultee relationship requires that both parties actively participate in personal and professional responsibilities. The roles and responsibilities of each must be clearly defined and formally agreed on in a contract. The test of the truly effective consultant is whether the consultee is able to capitalize on the insights, knowledge, and skills imparted and proceed independently and productively to upgrade the quality of services. Ultimately, the quality of consultative services should be reflected by clients, whose needs for and interest in play behavior are satisfied.

notes

[1] Gerald Caplan, *The Theory and Practice of Mental Health Consultation* (New York: Basic Books, 1970), p. 19.

[2] Adapted from Franklin B. McClung and Alstair Stunden, *Mental Health Consultation for Programs for Children: A Review of Data Collected for Selected U.S. Sites,* Public Health

Service Publication #2066 (Washington, D.C.: U.S. Government Printing Office, n.d.).

[3] Jesse S. Nirenburg, "Persuasive Communication—When You Consult with People," in *Teaching the Consultative Process* (Ithaca, N.Y.: Cornell University, New York State School of Industrial and Labor Relations, 1966), p. 1.

[4] Adapted from H. Curtis Mial,"What Is a Consultant?" *Public Relations Journal* (November 1959).

_____ *suggested references* _____

CAPLAN, G., *The Theory and Practice of Mental Health Consultation*. New York: Basic Books, 1970.

LEVINE, D. L., "The Field Consultant's Role: Purpose and Process," *Florida State University Research Reports in Social Science*, 5, no. 1 (February 1962), 14–27.

MANNINO, F. V., *Consultation in Mental Health and Related Fields: A Reference Guide*. Public Health Service Publication #1420. Washington, D.C.: U.S. Government Printing Office, 1969.

MANNINO, F. V., AND M. F. SHORE, *Consultation Research in Mental Health and Related Fields*. Public Health Service Publication, Monograph #79. Washington, D.C.: U.S. Government Printing Office, 1971.

NIRENBURG, J. S., "Persuasive Communication—When You Consult with People," in *Teaching the Consultative Process* (Ithaca, N.Y.: Cornell University, New York State School of Industrial and Labor Relations, 1966.

SCHEIN, E. H., *Process Consultation: Its Role in Organization Development*. Reading, Mass.: Addison-Wesley Publishing Co., 1969.

WILLIAMS, M., "The Problem Profile Technique in Consultation," *Social Work*, 16, no. 3 (July 1971), 52–59.

appendixes

instruments for evaluating the abilities of the physically handicapped child

introduction

These materials have been prepared to assist anyone who needs to evaluate the various abilities of the physically handicapped child. The physically handicapped child is defined for the purpose of these materials as *a child with severe speech, hearing, vision, and/or motor impairments.*

format

The instruments are divided into six major categories on the basis of test classification:

I. Intelligence Tests
   A. Individual
   B. Group
II. Achievement Tests
III. Developmental Scales
   A. General
   B. Behavioral
   C. Language
IV. Sensory-Motor Tests
   A. General
   B. Auditory-Perceptual

Used with permission of the author, Linda G. Geldman, Evaluation Research Center, University of Virginia.

    C. Visual-Perceptual
V. Attitudes
VI. Miscellaneous

    Each category is preceded by introductory remarks. For each test instrument, a capsule description, plus the means for obtaining the test, are provided. A list of publisher's addresses may be found at the end of appendix A. No attempt is made to evaluate each test, since the main intention is merely to describe what is available for testing physically handicapped children. Instruments are listed in alphabetical order.

    Due to the amount of overlap and cross-referencing, the tests have not been presented according to handicap. An index has been provided, however, which lists the instruments designed for specific handicapped populations. The index also permits the user to select tests appropriate for the multiple-handicapped. To select an intelligence test, for example, for a child with cerebral palsy, severe hearing loss, and speech impairment, the user can locate those tests that are repeatedly found in the three appropriate categories—motor impairment, hearing impairment, and speech impairment. One test selection might be the Colored Progressive Matrices.

list of instruments described

I. Intelligence Tests
    A. Arthur Adaptation of the Leiter International Performance Scale
    B. Chicago Nonverbal Examination
    C. Children's Picture Information Test
    D. Colored Progressive Matrices and Advanced Progressive Matrices
    E. Columbia Mental Maturity Scale, Revised
    F. English Picture Vocabulary Test
    G. Goodenough-Harris Drawing Test
    H. Hiskey-Nebraska Test of Learning Aptitude
    I. Kahn Intelligence Tests: Experimental Form
    J. Nonverbal Intelligence Tests for Deaf and Hearing Subjects
    K. Ohwaki-Kohs Tactile Block Design Intelligence Test for the Blind
    L. Ontario School Ability Examination
    M. Peabody Picture Vocabulary Test
    N. Performance Test of Intelligence: A Series of Nonlinguistic Tests for Deaf and Normal Children, Third Edition
    O. Pictorial Test of Intelligence
    P. Quick Test
    Q. Stanford-Binet Intelligence Scale
    R. Stanford-Ohwaki-Kohs Block Design Intelligence Test for the Blind: American Revision of the Ohwaki-Kohs Test

S. Van Alstyne Picture Vocabulary Test
T. Wechsler Intelligence Scale for Children
U. Williams Intelligence Test for Children with Defective Vision

II. Achievement Tests
   A. Colorado Braille Battery: Literary Code Tests
   B. Colorado Braille Battery: Nemeth Code Test
   C. Peabody Individual Achievement Test

III. Developmental Scales
   A. General
      1. Bayley Scales of Infant Development
      2. Denver Developmental Screening Test
      3. Gesell Developmental Tests
      4. Blum-Fieldsteel Development Charts
      5. Preschool Attainment Record, Research Edition
   B. Behavioral
      1. Child Behavior Rating Scale
      2. Maxfield-Buchholz Scale of Social Maturity for Use with Preschool Blind Children
   C. Language
      1. Utah Test of Language Development, Revised Edition
      2. Verbal Language Development Scale

IV. Sensory-Motor Tests
   A. General
      1. Detroit Tests of Learning Aptitude
      2. Illinois Test of Psycholinguistic Abilities
      3. Psychoeducational Profile of Basic Learning Abilities
      4. Screening Tests for Identifying Children with Specific Language Disability
   B. Auditory Perceptual Development
      1. Goldman-Fristoe-Woodcock Test of Auditory Discrimination
      2. Screening Test for Auditory Perception
      3. Tests of Listening Accuracy in Children
   C. Visual-Motor Perceptual Development
      1. Bender-Gestalt Test
      2. Bender Visual-Motor Gestalt Test for Children
      3. Developmental Test of Visual-Motor Integration
      4. Marianne Frostig Developmental Test of Visual Perception, Third Edition
      5. Meeting Street School Screening Test
      6. Memory-for-Designs Test
      7. Primary Visual-Motor Test
      8. Purdue Perceptual-Motor Survey
      9. Southern California Figure-Ground Visual Perception Test
     10. Southern California Kinesthesia and Tactile Perception Tests
     11. Southern California Motor Accuracy Test
     12. Southern California Perceptual-Motor Tests

V. Attitudes
   A. Attitude to Blindness Scale

      B. Attitude Toward Disabled People Scale
      C. Handicap Problems Inventory
VI. Miscellaneous
      A. Color Blindness
           Test for Color Blindness
      B. Reading Readiness
           Roughness Discrimination Test
      C. Vision
           Stycar Vision Test

intelligence tests

The Stanford-Binet Intelligence Scale and the Wechsler Intelligence Scale for Children are frequently used with the severely handicapped child with makeshift, informal adjustments to assess the child's response capacities. Verbal items of the Stanford-Binet and WISC are given to those with motor impairment or defective vision. Performance items (nonverbal) are often administered to those with speech or hearing handicaps. Testing procedures are modified.

Certain tests have been designed and developed for specific handicapped populations. For the deaf, the measures of general intelligence are typically nonverbal performance tests. The validity of these tests should be carefully assessed by the user, since in our culture "intelligence" largely depends on linguistic skills.

Oral tests are most readily adapted for children with defective vision. Some performance tests use the tactile sense.

Intelligence tests for motor-impaired children consist largely of two types: (1) picture vocabulary tests, and (2) pictorial classification tests. The picture vocabulary tests that are quick and easy to administer should be used only as screening devices. The obtained IQ score is narrowly based only on receptive vocabulary. The pictorial classification tests generally assess reasoning ability, again only a single unit of the construct called intelligence.

Intelligence tests for children with severe speech impairment include the performance tests, picture vocabulary, and pictorial classification tests.

As with nonhandicapped children, a battery of tests should be given if possible, rather than a single index of intelligence. The objective should be to obtain as complete a picture as possible of the total functioning of a child. A diagnostic picture of the child's strengths and weaknesses, covering many areas, is usually of more help in the classroom than an IQ score alone.

I. Intelligence Tests
  A. Individual

    1. *The Arthur Adaptation of the Leiter International Performance Scale* is designed for children from ages two to thirteen. This is a nonverbal scale suitable for testing for deafness and delayed speech or language problems. The scale consists of five tests:

        Knox Cube Test
        Seguin Form Board Test
        Arthur Stencil Design Test I
        Porteus Maze Test
        Healy Picture Completion Test II

    Several of the tests have no verbal directions. The scale yields a measure of general intelligence, examining thinking and reasoning skills. It may be obtained from the Psychological Corporation.

    2. *The Chicago Nonverbal Examination,* by Andrew Brown, Seymour Stein, and Perry Rohrer, is specifically designed for those handicapped in the use of the English language, including deaf and hard-of-hearing children. IQ's are derived for those aged six to adult. The authors state that not even for handicapped children does this test substitute for individual verbal tests like the Stanford-Binet, but is to supplement them and confirm results. Available from the Psychological Corporation.

    3. *The Columbia Mental Maturity Scale, Revised,* by Burgemeister, Blum, and Lorge, for children aged three to twelve. The CMMS requires no verbal response from the child and minimal motor response. On this test of reasoning ability, the child is presented with cards with a number of designs or pictures printed on them. The child must indicate (point, eye blink, etc.) the picture that does not belong with the others. Untimed. Available from Harcourt Brace Jovanovich, Inc.

    4. *The Colored Progressive Matrices,* 1965, by J. C. Raven, is designed for children aged five to eleven who for any reason cannot speak or understand English, or who have physical disabilities—cerebral palsy, aphasia, deafness. This test is untimed and assesses the intellectual capacity to reason or "the degree to which a person can think clearly." After age eleven, *The Advanced Progressive Matrices* can be used. Both tests are untimed and may be obtained from the Psychological Corporation.

    5. *The English Picture Vocabulary Test,* 1966, by M. A. Brimer and L. Dunn, is a test of listening vocabulary, derived from the Peabody Picture Vocabulary Test, and designed for the physically handicapped aged five through eleven (1 form, 2 levels). The subject must make some minimal movement to indicate the correct picture. Untimed. Available from Educational Evaluation Enterprises.

    6. *The Goodenough-Harris Drawing Test,* 1963, by Florence Goodenough and Dale Harris, yields a measure of intelligence by assessing conceptual maturity or cognitive development through a drawing task.

Children ages three to fifteen are asked to draw a man and then a woman. Untimed. Available from Harcourt Brace Jovanovich, Inc.

7. *The Hiskey-Nebruska Test of Learning Aptitude,* 1966, by Marshall S. Hiskey, and available from the author. This test is designed for the deaf and the hearing and includes both verbal and pantomime directions and two sets of norms. It yields mental age scores for the hearing population and "learning age" scores for the deaf. It taps components necessary for school learning of deaf children: memory, picture identification, picture association, and spatial reasoning.

8. *The Kahn Intelligence Tests: Experimental Form,* 1960, by Kahn, serves a population of age one month to adult, and is designed in particular for the verbally or culturally handicapped. It contains a scale for use with the deaf, and a scale for use with the blind. The entire test consists of a main scale plus six optional scales. Available from Psychological Test Specialists.

9. *The Nonverbal Intelligence Tests for Deaf and Hearing Subjects,* 1958, by J. T. Snyders and N. Snyders-Oomen. This individual intelligence test is suitable for deaf children ages three to sixteen. It may be obtained from Swets and Zeitlinger.

10. *The Ohwaki-Kohs Tactile Block Design Intelligence Test for the Blind,* 1965, by Yoshikaze Ohwaki, is designed for blind people aged six and over. It yields a ratio IQ. This test is an adaptation of the Kohs Block Design Test. The English translation may be obtained from Western Psychological Services.

11. *The Ontario School Ability Examination,* 1936, by Harry Amoss. This is an individual intelligence test for children ages three to fifteen who are deaf, nonnative English speakers or handicapped in language development. Available from Ryerson Press.

12. *The Peabody Picture Vocabulary Test,* 1970, by Lloyd M. Dunn. For children two and one-half to eighteen years of age. Two forms are available on this untimed test of listening vocabulary. No verbal response is required from the subject, only minimal movement to point out the correct picture. MA and IQ scores. Available from the American Guidance Service, Inc.

13. *The Performance Test of Intelligence: A Series of Nonlinguistic Tests for Deaf and Normal Children, Third Edition,* 1944, by J. Drever and M. Collins. Suitable for children ages five to six and seven to sixteen. This series, like the Arthur Adaptation of the Leiter International Performance Scale, is composed of modifications of other tests on the market. Test materials available from A. H. Baird and test manual from Oliver and Boyd, Ltd.

14. *The Pictorial Test of Intelligence,* 1964, by Joseph L. French, is designed for the physically handicapped as well as normal children from ages three to eight. The PTI yields seven scores: picture vocabulary, form discrimination, information and comprehension, similarities, size and number, immediate recall, and total. This test of intellectual functioning requires only sufficient command of English to understand very simple instructions. No verbal responses are

required of the child. The child responds in multiple-choice fashion, pointing to one of four pictures on test cards. Available from Houghton Mifflin Company.

15. *The Quick Test*, 1962, by R. B. Ammons and C. H. Ammons. This is another test of picture vocabulary designed to give a quick screening of verbal intelligence of children aged two and over. While standardized on a normal population, the test was designed for the severely physically handicapped. Any yes-no signal makes testing possible, since the examiner points to four drawings in turn on a plate. Three forms are available from Psychological Test Specialists.

16. *The Stanford-Binet Intelligence Scale*, Third Revision, 1960, for children aged two and over. A highly verbal scale that yields a singular index of intelligence. This test has been around a long time and has been the standard against which all other tests have been measured. Available from Houghton Mifflin Company. The Stanford-Binet may be used informally to supplement results of other testing with the physically handicapped.

17. *The Stanford-Ohwaki-Kohs Block Design Intelligence Test for the Blind: American Revision of the Ohwaki-Kohs Test*, 1966, by Richard M. Swinn and William L. Dautermur. For the blind and partially sighted, aged sixteen and over. The test materials are the same as in the Ohwaki-Kohs test. Available from Western Psychological Services.

18. *The Van Alstyne Picture Vocabulary Test*, 1961, by Dorothy Van Alstyne. Age range of two to seven years. This is another picture vocabulary test suitable for children with verbal or motor impairments, since no oral responses and minimal physical responses are required from the child. The child indicates the picture that illustrates the word or phrase presented orally by the examiner. Available from Harcourt Brace Jovanovich, Inc.

19. *The Wechsler Intelligence Scale for Children*, 1949, by David Wechsler, for children aged five to fifteen. Available scores are: verbal (information, comprehension, arithmetic, similarities, vocabulary, digit span [optional], total); performance (picture completion, picture arrangement, block design, object assembly, mazes [optional], coding, total); total. Available from the Psychological Corporation. Many studies have been done and are available on the application of the WISC to special populations—blind, deaf, etc. See the listing Oscar K. Buros, ed., *Mental Measurements Yearbook*, 7th ed., 2 vols. (Highland Park, N.J.: Gryphon Press, 1972).

20. *The Williams Intelligence Test for Children with Defective Vision*, 1956, by M. Williams. For children aged five to fifteen. This test may be obtained from the University of Birmingham Institute of Education.

B. Group. Four intelligence tests may be used in the small-group situation:
   1. Chicago Nonverbal Examination
   2. Goodenough-Harris Drawing Test
   3. Colored Progressive Matrices
   4. Quick Test

achievement tests

Few achievement tests seem to be designed for use with special groups. Standard batteries for measuring general educational achievement in the areas most commonly covered by academic curricula can often be used intact or adapted for the handicapped. Children with hearing and speech difficulties alone should be able to handle the traditional booklet and answer sheet test batteries. Modifications of test procedures will be necessary for other groups. For a motor-impaired child, for example, an examiner may be required to record the child's answers. For the easily fatigued, testing may have to take place over an extended period.

II. Achievement Tests
   A. *The Colorado Braille Battery: Literary Code Tests,* 1966, by R. Woodcock and S. E. Bourgeault, has three levels. It is useful for blind children in grades one and over. The test gives four scores: letters, punctuation, word form, and total. Available from American Printing House for the Blind.
   B. *The Colorado Braille Battery: Nemeth Code Test,* 1966, also by Woodcock and Bourgeault, examines knowledge of the braille mathematics code and is useful for blind children in grades four and over. Also available from American Printing House for the Blind.
   C. *The Peabody Individual Achievement Test,* 1970, by L. Dunn and F. Markwardt, Jr. is an untimed, power battery. Useful for children in grades kindergarten through twelve, this test takes an average of thirty to forty minutes to administer. Six scores are obtained: math, reading recognition, reading comprehension, spelling, general information, and total. The test is useful with the physically handicapped, since it simply requires a pointing (or eye blink, nod, "Yes-no," etc.) to select one of four pictures on three of the subtests. On general information and reading recognition subtests, a verbal response is necessary. The test may be obtained from the American Guidance Service, Inc.

developmental scales

A number of developmental scales have been included in this survey of instruments for the evaluation of the physically handicapped child. These scales are useful for obtaining a picture of the relative strengths and weaknesses in the total development of the child. A child may have a known language disorder, for example, but the examiner may still want to evaluate gross motor behavior, fine-motor adaptive behavior, or personal-social behavior in comparison to the normal developmental pattern. The scales also may be useful in identifying secondary sensory, motor, or emotional difficulties. Several of these scales were designed for a physically handicapped population.

III. Developmental Scales
  A. General
  1. *The Bayley Scales of Infant Development,* 1969, by N. Bayley. This scale is useful in assessing the developmental progress of infants aged two to thirty months. It may aid in recognizing sensory and neurological deficiencies and emotional disturbances. The scale has three sections. The mental section consists of 163 items that examine responses to visual and auditory stimuli, manipulation and play with objects, responses involving social interaction, discrimination of shapes, memory or object constancy, and simple problem solving. The motor section consists of eighty-one items that examine the progression of gross motor abilities as well as those involving finer motor coordination. A thirty-item behavior rating scale looks at emotional and social behaviors, activity levels, attention span, and persistence. Available from the Psychological Corporation.
  2. *The Denver Developmental Screening Test,* 1970, by Frankenberg and Dodds. Useful with children aged two weeks to six years. This rapid screening test (fifteen to twenty minutes) is useful for the detection of serious developmental delays in children. It can give an idea of relative strengths and weaknesses in development. Yields four scores: gross motor, fine-motor adaptive, language, personal-social. Available from Ladoca Project and Publishing Foundation, Inc.
  3. *The Gesell Developmental Tests,* 1965, by Ilg and Ames, tests general developmental levels. For children aged five to ten. Available from Programs for Education, Inc.
  4. *The Blum-Fieldsteel Development Charts,* by Blum and Fieldsteel. These charts are based on the norms and observational method of the Gesell Developmental Tests. Entries made on the charts indicate the performance of specific activities, and constitute a record of the child's motor and functional development, which may readily be compared to the normal developmental pattern. Useful for mapping the progress of the physically handicapped from six months to seven years old.
  5. *The Preschool Attainment Record, Research Edition,* 1967, by Edgar A. Doll, for children aged six months to seven years. Yields nine scores: ambulation, manipulation, rapport, communication, responsibility, information, ideation, creativity, and total. Designed to measure the physical, social, mental, and language attainments of children for whom verbal intelligence tests are not appropriate. These include children with sensory or neuromuscular impairments and speech or language disabilities. The test is well adapted for testing blind, deaf, aphasic, cerebral palsied, autistic, mentally retarded. A specimen set may be obtained from American Guidance Service, Inc.
  B. Behavioral
  1. *The Child Behavior Rating Scale,* 1962, by Russell N. Cassel. Teachers or parents can use this scale to rate children in grades kindergarten through three. Six adjustment scores are obtained: self, home, social, school, physical, and total. The author states that this test is in-

tended for use with "preschool children, primary grade children and children unable to read or handicapped in completing the conventional paper-and-pencil personality tests." No data are given, however, on the handicapped child. Available from Western Psychological Services.

2. *The Maxfield-Buchholz Scale of Social Maturity for Use with Preschool Blind Children*, 1958, by K. Maxfield and S. Buchholz. For children from infancy to six years old. Available from the American Foundation for the Blind, Inc.

C. Language

1. *The Utah Test of Language Development, Revised Edition*, 1967, by M. Mecham, J. Jex, and J. Jones, for children aged one and one-half to fourteen and one-half years. This test has fifty-one items to measure the expressive and receptive language skills of the normal and handicapped child. Untimed. Available from Communication Research Association, Inc.

2. *The Verbal Language Development Scale*, 1959, by M. Mecham, for children from birth to fifteen years old. A language-age equivalent is obtained from this fifty-item checklist. The scale is an extension of the communication section of the Vineland Social Maturity Scale. Available from American Guidance Service, Inc.

sensory-motor tests

The physically handicapped child often does not have one problem that can be isolated. There may be neurological deficiencies secondary to the main handicap. These are often found in the sensory-motor areas. Some of the following instruments show indices of organicity or minimal brain damage. Others examine auditory perception and visual-motor perception and execution. Several of the tests are intended for children with severe neuromuscular involvement.

IV. Sensory-Motor Tests

A. General

1. *The Detroit Tests of Learning Aptitude*, 1968, by Harvey J. Baker and Bernice Leland. Twenty subtests comprise this test for children aged three and over, but the examiner selects a range of subtests to administer. The subtests selected will vary according to the individual needs of the child. Scores available are: pictorial absurdities, verbal absurdities, pictorial opposites, verbal opposites, motor speech and precision, auditory attention span (for unrelated words, for related syllables), oral commissions, social adjustment A, visual attention span (for objects, for letters), orientation, free association, memory for design, number ability, social adjustment B, broken pictures, oral directions, likenesses and differences, total; individual age-

equivalent scores are obtained. The test is available from Bobbs-Merrill Company, Inc.

2. *The Illinois Test of Psycholinguistic Abilities*, 1968, by Samuel Kirk, James McCarthy, and Winifred Kirk, for children aged two to ten years. This is a diagnostic instrument that examines language, perception and short-term memory abilities. Scores available are: auditory reception, visual reception, visual sequential memory, auditory association, auditory sequential memory, visual association, visual closure, verbal expression, grammatical closure, manual expression, auditory closure (optional), sound blending (optional), total. Available from University of Illinois Press, Champaign.

3. *The Psychoeducational Profile of Basic Learning Abilities*, 1966, by Robert E. Valett, for children ages two to fourteen with learning disabilities. Examines five areas: motor integration and physical development, perceptual abilities, language, social-personality adaptivity, general intellectual functioning. Available from Consulting Psychologists Press, Inc.

4. *Screening Tests for Identifying Children with Specific Language Disability*, 1970, by Beth Slingerland, for children in grades one to four. This test is used to identify children with disabilities in reading, handwriting, spelling, and speaking. Available from the Educators Publishing Service, Inc.

B. Auditory Perceptual Development

1. *The Goldman-Fristoe-Woodcock Test of Auditory Discrimination*, 1970, for children aged four and over. The purpose of this test is to identify and assess the child's ability to distinguish among speech sounds, under two conditions: quiet and background noise. Available from the American Guidance Service, Inc.

2. *Screening Test for Auditory Perception*, 1969. Experimental edition by G. Kinnell and J. Wahl for children in grades two to six. This screening instrument, for children who may have inadequate auditory perceptual abilities, yields six scores: vowels, consonants, rhyming words, sound patterns, word differences, total. It may be given in a group as well as individually. From Academic Therapy Publications.

3. *Tests of Listening Accuracy in Children*, 1969, by M. Mecham, J. Jex, and J. Jones. This is a screening device for children aged five to nine in the area of auditory discrimination. It requires only a pointing response from the child; the child identifies the picture (out of three) named by the examiner. The test is available from Brigham Young University Press.

C. Visual-Motor Development

1. *The Bender-Gestalt Test*, 1969, by Lauretta Bender. This is a brief copying task that evaluates perceptual-motor functioning. Available from the American Orthopsychiatric Association, Inc.

2. *The Bender Visual-Motor Gestalt Test for Children*, 1962, an adaptation of the above by Aileen Crawson. From Western Psychological Services. Also, Grune and Stratton, Inc.

3. *The Developmental Test of Visual-Motor Integration*, 1967, by R. Beery

and N. Buktenica, for children aged two to fifteen. This test of visual-motor integration can be used in groups. It consists of twenty-four geometric forms to be copied in a test booklet. From the Follett Educational Corporation.

4. *The Marianne Frostig Developmental Test of Visual Perception, Third Edition*, 1966, for children aged three to eight. This test of visual perception yields seven scores: eye-motor coordination, figure-ground discrimination, form constancy, positions in space, spatial relationships, total, perceptual quotient. For groups or individuals. The test may be obtained from Consulting Psychologists Press, Inc.

5. *The Meeting Street School Screening Test*, 1969, by Peter Hainsworth and Marian Siqueland. For grades kindergarten to one. Useful in identifying children who will have learning difficulties. Examines motor patterning, visual-perceptual-motor functioning, and language. From Crippled Children and Adults of Rhode Island, Inc.

6. *The Memory-for-Designs Test*, 1960, by Frances Graham and Barbara Kendall. A widely used visual-motor test in which the child (aged eight and one-half and over) reproduces straight-line designs from memory. Available from Psychological Test Specialists.

7. *The Primary Visual-Motor Test*, 1970, by M. R. Haworth, is a downward extension of the Bender-Gestalt Test, intended for children aged four to eight. From Grune and Stratton, Inc.

8. *The Purdue Perceptual-Motor Survey*, 1966, by Eugene Roach and Newell Kephart. For children aged six to ten. This is a survey to identify children who lack the perceptual-motor abilities necessary for acquiring academic success. Activities involved are: rhythmic writing, walking board, jumping, identification of body parts, imitation of movements, obstacle course chalkboard, angels in the snow, ocular pursuits, developmental drawing. Available from the Charles E. Merrill Company.

9. *The Southern California Figure-Ground Visual Perception Test*, 1966, by A. Jean Ayres. This test for children aged four to ten examines the figure-ground perception of the child. $15 from Western Psychological Services.

10. *The Southern California Kinesthesia and Tactile Perception Tests*, 1966, also by A. Jean Ayres, for children aged four to eight. This test does not require any verbal response and examines the child's use of tactile and kinesthetic information. Six scores: kinesthesia, manual form perception, finger identification, graphthesia, localization of tactile stimulation, double tactile stimuli perception. Available from Western Psychological Services.

11. *The Southern California Motor Accuracy Test*, 1964, again authored by A. Jean Ayres. This test measures the fine discrimination and accuracy of the visually directed hand use of a pencil. It is for children aged four to seven, especially for those with neuromuscular immaturity or sensorimotor involvement (involuntary motor, gross tremor, spasticity, etc.). Available from Western Psychological Services.

12. *The Southern California Perceptual-Motor Tests,* 1969, by A. Jean Ayres. Evaluates the perceptual-motor functioning of children aged four to eight. Few verbal responses are required. Six tests: imitation of postures, crossing midline of body, bilateral motor coordination, standing balance with eyes open, standing balance with eyes closed. From Western Psychological Services.

attitudes

Several attitude scales pertain to the physically handicapped. All are self-report instruments in which the subject reports his or her own opinions directly. They are suitable for adolescents and adults.

V. Attitudes
   A. *The Attitudes to Blindness Scale,* 1958, by Cowen, Underberg, and Verillo. A four-point response scale with thirty items. The higher the score, the more unfavorable the attitude toward blindness. Available from the Journal Press.
   B. *Attitude Toward Disabled People Scale,* 1960, by Yuker, Block and Campbell. The ATDP attempts to measure attitudes toward disabled people in general. Each statement suggests that disabled people are either the same as or different from physically normal. With disabled subjects, high scores are interpreted as self-acceptance; for nondisabled, high scores are interpreted as a favorable attitude toward disabled persons. Available from Human Resources Foundation.
   C. *The Handicap Problems Inventory,* 1960, by George Wright and H. H. Remmers, for teenagers and adults. It is a checklist of 280 problems attributable to physical disability. Scores represent a quantification of the impact of the disability on the person as the person sees it. From the Purdue Research Foundation.
VI. Miscellaneous
   A. Color Blindness
      Test for Color Blindness, 1970, by Shinobu Shihaca, for children aged four and over. Examines congenital color-vision deficiency. Four editions of this test are available from Graham-Field Surgical Company, Inc.
   B. Reading Readiness
      The Roughness Discrimination Test, 1965, by C. Nolan and J. Morris. This is a test for blind children in grades kindergarten to one, of the tactual ability for predicting Braille reading readiness. From American Printing House for the Blind.
   C. Vision
      The Stycar Vision Test, 1970, by Mary Sheridan. Three levels. For normal and handicapped children aged six months to five to seven years. This test may be used with nonspeaking, severely handicapped children. Available from NFER Publishing Company, Ltd.

          12. Pictorial Test of Intelligence
          13. Quick Test
          14. Van Alstyne Picture Vocabulary Test
    B. Achievement
        Peabody Individual Achievement Test (in part)
    C. Development: General
        Preschool Attainment Record, Research Edition
    D. Development: Language
          1. Utah Test of Language Development, Revised Edition
          2. Verbal Language Development Scale
          3. Screening Tests for Identifying Children with Specific Language Disability
IV. Tests Specifically for the Motor Impaired
    A. Intelligence
          1. Children's Picture Information Test
          2. Colored Progressive Matrices and Advanced Progressive Matrices
          3. Columbia Mental Maturity Scale, Revised
          4. English Picture Vocabulary Test
          5. Peabody Picture Vocabulary Test
          6. Pictorial Test of Intelligence
          7. Quick Test
          8. Van Alstyne Picture Vocabulary Test
    B. Achievement
        Peabody Individual Achievement Test
    C. Development: Behavioral and General
          1. Child Behavior Rating Scale
          2. Preschool Attainment Record, Research Edition
          3. Utah Test of Language Development, Revised Edition
    D. Development: Visual-Motor
          1. Southern California Kinesthesia and Tactile Perception Tests
          2. Southern California Motor Accuracy Test
    E. Attitudes
          1. Attitude Toward Disabled People Scale
          2. Handicap Problems Inventory
    F. Vision
        Stycar Vision Test

publisher's index

1. Academic Therapy Publications, 1539 Fourth Street, San Raphael, California 94901

2. American Foundation for the Blind, Inc., 15 West 15th Street, New York, New York 10011

3. American Guidance Service, Inc., Publishers' Building, Circle Pines, Minnesota 55014

4. American Orthopsychiatric Association, Inc., 1790 Broadway, New York, New York 10019

5. American Printing House for the Blind, 1839 Frankfort Avenue, Louisville, Kentucky 40206

6. Baird, A. H., Instrument Maker, 33–39 Lothian Street, Edinburgh I, Scotland

7. Bobbs-Merrill Company, Inc., 4300 W. 62nd Street, Indianapolis, Indiana 46268

8. Brigham Young University Press, 205 University Press Building, Provo, Utah 84602

9. Communication Research Associates, Inc., P.O. Box 11012, Salt Lake City, Utah 84111

10. Consulting Psychologists Press, Inc., 577 College Ave., Palo Alto, California 94306

11. Crippled Children and Adults of Rhode Island, Inc., Meeting Street School, 333 Grotto Avenue, Providence, Rhode Island 02906

12. Educational Evaluation Enterprises, 5 Marsh Street, Bristol I, Gloucester, England

13. Educators Publishing Service, Inc., 75 Moulton Street, Cambridge, Massachusetts 02138

14. Follett Educational Corporation, 1010 W. Washington Boulevard, Chicago, Illinois 60607

15. Graham-Field Surgical Company, Inc., 32–56 Sixty-second Street, Woodside, New York 11377

16. Grune and Stratton, Inc., 757 Third Avenue, New York, New York, 10017

17. Harcourt Brace Jovanovich, Inc., 757 Third Avenue, New York, New York 10017

18. Hisky, Marshall S., 5640 Baldwin, Lincoln, Nebraska 68508

19. Houghton Mifflin Company, Educational Division, 1 Beacon Street, Boston, Massachusetts 02107

20. Human Resources Foundation, Albertson, New York 11507

21. Ladoca Project and Publishing Foundation, Inc., East 51st Avenue and Lincoln Street, Denver, Colorado 80216

22. Merrill, Charles E., Publishing Company, 1300 Alum Creek Drive, Columbus, Ohio 43216

23. NFER Publishing Company, Ltd., 2 Jennings Buildings, Thames Avenue, Windsor, Berkshire, SL4 1Qs, England

24. Oliver and Boyd, Ltd., Tweedale Court, 14 High Street, Edinburgh I, Scotland

25. Programs for Education, P.O. Box 85, Lumberville, Pennsylvania 18933

26. Psychological Corporation, 364 East 45th Street, New York, New York 10017

27. Psychological Test Specialists, P.O. Box 1441, Missoula, Montana 59801

28. Purdue University, Purdue Research Foundation, Building D, South Campus Courts, Lafayette, Indiana 47907
29. Swets and Zeitlinger, Keizersgrucht, 471 and 487, Amsterdam-C, Holland
30. University of Birmingham Institute of Education, 5 Great Charles Street, Birmingham 3, England
31. University of Illinois Press, 54 East Gregory, Champaign, Illinois 61801
32. Western Psychological Services, 12031 Wilshire Boulevard, Los Angeles, California 90025

assessment instruments useful in therapeutic recreation

I. Mental Status
  A. Minnesota Multiphasic Personality Inventory
       Source: Western Psychological Services
               12031 Wilshire Boulevard
               Los Angeles, California 90025
       Assistance in diagnosing patients within various psychiatric disorders, including identification of feelings, behaviors, and attitudes.
  B. Fidler Battery
       Gail Fidler and Joy W. Fidler, *Occupational Therapy* (New York: Macmillan Publishing Co., Inc., 1963)
       or
       Source: American Occupational Therapy Association
               6000 Executive Boulevard
               Rockville, Maryland 20852
       Used to develop rapport with client and assess intellectual, physical, emotional, and social development.
II. Activities of Daily Living
  A. Activities-of-Daily-Living Test, for moderately to severely handicapped
       Helen S. Willard and Clare S. Spackman, *Occupational Therapy*, 4th ed. (New York: J.B. Lippincott Company, 1970)
       Assesses daily living skills as well as home facilities and barriers
  B. Activities of Daily Living, for bilateral and single upper-extremity amputation assessment
       Source: Edward Gordon, M.D.
               Director, Department of Physical Medicine
               Michael Resse Hospital
               Chicago, Illinois

Compiled by therapeutic recreation students, Michigan State University, 1976.

C. Trainable Mentally Retarded Performance File, for severely and moderately retarded
   Source: Reporting Services for Exceptional Children
           563 Westview Avenue
           Ridgefield, New Jersey 07657

III. Mentally Retarded
   A. Cain-Levine Social Competency Scale
      Source: Consulting Psychologists Press
              577 College Avenue
              Palo Alto, California 94306
      Authors: Leo Cain, Samuel Levine, Freeman Elzey,
              San Francisco State University
              San Francisco, California 94132
      Assesses self-help, initiative, social skills, and communications.
   B. Vineland Worksheet
      Source: College of Education
              Department of Elementary and Special Education
              Michigan State University
              East Lansing, Michigan 48824
      Assesses self-help, locomotion, occupation, communication, self-direction, and socialization.

IV. Physical Assessment
   A. Amputee Assessment Form
      Source: Ingham County Medical Hospital
              Physical Therapy Department
              401 West Greenlawn
              Lansing, Michigan, 48910
      Assesses physical abilities, problems with prosthetic devices, and adjustments to artificial limbs.
   B. Behavioral Characteristics Progression (BCP)
      Source: Vort Corporation
              P.O. Box 11132
              Palo Alto, California 94306
      Author: Santa Cruz County
              California State Department of Education
      Used as an assessment, instructional, and communication tool. Identifies behavioral characteristics, aids in developing appropriate objectives, and offers a historical recording device.
   C. Movement Pattern Checklist and Profile Sheet
      Godfrey, Barbara B. and Newell C. Kephart, *Movement Patterns and Motor Education* (Englewood Cliffs, N.J.: Prentice-Hall, Inc., 1969)
      Used with children to evaluate and summarize some gross-motor skills and movements, such as jumping, hopping, pushing, and pulling.
   D. Preliminary test for "physical loss of function"
      Source: Oscar Boismier
              Olin Health Center
              Michigan State University
              East Lansing, Michigan 48824

Tests for muscle strength, joint ROM, joint instability, atrophy of muscle, edema, and ambulation.

V. Recreational Assessments

A. Mirenta Leisure Interest Finder (component of the Milwaukee Leisure Counseling Model)

Source: "Leisure Counseling"
Dr. Joseph Mirenta
Milwaukee Public Schools
Division of Municipal Recreation and Adult Education
P.O. Drawer 10–K
Milwaukee, Wisconsin 53201

Identifies degrees of interest in a variety of leisure activities.

B. Leisure Competency Interview Questionnaire

Source: Leisure Services Department
State Technical Institute and Rehabilitation Center
Alber Drive
Plainwell, Michigan 49080

Assesses past and present leisure involvement to determine areas of concentration in leisure planning.

C. Emerging Leisure Counseling Concepts and Orientations

Source: Chester F. McDowell, Jr.
Assistant Visiting Professor
University of Oregon
Department of Recreation and Park Management
Eugene, Oregon 97403

Provides a leisure-counseling model.

D. McKechnie Model (Leisure Activity Blank)

Source: George E. McKechnie
Assistant Professor of Psychology
Arizona State University
Tempe, Arizona 85281
or

George E. McKechnie, "Psychological Foundations of Leisure Counseling: An Empirical Strategy," *Therapeutic Recreation Journal*, 8 no. 1 (1974), 4–16.

Activity checklist to provide the counselor with psychological patterns and interrelationships of leisure activities.

VI. Social Assessments

A. Interpersonal Perception Method

Source: NFER Publishing Company, Ltd.
2 Jennings Buildings, Thames Avenue
Windsor, Berkshire, SL4 1Qs, England

Authors: R. D. Laing, H. Phillipson, and A. R. Lee

Using a dyadic encounter, the test focuses on self-perception and perception of the other member in the dyad.

B. Children's Minimal Social Behavior Scale

Source: Raymond A. Ulmer
1623 North Laurel Avenue, Apt. 238
Los Angeles, California 90046

Authors: Raymond A. Ulmer, and Martha Lieberman
Structured interview with examiner to derive scores on responses to social stimulus.

C. Fundamental Interpersonal Relations Orientations—Behavior (FIRO-B)
Leo F. Ryan, *Clinical Interpretation of the FIRO-B*, rev. ed. (Palo Alto, Calif.: Consulting Psychologists Press, Inc., 1977)
Author: William Schutz
Measures three dimensions of interpersonal relationships: inclusion, control, and affection.

D. Sociogram
Robert M. Goldenson, *The Encyclopedia of Human Behavior* (Garden City, N.Y.: Doubleday and Company, Inc. 1970)
Used on adolescents or adults to diagram social relationships within a group.

E. Social and Emotional Development, for trainable mentally retarded
Source: Trainable Program Coordinator
      Beekman Center
      2901 Wabash Road
      Lansing, Michigan 48910
Used individually to assess interpersonal relationships, personality, behavior, and independence.

VII. Blind and Deaf

A. Identification of Orientation and Mobility Skills Relating to Developmental Tasks for Young, Blind Children
Source: Department of Special Education
      California State College at Los Angeles
      Los Angeles, California 90032
Deals with developmental tasks, orientation and mobility skills, and learning necessary for performing these skills and tasks.

B. Manual for the Assessment of "Deaf-Blind" Multiple-handicapped Children
Source: Michigan School for the Blind
      Lansing, Michigan 48906
Assesses self-help, gross motor development, social development, fine-motor development, communication, and cognition.

C. Program Development in Recreation Service for the Deaf-Blind
Source: Recreation Education Program
      College of Liberal Arts
      University of Iowa
      Iowa City, Iowa 52242
Assesses locomotor skills, pretumbling skills, balance and coordination, ball skills, trapeze skills, doorway-chinning-bar skills, and aquatic activities.

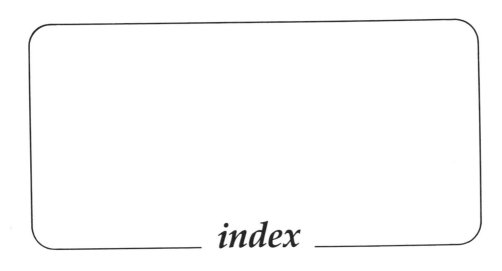

index